Chris van Uffelen, Markus Golser
Paris | The Architecture G

Edited by Markus Sebastian Braun

Chris van Uffelen, Markus Golser

Paris | The Architecture Guide

Edited by Markus Sebastian Braun
Photographs by Chris van Uffelen

The Deutsche Bibliothek is registering this publication in Deutsche National-bibliographie; detailed bibliographical information can be found on the internet at http://dnb.ddb.de

ISBN 978-3-03768-002-5

Copyright 2009 by Braun Publishing AG
www.braun-publishing.ch

1st Edition 2009

Translation:
Übersetzungsdienst Marcel Saché: 1–3, 5–40, 42–48, 50–83, 85–94, 96–102, 104–107, 109–114, 116–118, 120–122, 125, 126, 128–130, 132–141, 143, 144, 146–151, 156, 158, 159, 161–168, 170–182, 185–188, 192–194, 196, 197, 199–204, 207, 210–212, 215, 216, 219–222, 226, 229, 232, 234, 236, 237, 240, 241, 250, 253–255, 257–261, 263, 265–273, 277, 278, 281–284, 286, 288–290, 292, 295, 297, 301, 302, 307, 312, 315, 316, 319–323, 327–333, 335, 336, 338–340, 343, 346, 347, 349, 350, 352, 358, 360–362, 364, 367, 370, 372–374, 376, 377, 380–382, 384, 387, 391–398, 401
Übersetzungsdienst Marcel Saché / edited by Alice Bayandin: 4, 41, 49, 95, 103, 108, 115, 119, 123, 127, 131, 142, 145, 152–155, 157, 160, 183, 184, 189–191, 195, 198, 205, 206, 208, 209, 213, 214, 217, 218, 223–225, 228, 231, 233, 235, 238, 239, 245–249, 251, 252, 256, 262, 275, 276, 285, 287, 291, 293, 298, 305, 306, 310, 311, 314, 324, 334, 353, 356, 363, 365, 366, 368, 369, 371, 383, 388, 402, 404, 409
Alice Bayandin: Preface, 84, 124, 169, 227, 230, 242–244, 264, 274, 279, 280, 294, 296, 299, 300, 303, 304, 308, 309, 313, 317, 318, 325, 326, 337, 341, 342, 344, 345, 348, 351, 354, 355, 357, 359, 375, 378, 379, 385, 386 389, 390, 399, 400, 403, 405–408, 410, 412–495, Appendix
Design: port-d Burgold & Neumann GbR
Layout: Natascha Saupe, Georgia van Uffelen
Cover design: Michaela Prinz, Berlin
Reproduction: Bild1Druck GmbH, Berlin

Contents

Preface

France can be compared to a nested doll, a matryoshka of sorts. Île-de-France lies at the center of the country, Paris forms the center of Île-de-France, and Île de la Cité is the center of Paris. This small core of the Seine island was settled by the Romans, this is where the Merovingians built their castle, and where the expansion of the Gothic style, the first monogenic style to come after Roman antiquity, started out on its way to reach the rest of Europe.

After producing the Gothic style, France was not only concentrically structured, but was also centrally organized. Practically all developments in the country, political or architectural – which carry the same weight in the context of this book – originated in Paris, preserving a full spectrum of first-class monuments here. Of all European metropolises, only Rome can look back at a distinctly longer history. However, Rome's cultural influence in Italy was and remains much stronger than the influence of Paris in France. At the time when Paris was already a cultural center of the country and all of Europe, Berlin and Amsterdam were little more than just villages. In the course of the centuries French rulers moved from Île de la Cité to the Louvre, than to Versailles – in the meantime already swallowed up by the greater Paris – until they were finally abolished. Today, the Seine island is shared by the Justice Palace and Notre Dame, and the residents of Paris rarely find themselves wandering here even by mistake. In the meantime, they circulate in the city's new centers and are for the most part no longer really Parisians. Every day, thousands of so-called Parisians invade the 20 arrondissements from the equally urbane 'suburbia.' Life in the inner city is expensive, and in the course of the last decades the population here has changed dramatically. Primarily, it is the upper middle classes that remain in the city. The bourgeoisie ride their bicycles around the central districts (unthinkable ten years ago) and enjoy the highly dense cultural milieu, which has accrued due to their disproportional high presence in the overall population. The Grands Projets, the buildings representative of those erected by the presidents, attest to this shift. The closer one comes to the expressway that encircles the city, the Boulevard Périphérique, the higher is the proportion of the working classes who live there; upon crossing it, a new world is revealed. To say that today the ring separates the free, urban middle classes from the "low situated" under classes, as the city gate did during the Early Modern period, may be an exaggeration, but it reflects the facts. This is where, administratively speaking, Paris ends, and it is only for truly unusual projects that its leadership crosses the borders of the 20 districts. But this is also where the future of the "matryoshka" and its great architectural potential, but also the immense urban planning challenge lies. The residents of the banlieue (the cursed zone) who legitimately see themselves as residents of Paris due to their dependency on the inner city must become true cohabitants of the metropolis. This challenge has been accepted with the urban planning competition for "Grand Paris" initiated in 2008 which invited, among others, Jean Nouvel, Christian de Portzamparc, MVRDV and LIN-Finn Geipel/Giulia Andi.

Chris van Uffelen

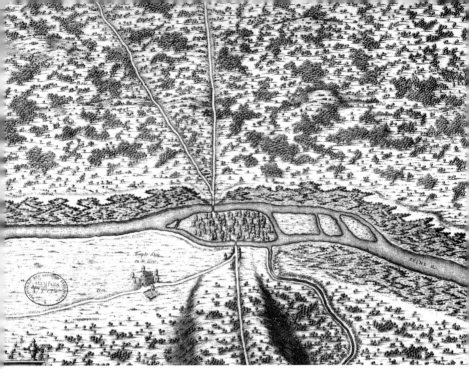

Origins in antiquity and the medieval city center (1)

The history of Paris is inseparably inter-twined with that of the Seine River. The Seine valley has been inhabited since the Stone Age. In the third century BC, the Celtic tribe of the Parisii, who lived from fishing and extensive trade, settled on the islands in the Seine. They founded their chief city, Lucotesia (from "louk-teih", swampy place), on what is now the Île de la Cité. The oldest historic and archaeological records of the city go back to 58 BC, when Julius Caesar began the conquest of Gaul. In 52 BC, the Romans reached the city on the Seine to find it destroyed and abandoned by the Celtic inhabitants. The Romans re-founded Lute-tia, extending it on the south bank of the Seine, with the heart of the settlement on the hillsides of Mont Sainte-Geneviève.

Remains of a Roman forum have been excavated near the present-day Panthéon (Sainte-Geneviève, no. 123). Nearby were an amphitheater (Arènes de Lutèce, no. 2) and an extensive bath complex (Thermes de Cluny, no. 3), with water supplied through an aqueduct (Roman Aqueduct, no. 4). In the fourth century AD, the city was named "Civitas Parisiorum" after the Celtic tribe that had originally inhabited the site. At the end of the 5th century, the Merovingian Franks conquered the Gallo-Roman settlement. Their king, Clovis (481–511), made Paris the capital of the Frankish kingdom. After the city's first bishop, St. Dionysus, had paid with his life for his efforts to spread Christianity among the population in the third century, Clovis' baptism brought his subjects over to the new faith.

The Abbey of Saint-Denis (no. 11) was built over the grave of Dionysus, and be-came a national monument as the burial place of the kings of France. Several ab-beys founded at that time near the city became the centers of small settlements or "bourgs", later called "faubourgs". In spite of a population of over 20,000, Paris lost its political importance under the Carol-ingian dynasty. It was not until the reign of Hugo Capet (987–996) that the city be-came the royal residence once more. The Capetians erected their royal palace on the Île de la Cité, at the site of the present-day Palais de Justice (no. 16), and the settle-ment rapidly expanded on both banks of the Seine. The first systematic attempt

left: Lutèce or first plan of Paris by Jean-Baptiste Bourguignon d'Anville, 1705 (detail)

right: The Louvre with the Saint-Chapelle, calendar picture from June from the "Très Riches Heures" of the Duc de Berry, In the beginning of 15th century (detail)

at urban planning for Paris was made under Philippe II. August (1180–1223). The king's extensive building program included not only the Covered Market, but also stone bridges, paved roads, numerous wells, and fortifications that were raised in a generous ring around the city. The city wall encompassed the castle built in 1200 on the right bank that would later become the Louvre (no. 49). The waters of the Seine separated the walled city into three zones.

The central part, the Île de la Cité, was the political and religious center of the city. On the north bank, 'la ville' had become a thriving commercial center. The southern borough, l'université, had been home to the teachers and students of the cathedral's colleges since the early 12th century. United in 1210, the colleges were an early model for universities to come. A college for poor students founded in 1257 by the canon of Paris, Robert de Sorbon, grew into the Sorbonne, in which 20,000 students were enrolled by the end of the 13th century. After the construction of Saint-Denis Basilica in 1140, numerous buildings were built in the new Gothic style (The Gothic Period), and Notre Dame (no. 19) became the model for many other churches, both in Paris and elsewhere. The Sainte-Chapelle (no. 34) marked a dramatic climax in the transparency of the High Gothic style. Like an oversized reliquary, this building epitomizes a brilliant period of Parisian history under Louis IX (Saint Louis, 1226–1270).

With a population of some 100,000, Paris had become the largest and most important city in all of western and central Europe. Its role as the political and cultural center of the continent ended with the extinction of the direct line of the Capetian dynasty, however. King Edward III of England claimed the throne of France, launching the Hundred Years' War (1339–1453).

The relatively rare late Gothic churches show a conservative architecture, usually recapitulating Notre Dame rather than keeping pace with the more advanced developments in England, Bohemia and southern Germany. Not until the 17th century did Paris regain its crucial importance for the progress of European architecture.

Arènes de Lutèce (2)
around 100
49, rue Monge; 6, rue des Arènes / 5e

One of the few relics of Roman Lutetia was discovered during excavations in 1869. From the ruins, archaeologists reconstructed an ancient multi-purpose building that had been used for theatrical performances, animal shows and gladiator fights. The arena seated 17,000, thus allowing almost the entire population of the Roman settlement to watch the spectacles. A complex system of passageways led to the seating recessed in the hillside of Mons Luticius around the oval arena. Wide corridors led to gates at the narrow ends of the arena, with cages for wild animals beside them. Comedies and dramas were played on the stage in the eastern part of the arena, and the postscenium, whose foundations remain, featured a rich decoration. Niches behind the postscenium served as dressing rooms for the actors.

Thermes de Cluny (3)
around 200
6, place Paul-Painlevé / 5e

Roman cities included not only temples, forums, theatres and amphitheatres, but also extensive public baths. With their luxurious furnishings and complex room arrangements, such buildings were among the most demanding for Roman architects. Significant vestiges of Lutetia's largest bath complex have been preserved. The frigi-

darium, or cold room, has been integrated in the Hôtel de Cluny (no. 31) since the mid-19th century. On its north wall, consoles shaped as merchant ships laden with weapons support the groin vault, which may indicate that the baths were built on behalf of the local inland shipping association. North of the frigidarium is the bathing pool, which is about ten meters long. Three rooms with heated floors south of the frigidarium formed the caldarium, or hot bath. In the tepidarium, or lukewarm bath, two walls show the remains of alternating semicircular and rectangular niches. The rectangular halls north of the frigidarium, of which only the foundations remain, were probably used for relaxation, entertainment and athletic activities.

Aqueduc romain (4)
around 200
between Arcueil and Cachan
(Val-de-Marne)

10

An aqueduct conveyed water over fifteen kilometers from the Rungis plateau to the baths at Lutetia. A small section of the conduit built in the late 2nd or early 3rd century AD remains near Arceuil, south of Paris. Today a suburban area, Arceuil takes its name from the ancient aqueduct that crossed the Bièvre valley here.

In the early 17th century the queen mother and regent Maria de' Medici prompted the restoration of antique aqueducts to, among other reasons, supply the fountains of the Palais du Luxembourg. The work started in 1613 and was finished in 1623 under Ludwig XIII. In the 19th century the aqueduct was expanded by an engineer named Eugène Belgrand.

Saint-Germain-des-Prés (5)
542–558, 990–1014, 1150–1163, 1819–1825
place Saint-Germain-des-Prés, rue Bonaparte, rue de l'Abbaye / 6e

In 558, Germanus, the bishop of Paris, consecrated the church to the Holy Cross and Saint Vincent. The original building was provided with rich furnishings, and was meant to house the tombs of the Merovingian dynasty. This honor soon fell to Saint-Denis Abbey (no. 10), however.

In 754, after Germanus had been canonized, the abbey took him as its patron saint. After repeated attacks by the Normans, the abbey was rebuilt in the Early Romanesque style. As its coarsely hewn blocks indicate, the west tower is the oldest part of the church, and hence the oldest church tower in Paris. Massive buttresses and round-arched windows give the exterior a closed, defensive appearance.

The basilica nave and the transept were built in the late 11th century. They still have the plain walls and massive structures that characterize the Romanesque period, but the choir, consecrated in 1163, shows the latest trend in the French architecture of the time: the Gothic style. The choir ambulatory with radiating chapels is in keeping with the plans of Early Gothic buildings, notably Noyons cathedral. In the choir, ten compound piers and their imposts support the slender ribs of the vault. The walls between the columns are largely open.

Filets unite the triforiums and the large clerestory windows. The nave, which originally had a flat ceiling, was given a ribbed vault and Gothic-arched windows in the 17th century to match the Early Gothic choir. The complete interior decoration, painted in the 19th century, masks the spatial characteristics of the medieval building.

11

Île-de-France
The Gothic island in Romanesque Europe (6)

About the middle of the 12th century, Paris and the surrounding crown lands became the cradle of Gothic architecture. The abbey church of Saint-Denis (no. 11) is considered the seminal Gothic building. Abbot Suger, an important figure both in politics and in the clergy, ordered a new building on the site of the previous Merovingian church in about 1130–1135. While the façade, which was built first, is still characterized by the fortress-like weight of Norman architecture, the choir, built about 1140–1144, shows the advent of a new architectural style. The Gothic style reduces the plain wall and vault surfaces of massive Romanesque buildings, with at most a few decorative elements, to a fragile-looking skeleton of columns, piers and ribs. The Gothic arch that ultimately becomes prevalent transfers the weight of the vault to flying buttresses outside. In addition to increased loft, the concentration on the skeletal structure also permits the replacement of large wall areas with glazed windows. Gothic buildings owe their beauty not least to the visible lines of force in the piers and buttresses. In the first Gothic works, the individual elements used – piers, ribbed vaults, and flying buttresses – were all borrowed from the architectural repertoire of the French Romanesque period. Thus, the new style is not the result of new developments, but evolved from the integration of existing forms in an overall system by particular structural principles.

For this reason, recent studies have re-evaluated the Early Gothic as a late Romanesque movement specific to the French crown lands.

Because only the choir of Saint-Denis Basilica is in the early Gothic style – and even that was later drastically modified – art historians consider Sens cathedral the earliest building completely conceived in the Gothic style. The floor plan of this three-nave basilica begun in 1140 became almost compulsory for later Gothic churches.

It features aisles that continue east of the transept, usually forming an ambulatory. Characteristic early Gothic elevations are composed of four levels – arcade, gallery, triforium and clerestory – as seen in the cathedrals of Noyon (c. 1148), Laon (c. 1155), Soissons (1176) and Paris (1163, no. 19). Chartres cathedral (1194) marks the transition to the High Gothic period, characterized by a three-story elevation, four-ribbed vaults, and a more elaborate system of forms.

Its openings prefigure the division of large window areas through tracery. This first invention of the Gothic style is fully developed at the cathedrals of Rheims (1211) and Amiens (1220).

The Gothic tracery window evolved from initially simple forms to the richer designs of the Rayonnant (1270–1370) and Flamboyant (from 1370 on) styles. The quest for ever greater heights with increasingly skeletal walls characterizes the High Gothic. The results were increasingly translucent "glass boxes," as exemplified by Beauvais cathedral (1225) and the Sainte-Chapelle (no. 34) in Paris (1241).

Initially limited to the crown lands around Paris, the modern forms of the Gothic style were emulated in other regions from the end of the 12th century on. The Cistercian monks, who played a key role in the dissemination of the new style, are sometimes called the "Missionaries of the Gothic".

13

left: Notre Dame in Paris, south transept   *bottom: Cathedral of Auxerre, tenpartite vault*

Saint-Martin-des-Champs (7)
1060, 1079, 1130–1142
292, rue Saint-Martin / 3e

This church takes its name from an Early Romanesque monastery dedicated to Saint Martin and built outside the city in 1060 under Henry I. His son Philip I ceded the monastery to the Cluny abbey, which made it one of its most powerful priories. He also had a new church built, whose choir ambulatory is still preserved. The present church dates from the mid-13th century, however. The transition from the Romanesque to the Gothic style is evident in the choir with ambulatory and radiating chapels – a floor plan that is rooted in French Romanesque architecture and was practically de rigueur in Gothic cathedrals. Here, however, the choir's floor plan is asymmetric to accommodate the adjoining structures.

The bays of the ambulatory are irregular, with trapezoidal and triangular sections. The radiating chapels open laterally on one another, forming a second ambulatory. The substantial deviation from the main axes necessitates piers and pilasters with different cross-sections. Their composition corresponds to the functionally distinct ribs and arches of the vault. Moreover, the choir and the central chapel with its triconch floor plan feature the earliest ribbed vaults in Paris, while the ambulatory and the side chapels have simple groin vaults. Decorative elements that emphasize the hierarchy of the structural elements distinguish Saint-Martin-des-Champs from Saint-Denis Basilica (no. 11), which was built only a few years later. The choir of Saint-Denis also has laterally interconnected chapels that form a second ambulatory, but it integrates the new patterns in a logical system that underlines the force vectors of the structure. A plain-sloped roof covers and unites the ambulatory and the radiating chapels. Segmental arches bridge the recesses between the chapels to support the eaves. The triconch apse protrudes distinctly, and the building's profile rises in steps from here to the clerestory and to the gable of the Gothic nave. The single-aisle nave with a late 19th-century wooden barrel vault is an extremely austere work in the rayonnant style. The bottom two stories of the southeast tower are the oldest part of the church, and date from the early 12th century. The west front was remodeled in the 18th and 19th centuries.

Saint-Pierre-de-Montmartre (8)
1134–1147
2, rue du Mont-Cenis,
place du Tertre / 18e

The mighty proportions of the nearby Sacré-Cœur (no. 209) underscore the simplicity of this Romanesque church. Several sacred buildings, including a Roman temple and an abbey founded in 1134, stood on this site. The cloister of Montmartre was demolished during the French Revolution, however, and its last abbess died on the guillotine in 1793.

The three-aisle basilica with a tri-conch apse to the east was consecrated by Pope Eugene III in 1147. Its sturdy, almost chunky forms are characteristic of village churches of the period. The marble columns in the choir and on the west wall are remnants of a pre-existing Merovingian church.

Le rempart de Philippe Auguste (10)
1190–1215
in Lycée Charlemagne: 14, rue Jardins Saint-Paul, rue Clovis / 4e, 5e

Before embarking on the Third Crusade, King Philippe Auguste (1180-1223) ordered the construction of a wall around Paris to protect his capital city in his absence. The large-scale circle of fortifications also en-veloped areas that were undeveloped at the time. Seventy towers reinforced a ten-me-ter high wall. Remnants of two towers are still visible behind the Saint-Paul ct Saint-Louis church (no. 57) as part of the Lycée Charlemagne. Moreover, a cross-section of the approximately ninety-centimeter thick wall is visible between two houses in Rue Clovis. Down to the river, a bastion that was to become the Louvre (no. 49) further protected the city. Two 17th-century gates, Porte Saint-Denis (no. 85) and Porte Saint-Martin (no. 86), stand on the site of two of the twelve original gates.

15

Saint-Julien-le-Pauvre (9)
around 1165–1240, 1651
1, rue Saint-Julien-le-Pauvre / 5e

As early as 582, Gregory of Tours men-tions Saint-Julien-le-Pauvre as one of only six churches in the city. In 1165, a basilica was built on the foundations of the Merovingian structure. Practically hidden by houses and trees, the incon-spicuous three-apse church is rooted in the Romanesque tradition, but the sturdy columns and sexpartite ribbed vaulting ascribe the building to the Early Gothic. In 1651, however, the original vaulting was replaced with a barrel vault and the nave shortened to the west.

Abbot Suger and the abbey church Saint-Denis (11)

The former abbey church, which was made a cathedral in 1966, is considered one of Europe's most important monuments, both historically and architecturally: it was the burial place of the Kings of France, and it marks the beginning of the Gothic period. The church stands on the spot chosen in the third century by Saint Dionysus, the first bishop of Paris, as his burial place. After his decapitation on Montmartre, according to legend, the bishop carried his head to this spot, singing all the way. In 623, the sanctuary that initially marked the site gave way to a larger church built under the Merovingian king Dagobert I, who decided that Saint-Denis would replace Saint-Germain-des-Prés (no. 5) as the royal burial crypt. Nearly all the French monarchs up to Louis XVIII (†1824) were buried here.

Abbot Suger (1081–1151), who wielded political power as the representative of Louis VII, presided over the building of the basilica as early as 1130 or 1135, and can thus be considered the founder of Gothic architecture. While the main façade, finished by 1140, is barely opened and still features Romanesque blind arcades, the choir built in the three years that followed already integrates typical Gothic design elements in a logical system that externalizes the structural principles of the building. The new style relieves the walls of their load-bearing function and thus allows large windows. Suger's intention of flooding the church with light was in keeping with the Neoplatonist mysticism of Dionysus the Areopagite – a figure popularly identified with Saint Dionysus of Paris

Both the choir and the ambulatory follow a plan that was already common in the Romanesque period. In Saint-Denis, however, the succession of radiating chapels forms a second ambulatory, whose walls are largely open with tall Gothic-arched windows. En délit piers and delicate columns support the arches and slender ribs of the ambulatory vault. The triforium and clerestory of the choir are the result of remodeling works begun around 1230, when a Gothic structure replaced the early medieval nave and transept. The three-part elevation recalls that of two cathedrals: Rheims, begun in 1211, and Amiens, begun in 1220. The double-pitched roofs of the aisles were an innovation, however. It critically contributes to improve the illumination and spatial impression of the interior. In Romanesque churches, the lean-to roof of the aisles meets the walls at the height of the triforium, making windows impossible. In Saint-Denis, however, the triforium is glazed and merges with the clerestory to form a continuous window area – a pattern followed in many later churches. At this point, the Gothic trend towards ever lighter walls pervaded the entire elevation, and would lead to such delicate glass boxes as the cathedrals of Beauvais, Metz, Strasbourg and Cologne. The filigree appearance of the nave and choir contrasts with the Romanesque solidity of the west façade, which resembles a castle due to the crenellation added in the 19th century. The transept fronts are about a hundred years younger, and characterized by rayonnant style also found on Notre Dame (no. 19).

After the desecration of the royal burial place during the French Revolution, the remains of the royal families were reburied in two tombs in 1817. Fortunately, the impressive series of non-royal sepulchers dating from the 13th to the 19th centuries was preserved. It provides a panorama of funerary sculpture from the High Gothic to the neo-Classical period.

17

Choir – the beginning of Gothic style

Façade – the late Romanesque structural element

Saint-Germain-l'Auxerrois (12)

between 1220 and 1300, 1420–1425,
1435–1439, 1500–1570
2, place du Louvre, rue de l'Arbre Sec / 1er

A church dedicated to Saint Germanus of Auxerre existed here as early as the 7th century. The choir tower built as part of a Romanesque construction in the 12th century has survived and harks back to the tower of Saint-Germain-des-Prés (no. 5) in terms of position and form. The construction work carried out in 1220 included the south aisle, the choir and its ambulatory, and the central portal adorned with sculptures. The remaining building components are Late Gothic additions. This applies in particular to the porch created by Jean Gaussel (1435–1439) after Burgundian models. Inside the church, the columns and the walls are richly adorned.

The floor plan of Saint-Germain-l'Auxerrois follows that of Notre Dame (no. 19), as many churches in Paris also do. Like in the cathedral, a double ambulatory surrounds the choir to the east of the transept, and wide arcades lend the nave a somewhat sluggish rhythm. The tracery of the outer ambulatory and its radiating chapels already suggest the Renaissance. The portal added in 1570, through which the canons entered the choir, was also designed in the Renaissance style.

The church won notoriety only two years after its completion. On the eve of the 23 August 1572, its vesper bells gave the signal for the massacre of Protestants by the Catholic party at the court of Charles IX. In the following three days, more than three thousand Protestants were slaughtered (Saint Bartholomew's Day Massacre). Saint-Germain-l'Auxerrois was the Louvre's Chapel Royal and became the last resting place for numerous architects and artists appointed by the kings of France, including Louis Le Vau, Jacques Lemercier, Robert de Cotte, Ange-Jacques Gabriel, Jean-Baptiste Chardin and François Boucher.

Saint-Séverin (13)

between 1225 and 1230, 1489–1495,
1498–1520
1, rue des Prêtres-Saint-Séverin / 5e

Situated in the Latin Quarter, the church is supposed to have been built in the 6th century on the grave of the hermit Severinus, who died in 555. Following Carolingian and Romanesque extensions to the building, a new construction ensued in the early 13th century, of which the façade, the tower and the western part of the nave still remain. The church was damaged by fire prior to the termination of the construction works during the 15th century, however, and completed in the Late Gothic style between 1450 and 1520. A five-aisle basilica with side chapels joins a choir with ambulatory – a plan corresponding to that of Notre Dame (no. 19). However, the vertical dimension that characterizes Early Gothic churches is not present in Saint-Séverin. To the east, the plain Early

Gothic forms progressively give way to flamboyant elements. Delicate stellar and ribbed vaults span the choir, while twisted columns and ribbed sheaves sprouting out of them bestow a palm-like appearance upon the ambulatory.

Saint-Martin-des-Champs (14) (refectory)
between 1230 and 1235
292, rue Saint-Martin / 3e
Pierre de Montreuil (not verified)

The refectory of the former priory ranks among the most impressive examples of French Gothic abbatial architecture. Extremely slender columns with tapered shafts divide the interior into several naves. The barrel vaults rest on fluted columns, and the twin windows, the barrel bands and the composite capitals are typical Early Gothic elements that were already behind the times in the High Gothic period. Four years after the dissolution of the abbey in 1790, the freshly founded Conservatoire des Arts et Métiers, a major school for technology and industry, moved into the building. The former abbey was extensively renovated and extended on this occasion.

Saint-Maur saw its revival in 1631. In 1792, more than three hundred revolutionaries were murdered here. Large sections of the building were demolished in 1802. A few remnants still stand along the Square Laurent-Prache. Of the refectory – a work by architect Pierre de Montreuil, who also designed la Sainte-Chapelle (no. 34) – the large rose window has survived and is walled in the stairwell of a residential building.

Conciergerie, Palais de Justice (16)
1296–1313, 1350–1353, 1783–1786
quai de l'Horloge, quai de la Corse,
boulevard du Palais / 1er
Enguerrand de Marigny, Pierre
Desmaisons, Jacques-Denis Antoine,
Salomon de Brosse (Grande Salle)

The present-day palace of justice enjoys a long history dating back to pre-Christian times. After the Celts had fortified the island on the Seine River, the Romans settled on the left bank and built a stone wall around the island in the 3rd century to secure the governor's palace occasionally used by the Emperors Valentinus and Julianus Apostata. The site became the cradle of the French monarchy under the Merovingian dynasty.

Saint-Germain-des-Prés (15) (refectory)
between 1238 and 1245
16, rue de l'Abbaye,
3, place Saint-Germain-des-Prés / 6e
Pierre de Montreuil

Only a few parts of the mediaeval Saint-Germain-des-Prés abbey (no. 5) have survived. After the abbey's demise during the Religious Wars, the reform of

Under the Capetians, the royal residence reached the peak of its glory as Louis IX had la Sainte-Chapelle (no. 34) erected in the middle of the palace. However, the significance of the building complex declined after the Royal House moved to the Louvre (no. 49) in 1360. Henceforth, a concierge with judiciary power resided in the western section of the enormous complex.

The ground-floor rooms were converted into a prison in the early 15th century and Charles V consigned the complex to the Supreme Court of Justice in 1431. The building became notorious during the French Revolution as people were jailed here prior to being guillotined.

After the revolution, civil courts settled in the former royal residence. Damaged in several fires, today's palace of justice is the result of various extension and alteration work performed between the 17th and the 20th centuries. The oldest sections, most of which have been heavily restored, were built in the 14th century, however.

These include the large Salle des Gens d'Armes, which is divided by pillars that support cross-ribbed vaults. The adjacent Salle des Gardes is smaller but similar. The square kitchen fitted with four corner fireplaces was built in 1353 along with the adjoining clock tower. In the 19th century, a neo-Gothic wall built

to the north of the complex integrated this rectangular tower, as well as three medieval round towers.

Saint-Leu-Saint-Gilles (17)
1319, 1611, 1858–1861
92, rue Saint-Denis,
boulevard de Sébastopol / 1er
Victor Baltard

This High Gothic church is dedicated to two saints whose names are celebrated on September 1: Saint Leu, a bishop of Sens, and Saint Gilles, a hermit from southern Provence. The simple portico framed by columns is a remnant of the original building, the construction of which started in 1235. In the 16th century, the alteration of the six-bay hall built in 1319 resulted in a three-aisle basilica.

In 1860, the construction of Boulevard de Sébastopol required the shortening of the choir ambulatory built in 1611 and the remodeling of the east façade in the neo-Renaissance style. The strong contrast between the Early Gothic nave and the High Renaissance choir characterizes the interior. As no buttresses support the walls outside, it was necessary to reinforce the columns in the central aisle, which strongly emphasizes the importance of the bays and lends the nave a staccato-like rhythm.

Château de Vincennes   (18)
started in 1361
Vincennes / Val-de-Marne
Raymond du Temple (not verified)

This castle, built over four centuries, combines medieval military features and Baroque palatial elements to form an impressive ensemble. In the 11th century, the Crown acquired a forest – today's Bois de Vincennes – from the Saint-Maur Abbey. Louis IX (St. Louis, 1226–1270) had the forest fenced in to prevent disturbances during his hunting parties, and had a hunting lodge built. Philip VI (1328–1350) remodeled the small building into a castle. The 52-meter keep with round towers at either side was built at that time. Charles V (1364–1380) developed the castle into one of Europe's largest fortified dwellings. In 1379, he also had a royal chapel built here in the same Flamboyant Gothic style as the Sainte-Chapelle on the Île de la Cité (no. 34). Because the church was not completed until 1552, it also incorporates Renaissance elements, such as the pictures on the stained-glass windows in the choir.

Vincennes castle was later used to jail opponents of the Crown. Cardinal Mazarin commissioned Louis le Vau to convert it into a stately residence between 1654 and 1661. Louis XIV and Maria Theresa of Austria spent their honeymoon in le Vau's symmetrical buildings, called the King's and the Queen's Pavilions. The Sun King soon lost interest in Vincennes, however, and concentrated on his favorite residence, Versailles (no. 98). Napoleon converted the castle into an arsenal and his nephew, Napoleon III, had it restored by Viollet-le-Duc.

Notre Dame – a paradigm of Gothic architecture (19)

Like the Eiffel tower (no. 218), Notre Dame cathedral on the Île de la Cité is among Paris's major landmarks. Many people associate the building – the seat of the archbishop of Paris – with Victor Hugo's novel, or its film and theatrical adaptations, and with its mismatched protagonists, the hunchbacked bell-ringer Quasimodo and the beautiful gypsy Esmeralda.

Notre Dame is one of the most important Early Gothic works. Pope Alexander III was in attendance in 1163 when the bishop of Paris, Maurice de Sully, laid the cornerstone of a church that was intended to compete with Saint-Denis Basilica (no. 11). The cathedral was built from east to west over nearly one hundred years, incorporating and advancing the latest developments in French Gothic architecture. With a length of 127 meters and a vault height of thirty-five meters, Notre Dame outshone all the earlier cathedrals in the Île-de-France region by far.

The construction was made possible by the generous patronage of the burghers, the guilds and the crown, which counted on the superlative construction to add to its own prestige.

The plan is that of a five-aisle basilica, with the lateral aisles continuing across the transept as ambulatories. It is unusually compact due to the short transept arms, which barely extend past the walls of the nave and choir, and to the position of the side chapels between the buttresses. Yet this plan was to serve as the model for many Paris churches into the 17th century.

The choir ambulatory (1163–1182) features compound piers that support sexpartite ribbed vaults typical of the Early Gothic style.

However, the visual and structural coherence of the ensemble is evident only at the upper elements of the arcades, as the base is not typically Gothic. Furthermore, the plain wall surfaces of the

The nave towards the choir

gallery that replaces the triforium recall the cathedrals of Sens and Laon. The four-story elevation taken from those churches was altered in the course of the centuries. In 1240, the merging of the clerestory windows with the round windows of the gallery resulted in large, two-paneled tracery windows. Viollet-le-Duc restored the original design on the transept and the eastern bays of the nave, however.

The towers (1200–1250) owe their imposing aspect not least to a simple composition that integrates finely balanced vertical and horizontal elements. Their buttresses structure the façade into three vertical strips that echo the horizontal structure of the three portals, the royal gallery with a rose window between a pair of two-light windows, and the tracery arcade connecting the upper stories of the towers. Flying buttresses dominate the rest of the exterior.

The rose windows of the west front and the transept façades display the radial tracery that gives the Gothic rayonnant style its name. The sculptures, most of which had been removed before the French Revolution, were replaced during the restoration work directed by Viollet-le-Duc in the mid-19th century. Some of the originals are in the Hôtel de Cluny (no. 31).

23

Notre Dame – view of the early Gothic choir

Bastille (20)

started in 1370
place de la Bastille / 4e, 11e, 12e

DEMOLITION Charles V built the Bastille, or "small bastion" to reinforce the city walls, and his successor further developed the stronghold. By 1382, it had become a powerful fortress with eight towers.

Cardinal Richelieu was the first to use the Bastille as a prison for enemies of the Crown. Most of them were jailed without trial, but enjoyed exceptional conditions, including the right to have their own servants and to receive unlimited visitors. Among the political opponents and freethinkers jailed here were Voltaire, Mirabeau, Fouquet and the Marquis de Sade.

By 1789, the Bastille had become obsolete and its demolition was already planned. Nevertheless, on July 14, six hundred revolutionaries stormed the fortress – a hated symbol of absolutism. Although only seven petty prisoners were freed, the mob celebrated the event as a triumph. Bastille Day symbolically marked the outset of the French Revolution and became France's national holiday. The destruction of the building in the months that followed was another symbolic event. The only vestiges of the fortress are parts of the foundations visible in the Bastille metro station, numerous building stones re-used in the construction of the pont near Place de la Concorde (no. 121), and the partial outline of the fortress walls in the pavement at Place de la Bastille. On the occasion of the bicentennial of the Revolution in 1989, President François Mitterrand unveiled the nearby Opéra de la Bastille (no. 366).

Hôtel de Clisson (21)

around 1371
58, rue des Archives / 3e

Olivier de Clisson, commander in chief of the royal armies, had a mansion built here in 1371. Only the gateway remains from the original building, however, as the mansion was demolished in 1704 and replaced with the Hôtel de Rohan-Soubise (no. 99).

Two echauguettes of different diameters protuberate from the façade. The coat of arms of the Dukes of Guise, who purchased the building in 1553, hangs above the pointed arch of the portal. The medieval chapel has largely remained unaltered over the centuries, except for the paintings, by artists from the School of Fontainebleau, which have not been preserved.

Chapelle du Collège de Beauvais (22)

1375–1380
9, rue Jean-de-Beauvais / 5e
Raymond du Temple

In 1370, Jean de Dormans, bishop of Beauvais, founded a college for twelve scholars from his home village. If we consider the small number of students, the laying of the cornerstone by Charles V, the once opulent furnishings and the involvement of the greatest court artists

seem all the more surprising. The architect, for example, was none other than Raymond du Temple, who also worked on the Louvre (no. 49).

However, the building was demolished in 1881, so that the chapel consecrated in 1380 is the sole remnant of the former college. Its interior volume, polygonal choir and tracery works recall the Sainte-Chapelle (no. 34). The original wooden barrel vault that rests on sculpted corbels – a work by architect Jacques de Chartres – features elaborate foliage scrolls at its base. The Romanian orthodox community has been using the chapel since 1892. The iconostasis with silver-gilt icons is quite surprising in the Early Gothic interior.

11–13, rue François Miron (23)
before 1400, 1967
11–13, rue François-Miron / 4e

Presumably older than the "eldest house in Paris" (no. 71), these structures belong to the rare examples of half-timber houses in the French capital. The timber work which has been visible since the restoration in 1967, however, does not

correspond to the original condition as façades had to be entirely plastered for fire protection reasons in the Middle Ages. The residential houses are very narrow as only two windows open on to the street on each of the four or five floors. The triangular pediments indicate that the structures were erected in the 15th century as the construction of pediment houses was prohibited in Paris in the early 16th century.

Saint-Germain de Charonne (24)
around 1400, 1835–1839
4, place Saint-Blaise,
rue de Bagnolet / 20e

The late Gothic church rises at the point where in the year 429, while guarding sheep, six-year-old Genevieve is said to have met Germanus, then Bishop of Auxerre in Burgundy. The saint recognized the pious zeal of the child, gave her a copper cross and foretold her future sanctity.

The parish church of Charonne, formerly an autonomous village near Paris, stands on a hill at the center of a cemetery – a picturesque location in a city with several millions of inhabitants.

Only some columns are left over from the Romanesque church built in the 12th century. A rectangular choir and a massive 13th-century tower complement the nave erected in the 15th century.

Saint-Laurent (25)
1400–1429, around 1500, 1621
68, boulevard de Strasbourg / 10e

In 582, Gregory of Tours mentions a church dedicated to Saint Lawrence as one of city's six churches. Today's church includes a Romanesque tower and 15th-century additions: the five-

aisle nave with side chapels, the transept and the choir with its ambulatory. In the nave, the high position of the clerestory is the result of the exceptional height of the arcades.

The nave vaulting was added between 1655 and 1659. During the construction of Boulevard de Strasbourg in 1852–1865, a neo-Gothic façade with a richly adorned portal replaced the Renaissance front built in 1621 recalling that of Saint-Paul-Saint-Louis (no. 57).

Tour de Jean Sans Peur (26)
around 1407
20, rue Etienne-Marcel / 2e

The father of John the Fearless, the powerful Duke of Burgundy, had a mansion built in the French capital in 1375. However, only the tower of the building remains. The tympanum of its pointed-arch portal is adorned with the coat of arms of the House of Burgundy.

The plain tower, structured by simple cornices and irregularly distributed windows, shares certain similarities with the ducal palace built in Dijon, the Duke's capital, around the same time. Both buildings boast lavish interior decoration, however, including the branch-like patterns on the vault of the corkscrew staircase.

Maison du Nicolas Flamel (27)
1407
51, rue de Montmorency / 3e

The Parisian university scholar Nicolas Flamel and his wife Pernelle ordered the construction of this house – one of the oldest residential buildings in Paris – as a shelter for the homeless. As the inscription on the façade notes, the residents had to say the Lord's Prayer and a Hail Mary for the dead once daily in return for the roof over their heads.

Large rectangular doors and windows open on the first floor. Reliefs depicting prophets and angels with music instruments adorn the portions of wall between the openings, while high rectangular windows structure the upper stories.

Temple des Billettes (28)
(cloister)
1408–1427, 1755–1758
24, rue des Archives / 4e
Père Claude

In 1290, a Jew by the name of Jonathan allegedly tried to destroy a host, which subsequently started to bleed. Only nine years later, Philip the Fair handed over an Augustinian monastery built on the site of the miracle to the hospital monks known as "Les Billettes". A late Gothic

monastery was erected here in 1408 and complemented with a cloister in 1427.

Although modestly dimensioned and overlaid with clumsily shaped ribbed vaults, the Billettes cloister deserves attention as it is the only mediaeval covered walk preserved in the city. The original church was replaced between 1756 and 1758 by a plain building.

Saint-Nicolas-des-Champs (29)
1420–1480, 1576–1587, 1613–1615,
1745, 1823–1829
254, rue Saint-Martin, rue Réaumur / 3e

In the early 12th century, the Cluniac monks from the neighboring Saint-Martin-des-Champs abbey (no. 7) built a Romanesque church here. A new sacred building was erected between 1420 and 1620, so that today's church offers a panorama of the transition from the Late Gothic to the Renaissance style. The arches, for example, are pointed to the west, but round to the east. Moreover, the floor plan of the double choir ambulatory still recalls the Early Gothic style of Notre Dame (no. 19), while Renaissance architecture elements unfurl on the elevation. The ribbed vaults of the ambulatory rest on slender columns, but their crystalline clarity is far from the foliage scrolls common in Late Gothic works. The southern portal – designed

27

by Philbert Delormes, 1581 – is worth mentioning. The west façade featuring a main portal with an ogive arch is the oldest part of the building.

Hôtel de Sens (30)
1475–1507
1, rue du Figuier / 4e

Until 1622, Paris remained under the control of the archbishop of Sens, "primate of Gaul" according to a papal decree in the 12th century. Archbishop Tristan de Salazar underlined this special situation by building a stately residence in the capital of the kingdom of France. The various wings of the late Gothic building surround an irregularly shaped courtyard. Simple cornices frame the large mullioned windows on their upper part. The resulting up and down, as well as the lavishly adorned dormer windows, contributes to enliven the façades. Two watch turrets flank the fortified portal. Since 1961, the entirely refurbished building has been housing the Fornay library that concentrates on arts and crafts.

Hôtel de Cluny (31)
(Musée national du Moyen-Age)
between 1485 and 1510
6, place Paul-Painlevé / 5e

In 1330, Pierre de Chastellux, abbot of Cluny Abbey in Burgundy, bought the ruins of the Roman baths near the Sorbonne (no. 3) to have a college built there. Abbot Jacques d'Amboise had the modest building demolished after 1485 and replaced by an imposing residence. Together with the contemporary Hôtel de Sens (no. 30), the Hôtel de Cluny is a major example of profane architecture in Paris at the close of the Middle Ages. While the irregular floor plan and the lancet arches are still rooted in the Gothic style, the mullioned and transomed windows with simple profiles already show the influence of the Renaissance. The square chapel is particularly noteworthy for its exceptional quality: the ribs of its vault originate from a slim octagonal column and the apse features extensive glass surfaces. The almost entirely refurbished building has been housing the exquisite medieval collections of the Musée de Cluny since 1842.

Saint-Étienne-du-Mont (32)
1492–1626
1, place Saint-Geneviève / 5e
Etienne Viguier, Claude Guérin,
Victor Baltard

In the 13th century, monks of the Saint Geneviève monastery (Panthéon, no. 123) had established a parish church here. In the late Middle Ages, the rapid increase in the population made it necessary to build a larger building. The construction work started in 1492 in the east section but the west façade was not completed until 1622. Saint-Étienne-du-Mont, like many other buildings of the same period in Paris, features both Late Gothic and Renaissance stylistic elements. Although the floor plan follows that of Early Gothic cathedrals (Notre Dame, no. 19), the intricate forms of the Late Gothic are predominant in the interior decoration. In the nave, a pseudo-gallery extends between plain round columns. The choir screen, composed of a basket-handle arch and two spiral stairs, is particularly noteworthy. Its original design and exquisite quality preserved it from destruction, and it is the only jube that still exists in Paris. The keystone of the crossing, which hangs downwards on almost six meters, is another particular-

ity of the church. The west façade shows a rich mannerist décor. The philosopher Blaise Pascal and the dramatist Jean Baptiste Racine are buried in this church.

Saint-Gervais-et-Saint-Protais (33)
1494–1621
2, rue François-Miron / 4e
Salomon de Brosse, Clément II Métezeau

Like many other sacred buildings in Paris, this church dedicated to two martyrs of the Diocletian period combines an Early Gothic floor plan similar to that of Notre Dame (no. 19) with various Renaissance stylistic elements. In spite of the unusually long construction time, the Gothic interior appears to be homogenous. Stellar vaults extend from the middle ship to the ambulatory with radiating chapels. The main façade, built in 1616 to plans by Salomon de Brosse and Clément II Métezeau, shows the influence of Early Classicism and became a model for many Parisian church fronts. On the three-story façade topped with a segmental pediment, pairs of fluted columns feature capitals that integrate elements from the three Classical orders: Doric on the base, Ionic in the middle, and Corinthian at the top. This arrangement – also found at the Saint-Roche (no. 72) and Saint-Paul-Saint-Louis churches (no. 57) – was first used in the region on the Anet château built in 1547–1552 to plans by Philibert Delorme.

29

Sainte-Chapelle – the glass casket of the kings (34)

In the Middle Ages, the "Holy Chapel" was the heart of the Royal palace – a magnificent complex developed on the left bank by Louis IX (today's Palais de Justice, no. 16).

Two major transactions of the mediaeval reliquary trade led to the construction of a Chapel Royal. The first of them was the acquisition of Jesus Christ's crown of thorns by the king of France from Baldwin II, the Byzantine emperor, for 135,000 pounds.

As the relic arrived in Paris in 1239, Louis IX humbly laid it to rest in Notre Dame (no. 19). Only when crucifixion nails and wooden particles from the Holy Cross were purchased thanks to the intervention of the Knights Templar did the King, who was eventually canonized, decide to build a chapel to house the relics.

Their transferal from the cathedral to the royal palace – a private building – empowered the belief that Christ himself had crowned the Kings of France, as claimed by Pope Innocent IV in 1244.

Despite its being used as an archive for a while, the Early Gothic building consecrated on 26 April 1248 has remained largely unaltered over the centuries.

Slender columns which support a high ribbed vault structure the lower chapel dedicated to the Virgin Mary. The narrow aisles form an ambulatory that surrounds the choir. Even though the ceilings are low here, an opulently painted and gilded decoration creates an exquisite atmosphere.

The decoration achieves unparalleled splendor in the upper chapel, which was reserved for the Royal Family and ecclesiastic dignitaries. The slender ribbed vaulting rests upon delicate compound columns.

Above the plinth and its blind arcade, high tracery bays extend between the columns to reach the ceiling. Details in the design of the windows suggest that they were created by an artist who had previously worked on Amiens cathedral. On the exterior, fourteen buttresses and a system of ring anchors and iron reinforcements make the building's filigree structure possible.

The atmosphere inside the upper chapel, which mediaeval chroniclers described as "paradisiacal" is the result of the stained-glass windows that fracture the incidental light into a rich play

Inside the upper chapel

of colors dominated by shades of blue and red. A total of 1134 scenes illustrate the Bible Story on an area of approximately 620 square meters. About two thirds of the panes are originals from the 13th century; the remainder were reconstructed in the 19th century during refurbishment works that also included all paintings and sculptures.

Life-size figures of the twelve apostles guard the compound columns. Their position inside the building – unusual by French standards – as well as the edifice's short length (only thirty-three meters) and meticulous interior decoration cast la Sainte-Chapelle as a monumental reliquary.

Despite the exquisite quality of both the architecture and the interior decoration, the building costs were lower than the purchase price of the relics preserved today at Notre Dame (no. 19).

Sainte-Chapelle, a monumental reliquary

Tour Saint-Jacques (35)
1508–1522
place de la Tour Saint-Jacques,
rue de Rivoli / 4e
Jean de Félin, Théodore Ballu

The Late Gothic tower is the last remnant of a church built in the 11th century in the heavily-populated Grand Châtelet borough, on a pilgrims' way to Santiago de Compostela.

As the parish church of the butchers' guild, the building was altered in the 13th and 14th centuries, and Jean de Félin added the elegant steeple tower between 1508 and 1522. Four corner buttresses strengthen the steeple. High lancet openings enable the sound of the bells to propagate outside. Intricate tracery reinforces the impression of lightness that radiates from the tower. During the French Revolution, the church was among the many medieval sacred buildings that were sold and pulled down to reuse the stones.

Saint-Merri (36)
1515–1612, 1743
78, rue Saint-Martin,
76, rue de la Verrerie / 4e
Martin Chambiges, Pierre Anglart,
Germain Boffrand

Near the end of his life, Medericus, the abbot of Saint-Martin Abbey in Autun, Burgundy, made a pilgrimage to the relics of Saint Germanus, former bishop of Paris. Marked by his malady, Medericus lived in a small cell on the outskirts of the city.

When he died there in the year 700, he was buried in a nearby chapel dedicated to Saint Peter. In 884, his relics were transferred to a church built on the site of his cell. Due to the increasing number of pilgrims to the grave of the patron of the Right Bank, it became necessary to extend the Late Carolingian building. The church of Saint-Merri, as it stands today, was built in 1515 to plans by Martin Chambiges. Its floor plan copies on a smaller scale that of Notre Dame (no. 19). In the nave, a rich frieze with animals and floral motifs separates the arcades from the clerestory with its large tracery windows. Various architecture elements – vaulting shafts without capitals, sharp-edged profiles and linear forms of the tracery – are typical of the Late Gothic style. The choir was redesigned in the 18th century.

Saint-Eustache   (37)
1532–1640, 1754, 1844
1, rue du Jour, rue Montmartre / 1er
Pierre Lemercier (not verified), Jean
Hardouin-Mansart de Jouy, Victor Baltard

Saint-Eustache, the former market trad-
ers' parish church, impressively combines Gothic and Renaissance architectural elements – a common synthesis in
French religious architecture of the late
16th and early 17th centuries. In 1213,
a chapel dedicated to Saint Agnes was
built near the Covered Markets.

In the late Middle Ages, the structure was extended and dedicated to
Saint Eustachius, a Christian martyr.
As the church grew too small, noblemen patronized the construction of a
new building, the cornerstone of which
was laid in 1532. The French Wars of
Religion interrupted the construction,
however, and the works only really begun in the 17th century. Nonetheless,
the original plans – probably by Pierre
Lemercier the Elder – remained almost
unaltered and were carried out without
far-reaching modifications. The church
was consecrated in 1637 prior termination of the construction works, and the
main façade was set up in early Classical

style between 1754 and 1788. Just like
Notre Dame (no. 19), Saint-Eustache is a
five-nave basilica with a transept ranging
within the alignments and a choir ambulatory that gives access to radial chapels.
The proportions, the side chapels, the flying buttresses and the verticality of the
interior also recall Notre Dame, whose
construction started in 1163.

Saint-Eustache, however, revisits the
late 12th-century design using forms related to the Renaissance. In the nave, for
example, the vaulting shafts have been
replaced by pilasters that end as fluted
pillars in the triforium and the clerestory, while Classical capitals replace the
Gothic composite capitals. Moreover,
pointed arches gave way to round arches with fascias, and aedicule-like frames
complement the triforium. At the same
time, however, Saint-Eustache also features typical Late Gothic elements such
as stellar vaults over bundled capitals
and tracery windows with flamboyant
forms.

The harmonious blending of elements
from two radically different styles confers
an outstanding position onto Saint-Eustache among Parisian architectural history. Viollet-le-Duc's verdict of a "Gothic
skeleton dressed in Roman rags held."

Absolutist splendor: Renaissance, Baroque and Palladian style (38)

The Hundred Years' War against England (1339–1453) and the resulting troubles, revolts, famines and epidemics lamed building activity in Paris at the end of the Middle Ages. Like his predecessors, Francis I (1515–1547) did not reside in his capital city. However, after his successful campaigns in Italy, he had Italian artists decorate the new Château de Fontainebleau, thus introducing the Renaissance and the Mannerist style in France. Pierre Lescot had a leading role among French Renaissance architects. His works inspired by classical models include the Hôtel Carnavalet (no. 40), the Fontaine des Innocents (no. 39) and the transformation of the Louvre (no. 49), beginning in 1546, from a medieval castle into a stately royal residence. But while the new style rapidly became popular for secular buildings, the late Gothic forms remained de rigueur for churches until the 17th century, even though Saint-Eustache (no. 37), Saint-Roch (no. 72) and Saint-Sulpice (no. 68), inspired by the Early Gothic style of Notre Dame (no. 19), began to incorporate some Renaissance elements.

Henry IV (1589–1610), the first king of the Bourbon dynasty, who acceded to the throne after the Wars of Religion, initiated urban development projects in the Renaissance style. Ensembles with regular shapes, unified façades and constant heights, such as Place des Vosges (no. 45) and Place Dauphine (no. 47), embodied the architecture ideal of the time and marked the birth of modern urban planning in France. At the same time, growing numbers of noblemen began to have city mansions built in the capital.

Numerous churches and convents were built in the city as the Counter-Reformation spread in the 17th century. The Saint-Paul-et-Saint-Louis church (no. 57), for example, begun in 1627, was the first of a series of sacred buildings patterned after Roman churches. However, the Val-de-Grâce (no. 67) remained one of the rare Paris churches to incorporate the dynamism, plasticity and wealth of ornament typical of the Italian Baroque. Indeed, French architecture of that time favored the monumentality of Baroque Classicism, a style

*right: "The Birth of Venus",
painting by François Boucher,
around 1750, (detail)*

inspired by ancient Rome and the Italian Renaissance (the Palais du Luxembourg, no. 52) is a perfect example here.

As in England and the northern Netherlands, Classicism proper developed on the basis of the writings and designs of Andrea Palladio, and culminated during the reign of Louis XIV (1643–1715), when it became compulsory for all royal commissions. As a result, the regularity of the rhythmical elements on the extension of Versailles (no. 98), built to plans by Le Vau and Hardouin-Mansart beginning in 1668, borders on monotony. Moreover, the fact that Perrault's Palladian building was preferred to Bernini's Baroque design for the east façade of the Louvre (no. 49) is evidence of the dogmatic character of Louis XIV's "state style". The Hôtel des Invalides (no. 85), originally conceived as the mausoleum of the Sun King, replaced the longitudinal dimension inherited from the Gothic tradition with a monumental and clearly structured central building. The hospice for disabled veterans that is part of the Invalides complex, as well as the Arsenal converted into a large hospital, are examples of Louis XIV's social welfare projects. Moreover, a comprehensive urban development project initiated by the Sun King provided for demolition of the medieval city walls and their replacement by a ring boulevard lined with trees, while massive triumphal arches replaced the former gates at Porte Saint-Denis (no. 86) and Porte Saint-Martin (no. 88).

Last but not least, prestigious aristocratic dwellings were built on monumental new squares such as Place des Victoires (no. 92) and Place Vendôme (no. 95). A new taste in architecture became fashionable after the death of Louis XIV. Under his successor Louis XV (1715–1774), the stately monumentality of Classicism gave way to the intimate elegance of the Rococo. This style's asymmetrical ornaments dominated the second quarter of the 18th century, but fell out of fashion after 1750, as rhythmic and decorative elements became ever rarer. This "bare Rococo" formed a transition to the neo-Classical achievements of Ange-Jacques Gabriel at Versailles and the Petit Trianon.

Fontaine des Innocents (39)
1547–1549
place Joachim-du-Bellay, rue Berger / 1er
Pierre Lescot (not verified)

Originally, this fountain was an extension to the Church of the Innocents. It was rectangular and served as a platform during parades coming from Rue Saint-Denis. After demolition of the church in 1788, the fountain was moved to today's Place des Innocents. On this occasion, 16th-century architect Pierre Lescot added a fourth arch to the original structure to form a square construction. The fountain was moved again in the 19th century, placed in the middle of a basin atop a pedestal shaped like a round flight of stairs, and topped with a cupola.

The spire-like construction as it stands today still features the ornaments of the original fountain. Pairs of fluted pilasters with Corinthian capitals flank each of the four round arches with fascias. Curiously, the entablature is only crimped in its lower part. It carries a shallow attic story crowned by delicate triangular pediments. Numerous reliefs by Jean Goujon adorn the walls between the structural elements. Particularly noteworthy are the nymphs that show the influence of the School of Fontainebleau: their vestment adapted from Classical models is reminiscent of works by Primaticcio and Rosso Fiorentino. Goujon also created the rectangular reliefs in the pedestal and the attic story, as well as the victories in the spandrels.

Hôtel Carnavalet (40)
(Bijouterie Georges Fouquet)
1548–1550, 1654
23, rue de Sévigné,
14–18, rue des Francs-Bourgeois / 3e
Pierre Lescot, Nicolas Dupuis,
François Mansart

Jacques de Ligneris, President of the Parliament, had this building erected between 1548 and 1550 by master mason Nicolas Dupuis to plans by Pierre Lescot. The complex consists of four wings grouped around a rectangular courtyard. Originally, all the façades were plain, except for that of the side wings with round arches, which were divided by pilasters adorned with bas-relief allegories of the Four Seasons and signs of the Zodiac, works by Jean Goujon. In 1648, François Mansart remodeled the building, giving it its present appearance: he added the central staircase and built the front and side wings higher.

Today the Hôtel Carnavalet houses the museum of the history of Paris. The museum's collection includes architectural elements and furnishings from 17th and 18th-century Parisian city mansions that have been demolished.

Palais des Tuileries   (41)
1564–1572
place du Louvre, quai des Tuileries / 1er
Philibert Delorme

DEMOLITION Rubbish heaps and brick-works were once found west of the Louvre (no. 49). In 1564, Catherine de' Medici had Philibert Delorme begin construction of a palace here. But after her court astrologer predicted she would soon die "near Saint-Germain," the widowed queen closed down the building site, which was not far from the church of Saint-Germain-l'Auxerrois (no. 12). After Catherine's death, Henry IV ordered the palace completed as an extension of the Louvre complex. Louis XVI, driven out of Versailles (no. 98) by the people of Paris in 1789, spent his last years in the Tuileries Palace. Napoleon and his successors also resided there from 1800 to 1848. In 1871, during the fall of the Paris Commune, rebels set fire to the complex. The reconstruction plans for the Castle Tuillerien failed in 1882 because of only one dissenting vote, but are being discussed again at present. The burnt-out ruins were finally demolished in 1883. Since then, the Louvre courtyard has remained open to the west on the Tuileries Garden, laid out by André Le Nôtre in 1664. In recent years, the architects Benech, Cribier and Roubeaud largely reconstructed the baroque garden, reversing 19th-century alterations. The orangery built by Louis Visconti on Place de la Concorde according to plans by Firmin Bourgeois (1853) and its counterpart, the Jeu de Paume (1851) have remained intact. Today, both are museums. The former ball house Jeu de Paume was redesigned by Antoine Stinco. The Musee de l'Orangerie was rebuilt in the 1960s by Olivier Lahalle, and in 2006 the Brochet Lajus Pueyo office executed the interior design.

Pont Neuf   (42)
1578–1607
Seine / 1er, 6e
Baptiste Androuet Ducerceau

The extension of the Louvre (no. 49) and the growing population of the Faubourg Saint-Germain made another bridge over the Seine necessary.

In 1578, Henry III laid the cornerstone of the "New Bridge" – now the oldest bridge in Paris. With a total length of 330 meters, the bridge spans both arms of the river near the northwest tip of the Île de la Cité. It was the first bridge in Paris that was not built upon, so that the view remained unobstructed from the Conciergerie (no. 16) to the new royal residence. The carriageway was lined by raised pavements that quickly became a popular place for a stroll. Vendors set up stalls in the semicircular bastions over the piers. On the island, the bridge widens to a bastion-like square on the west side.

Hôtel de Lamoignon /   (43)
Hôtel d'Angoulême
around 1600
24, rue Pavée / 4e
Jean-Baptiste Ducerceau (not verified),
Thibault Métezeau (not verified)

Like the Hôtel Carnavalet (no. 40) across the street, the Hôtel de Lamoignon, built fifty years later, is one of the most important Renaissance city mansions in Paris. Built for Henry II's illegitimate daughter Diane de France, duchess of Angoulême, the mansion changed hands several times after the princess death. The complex was expanded in the 18th and 19th centuries, and since 1968 it has housed the historical library of Paris.

The corps de logis, flanked by secondary wings, is an early example of a colossal order: pilasters unite the two main stories of the façade. The square corner turrets are reminiscent of medieval military architecture.

Bibliothèque de l'Arsenal (44)
around 1600, 1718–1725
1–3, rue de Sully / 4e
Philibert Delorme, Germain Boffrand

In 1594, Henry IV had an armory and gunpowder factory built on the outskirts of the city due to the risk of explosion. Under Louis XIII, the facilities were relocated to the Salpêtrière (no. 75) on the left bank. The royal foundry produced

not only weapons, but also bronze sculptures, in particular for Versailles Palace (no. 98). In the late 18th century, the building was converted into a library that became an important meeting place of French writers in the following decades. The elongated two-story structure owes its present form to numerous modifications of the original building. One bedroom, a staircase and an oratory still feature the rich interior decorations created between 1637 and 1640. From 1718 to 1725, Germain Boffrand redesigned the narrow northeast façade and added a rusticated portal topped with a window and its aedicular frame.

Place des Vosges (45)
1605–1612
place des Vosges / 4e
Androuet Ducerceau, Claude (de) Chastillon, Louis Métezeau

This geometric square of 108 meters on a side was built under Henry IV and originally called "Place Royale". It constitutes a unique ensemble made of thirty-six perfectly matching brick-and-stone façades. Red brick surfaces framed in light-yellow limestone quoins are a typical motif in Parisian secular architecture of the late Renaissance. The present name of the square honors the inhabitants of the Vosges mountains, who were the first to pay their taxes to the young Republic after the French Revolution.

40

Hôtel de Mayenne (46)
1606–1609, 1707–1709
21, rue Saint-Antoine / 4e
Jacques II oder Jean Androuet
Ducerceaus (Du Cerceau), Germain
Boffrand

This building, developed by Henri de Lorraine, duke of Mayenne, is one of the earliest examples of the city mansions built in Paris by aristocrats over the course of the 17th century: two low wings (communs) flank the main wing (corps de logis). On the street side, the wings end in corner pavilions connected by a low gateway which encloses the cour d'honneur.

Since Germain Boffrand remodeled the mansion in 1709, only the engravings by Jean Ducerceau convey an impression of the rich original façade that included Ionic pilasters and various types of pediments. The largely restored brick-and-stone corps de logis is typical of the late Renaissance

Place Dauphine (47)
1607–1619
place Dauphine (Île de la Cité) / 1er
Louis Métezeau (not verified)

This square was developed together with the Pont Neuf (no. 42) and named for the crown prince (the dauphin, later Louis XIII) born in 1601. To the west, its triangular shape follows the contours of the downstream end of the Île de la Cité.

Only the two buildings at the tip of the triangle remain of the original 16th-century development, however. The four-story brick-and-stone façades – similar to those around Place des Vosges (no. 45), which were built a few years earlier – feature a series of round arches on the ground

floor. Slab-shaped chimneys and dormer windows with round pediments enliven the rooflines.

Hôpital Saint-Louis (48)
1607–1612
40, rue Bichat,
2, place du Docteur-Fournier,
1, avenue Claude Vellefaux / 10e
Claude (de) Chastillon (not verified),
Claude Vellefaux

In 1607, Henry IV founded this hospital for the care of plague victims. The complex of four wings encloses a courtyard of 120 lateral length.

The two-story buildings connect eight tower-like pavilions and feature the brick-and-stone façade typical of the period. The chapel, a work by Claude Vellefaux, has a barrel-vaulted hall, a rib-vaulted transept and a semicircular apse.

Its buttresses and simple cross-sectional façade give it a strongly medieval flair.

41

The Louvre – from fortress to mega-museum (49)

Too often the Louvre, one of the world's premiere museums, is immediately associated with works like Leonardo's Mona Lisa, the Venus de Milo and the Winged Victory of Samothrace. However, these are just the most prominent pieces in a collection of 35,000 works of art covering 55,000 square meters – a treasure that attracts more than five million visitors a year. But before becoming a museum, the Louvre was a royal residence developed over several centuries, from the early Middle Ages until the court moved to Versailles (no. 98) in the late 17th century. The numerous enlargements performed over this long period make the Louvre a major ensemble of the Renaissance and the Baroque eras. Complementary building projects were undertaken even after the former royal palace had been converted into a museum in the 19th century.

Around 1200, King Philipp II August (1180–1223) had a fortress built to control traffic on the Seine. Four powerful corner towers reinforced this four-winged castle with a keep at its center. Charles V (1364–1380) had his ancestor's fortress converted into a more comfortable palace around 1370. Francis I (1515–1547) ordered a drastic enlargement and conversion of the medieval structure in 1528: he had the keep demolished and a part of the Louvre modernized. In 1546, he even decided to replace the existing buildings one after another with new structures built on the same foundations. Pierre Lescot designed the west wing that today represents the oldest example of the Renaissance style in Paris. However, this two-story structure was only built under the reign of the next king, Henry II (1547–1559). Because the king insisted on having a ballroom in the basement, the architect had to place the staircase at the extremity of the north wing, concealing it behind a projection of the façade. Another projection was added to the south for the sake of symmetry, so that three projections flanked by pairs of columns enliven the façade adorned with pilasters. Attic stories with segmental pediments top the projections. In 1555, an alteration of the original design extended the mezzanine story all along the façade, with exquisite bas-reliefs by Jean Goujon and his workshop.

Although the west wing clearly shows the influence of Sebastiano Serlio and various Italian artists of the School of Fontainebleau, it includes typical elements of the French Renaissance, such as the paired columns that adorn the projections, which are also found at the contemporary châteaux of Écouen and Anet. Moreover, there are no Italian models for the sculptures on the mezzanine story or the acanthus leaves on the cornice. Lescot also built a four-story pavilion to the south of the west wing to house the apartments of Henry II. Because this Renaissance building clashed with the neighboring palace, a mezzanine story was added around 1555. Construction of the south wing began under Henry II in a style that matches that of the west wing. The works continued under the reign of Charles IX (1560–1574), and the shell construction was completed under Henry III (1574–1589).

The ornamentation of the building was completed in 1594, and the same year Henry IV (1589–1610) decided to unify the appearance of the Louvre, quadrupling its total spread. But this expansion would only be completed in the 17th century because the king had in the meantime turned to a different project. In 1594, Henry IV decided to finish a gallery leading to the Seine, located at the start of a structural connec-

43

Between Seine and Place du Carrousel

The main entrance within the pyramid

View towards the former Tuileries Palace

tion to the Tuileries (no. 41), built in 1564 for Catherine de' Medici, and which was already begun in 1568 by Charles IX. The already completed access to the arcades was expanded by an additional story to become the so-called 'Petite Galerie,' whose original appearance received a touch of Jean Marot's style. This building, replaced by the 'Galerie d' Apollon' after a fire in 1661, was connected to the floral pavilion of the Tuileries by the 'Grande Galerie' running along the Seine. Contemporary sources point to Louis Métezeau und Jacques II as probable architects of this wing characterized by two bordering elevation systems.

Louis XIII (1610–1643) concentrated on the extension of the west wing already planned by his father. He entrusted the works to Jacques Lemercier, who designed the Baroque Clock Pavilion and a wing that copies the Renaissance style of Lescot's façade for the sake of symmetry. Louis XIV (1643–1715) developed three other wings in the same style, enclosing the Cour Carrée, or square courtyard. However, the king had the plans altered in 1665 before completion of the building works and an architecture competition organized for the

development of a more sumptuous façade to the east. The participation of international architects influenced French architecture for decades to come.

Gian Lorenzo Bernini, the architect of Saint Peter's Basilica in Rome, came to Paris at the invitation of Louis XIV and submitted two designs characterized by colossal pilasters and columns over a rusticated base. One variant was an oval pavilion flanked by two concave wings, while the other was based on a typically Baroque block. Although Bernini's designs made concessions to the French taste of the time, the king rejected them in favor of a project submitted by Claude Perrault, Louis Le Vau and Charles Lebrun that was implemented beginning in 1667. The French architects took over some elements of Bernini's second design, however, including the colonnades, the unstructured base and the "un-French" flat roof. The extension by Perrault and his colleagues also had a far-reaching influence on French architecture: Classicism thus affirmed its supremacy over the Baroque and became the official style of the French absolutist monarchy. From 1668 on, this style was reproduced with little alteration at Versailles (no. 98).

When the king and his court moved to the new palace in 1678, space became available in the Louvre, and was used to house academies and artists' workshops. In 1793, the revolutionary government converted the building into a Museum of the Republic, which became the Napoleon Museum ten years later. After his coronation as emperor in 1804, Napoleon ordered

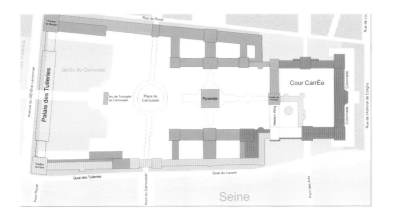

the construction of a pendant to Henry IV's Great Gallery along the new Rue de Rivoli, making the Tuileries Palace (no. 41) a three-winged ensemble. Furthermore, Napoleon had the Carrousel triumphal arch erected on the central axis of both the Louvre and the Tuileries. Napoleon III (1852–1870) had two similar structures built between the Cour Carrée and Place du Carrousel, thus closing the Louvre ensemble. As a fitting expression of his power, Napoleon III had Louis Visconti design the new buildings in the neo-Baroque style. A fire destroyed the Tuileries Palace during the Paris Commune in 1871, and the ruins were removed in 1882, opening a vista along the Champs-Élysées (no. 80) to Place de l'Étoile (no. 158). In the 1980s, President François Mitterand initiated the ambitious "Grand Louvre" project, aimed at further developing the historic ensemble.

Because all of the existing buildings were under preservation orders, the exhibition area could only be increased by building underground.

A glass pyramid provides the lobby and entrance areas with natural light, however. This design by the Chinese-born American architect Ieoh Ming Pei was highy controversial, and there were fears that it would impair the westward vista. Only gradually did the carefully inserted new additions built with the help of Michel Macary (SCAU) between 1982 and 1989 find acceptance.

Nevertheless, the public gradually accepted the modernist pyramid, partly because the excavation for the underground extension revealed remnants of the foundations of the city wall erected by Philip II August, the king who had begun the Louvre in the 12th century. The cycle was thus complete, and the modern Louvre had re-established contact with its origins. The redesign completed in the 1990s included underground workshops and laboratories of the Musée de France (Jérôme Brunet und Eric Saunier) as well as refitting of Cafés Richelieu (Jean-Marie Wilmotte) and Marly (Yves Taralon, Olivier Gagnère), both overlooking the Cour Napoléon. Under the current building conditions, the redesign of the Islam collection started in 2005 by Mario Bellini and Rudy Riccionti is very apparent. Lighting is provided by a "flying" carpet that appears to float over the Visconti courtyard. The independent Musée des Arts décoratifs located in the Marsan Pavilion was redesigned in 2008 by Oscar Tusquets, Bruno Moinard, Sylvain Dubuisson, Daniel Kahane and François-Joseph Graf. The associated restaurant "Saut du Loup" was created by Philippe Baisselier. The Office de tourisme in the Carrousel du Louvre was designed by soa architectes in 2008.

Saint-Joseph des Carmes (50)
1613–1620
70–72, rue de Vaugirard / 6e

The oldest settlement of the reformed Carmelite order in France owes its founding to an initiative of Pope Paul V, who sent monks to Paris in the early 17th century. In 1613, Marie de' Medici, the widow of Henry IV, laid the cornerstone for a church whose architecture was to reflect the order's and the queen's Italian origins.

The building is most likely the work of an Italian architect. Like Santa Maria della Vittoria, the church of the Carmelite headquarters in Rome, it features a transept and a drum cupola over the crossing, while the barrel vault rests on rectangular embedded piers.

Saint-Joseph des Carmes became an infamous prison during the French Revolution, when more than one hundred bishops and priests from all parts of France were jailed there. Those who refused to swear allegiance to the constitution were brutally murdered in the abbey garden.

Pont Marie (51)
1614–1635
Île Saint-Louis, quai des Celestins / 4e

In 1614, Cardinal de Richelieu ordered a channel filled in to make one island – Île Saint-Louis – out of two isles in the Seine. The Pont Marie was the first bridge to connect the island with the right bank. It was originally a five-span bridge bearing a row of houses on either side of the carriageway.

Two spans destroyed in a flood in 1658 were rebuilt by 1670, but without the houses. For the next century, the bridge had an unusual profile, with buildings on the half towards the bank and none on the half towards the island. It acquired its modern appearance in 1788, when the remaining houses were demolished after a royal edict had prohibited buildings on bridges.

Palais du Luxembourg (52)
1615–1631, 1799–1805, 1835–1841
15, rue de Vaugirard / 6e
Salomon de Brosse,
Jean-François Chalgrin, Alphonse de Gisors

After the assassination of Henry IV, Marie de' Medici, the queen widow, gave up her residence in the Louvre (no. 49). In 1612 she bought the city mansion of François de Luxembourg, which she had demolished and replaced with a splendid new palace.

The three-winged complex by Salomon de Brosse, begun in 1615, merges the French Renaissance tradition of palatial architecture with elements from Florence's Pitti Palace. It takes from the latter building the severe horizontal lines, the blind arcades on the ground floor, and the rusticated masonry of the columns and pilasters. Although the Luxembourg Palace was built on the threshold of the Classical period, these formal references mark the building as a late representative of Renaissance architecture.

The mighty Cardinal de Richelieu forced the queen widow to leave Paris before she could take up residence in her new palace, however. In the early 19th century, Jean-François Chalgrin remodeled the interior and the garden for Napoleon in the neo-Classical style. The Senate has met here ever since, while the lower house of the French parlia-

ment, the National Assembly, is located in the Palais Bourbon (no. 127).

Oratoire du Louvre (53)
1621–1630
145, rue Saint-Honoré, rue de Rivoli,
4, rue de l'Oratoire / 1er
Clément II Métezeau, Jacques Lemercier

In 1552 in Rome, Filippo Neri founded the Congregation of the Oratory, a religious order dedicated to teaching and preaching. In 1611, Pierre de Bérulle founded a similar order in Paris with the help of Marie de' Medici, the Congrégation de l'Oratoire de France. In 1621, Clément Métezeau the Elder began to erect a church for the new order to plans by Jacques Lemercier. Chapels surmounted by galleries complement the barrel-vaulted nave. An indepen-

dent oval choir where the monks once had their pews stands behind the semicircular apse.

Louis XIII made the oratory the royal chapel even before the building was completed. The church is oriented toward the Louvre, the royal palace, which is why the façade, built by Pierre Caqué between 1745 and 1750, does not stand parallel to the street.

Hôtel de Sully (54)
1625–1630
62, rue Saint-Antoine / 4e
Jean I Androuet Ducerceau

In 1624, Finance Inspector Mesme Gallet had Jean-Baptiste Ducerceau build one of the most superb city mansions in the Marais. Maximilien de Béthune, Duke of Sully, Henry IV's Minister of Finances, acquired the building in 1634, just a few years after its completion. Two side wings that end in lower pavilions near the street enclose the three-story corps de logis. On the street façade, a segmental pediment unites the pavilions' three vertical axes. The main façade features

an exceptionally lively structure: precisely cut rusticated ashlars frame the windows placed at different intervals. Triangular and segmental pediments top the windows, doors and dormer windows. The opulent sculptural decoration is unusual for Parisian buildings of the early Classical period. Another structure built in the garden in 1628, the Petit Hôtel de Sully, served as an orangery and an art gallery.

Saint-Nicolas du Chardonnet (55)
1625, 1656–1667
26, rue Saint-Victor / 5e
François Levé, Michel Noblet,
Charles Lebrun

In 1230 a chapel was built near the Seine on a field covered with thistles (French: chardons). Because many bargemen lived in the vicinity, the building was dedicated to their patron, Saint Nicholas. The tower built in 1625 recalls the original Gothic building, which was demolished and replaced in 1656 by a structure designed by François Levé and Michel Noblet. Although the choir was consecrated in 1667, the construction works were repeatedly interrupted and the neo-Baroque façade was not completed until 1934.

The church's floor plan – three naves, a short transept and an ambulatory with radial chapels – is common to many Paris churches. The attic story between the arcades and the base of the barrel vault is quite exceptional, however. The plain exterior appearance contrasts with the quality of the paintings that adorn the interior. These include works by Charles Lebrun, whose tomb is located in the choir.

Sainte-Marguerite (56)
1627 started, 1760–1765
36, rue Saint-Bernard / 11e
Victor Louis

In 1627, the priest of Saint-Paul-et-Saint-Louis (no. 57) personally financed the construction of a chapel for his parishioners living in the remote Faubourg Saint-Antoine.

The building became an independent parish church in 1712. Sainte-Marguerite is a plain three-nave basilica. Among its extensions, the chapel for the Poor Souls in Purgatory, built to plans by Victor Louis between 1760 and 1765, is particularly noteworthy. Its grisaille paintings simulate a Classical temple.

Saint-Paul-et-Saint-Louis (57)
1627–1641
99–101, rue Saint-Antoine / 4e
Étienne Martellange, François Derand

In 1534, Ignatius Loyola and several members of his Society of Jesus promised in Montmartre's Saint Denis chapel to devote their lives to serving the Church. Six years later, the Pope recognized the Jesuit order. Henceforth the Jesuits became the chief proponents of the Counter-Reformation, endeavoring to restore the authority of the Catholic church in the Protestant countries. A first Jesuit settlement was founded in Paris in 1580. The order, which supported the radical Catholic League during the Wars of Religion, was banned in 1595, but its influence grew rapidly after its reauthorization in 1603. In 1627, Louis XIII laid the cornerstone of Saint-Paul-et-Saint-Louis, the first Jesuit church in Paris, and Cardinal Richelieu celebrated the first Mass here in 1641. The construction of the church began on the basis of plans by Étienne Martellange. The floor plan recalls that of the Church of the Gesù, the mother church of the order in Rome.

However, the two-story façade – a work by François Derrand – features a strongly vertical structure in the French tradition. The façade of Saint-Gervais-Saint-Protais (no. 33) had introduced the three-story portico, borrowed from Renaissance palatial architecture, as a motif in Parisian church building a few years earlier.

Chapelle Sainte-Ursule-   (58)
de-la-Sorbonne
1627, 1635–1653
place de la Sorbonne / 5e
Jacques Lemercier

The various colleges of Notre Dame's (no. 19) school united to form a university as early as the 13th century. As many theological students of the time were indigent, Robert de Sorbon, who had been appointed Chaplain of Paris by Louis IX, provided a house and stables to poor masters and scholars. The house, soon named

"La Sorbonne" after its patron, became a college that grew rapidly and became independent. A first chapel, whose traces are still visible in the courtyard of the Sorbonne today, was built in 1326; a library opened in 1481.

The building later deteriorated, and Cardinal Richelieu commissioned Jacques Lemercier to develop a new structure in 1627. That three-winged building was eventually demolished to make room for an eclectic complex built to plans by Paul-Henry Nénot between 1885 and 1901 (La Sorbonne, no. 58). The University church built by Lemercier between 1635 and 1648 was preserved, however. It houses Richelieu's funeral chapel and his tomb, a work by François Girardon (1694).

Sainte-Ursule-de-la-Sorbonne has a cruciform floor plan with a short transept and a cupola over the crossing. Rectangular chapels flank the nave on either side. The shape recalls that of the Barnabite church of San Carlo ai Catinari in Rome, a work by Rosato Rosati whose construction began in 1612, when Lemercier was studying in the Eternal City. The dome of Sainte-Ursule-de-la-Sorbonne, surmounting a drum ringed with pilasters, also follows the Roman prototype.

Notre-Dame de Bonne-Nouvelle (59)
1628, 1823–1830
25, rue de la Lune, rue Beauregard / 2e
Etienne-Hippolyte Godde

Anne of Austria, the consort of Louis XIII, laid the cornerstone of a church dedicated to the Virgin Mary in 1628. Later the queen often came here to pray for the birth of an heir to the throne. After the birth of her son, the future Louis XIV, she founded the royal Val-de-Grâce abbey (no. 67) to thank God for fulfilling her prayers. The original church was demolished after the revolution, except for the tower. Étienne-Hippolyte Godde built today's neo-Classical basilica between 1823 and 1830. In the nave, Doric columns support a drum and a cupola with glassed openings.

Notre-Dame des Victoires (61)
1628–1629, 1629–1666, 1737–1740
1, place des Petits-Pères, rue Notre-Dame-des-Victoires, rue de la Banque / 2e
Pierre Le Muet, Libéral Bruant,
Robert Boudin, Gabriel le Duc,
Jean-Sylvain Cartaud

In 1629, Louis XIII laid the cornerstone of this church, built for the Augustinian friars, to commemorate his victory over the Protestants at La Rochelle. Pierre le Muet designed a single-nave structure with a transept, a deep choir and several side chapels. Despite the king's commitment, financial difficulties led to repeated interruptions of the construction works and to a change of architects. Sylvain Cartault finally completed the building in 1737–1740.

The well-proportioned main façade with Ionic pilasters in the ground floor

Sainte-Elisabeth (60)
1628–1645, around 1858
195, rue du Temple, rue Turbigo / 3e
Louis Noblet, Michel Villedo, Etienne-Hippolyte Godde

Marie de' Medici laid the cornerstone of this sacred building in 1628. The structure, by Louis Noblet, was to be the church of a Franciscan monastery that had been founded by the queen mother. Michel Villedo directed the building works and the church of Sainte-Élisabeth was consecrated in 1645. The two-story façade is composed of Doric and Ionic pilasters topped with a segmental pediment. In the barrel-vaulted central nave, Ionic pilasters support a frieze whose metopes are adorned with Christian motifs. The lateral naves feature old-fashioned ribbed vaults.

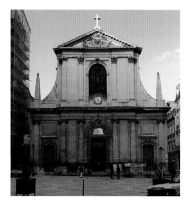

and Corinthian pilasters above is particularly noteworthy. The interior is lavishly decorated. Some 35,000 votive plaques on the walls and pillars are evidence that Notre-Dame-des-Victoires has been one of the most popular Marian pilgrimage churches in France since the 19th century.

Saint-Jacques-du-Haut-Pas (62)
1630–1643, 1676–1683
252, rue Saint-Jacques / 5e
Daniel Gittard (façade)

Augustinian friars from Alto Pascio in Tuscany built a hospice outside the city walls for pilgrims to Santiago de Compostela in the 13th century. In 1554, Henry II converted the building into a hospital for injured soldiers. Gaston, Duke of Orléans, a brother of Louis XIII, laid the cornerstone of today's church on the spot of the former hospice chapel in 1630. The building was not completed until 1683, however.

Among the church's outstanding features are the polygonal choir ambulatory after the Gothic pattern and the sober, well-lit nave with a singular alternating of barrel and dome vaults. The almost ascetic austerity of the façade, built by Daniel Gittard, can be interpreted as a counterpoint to the royal court's magnificence: like the Port-Royal convent, Saint-Jacques-du-Haut-Pas was a stronghold of Jansenism, a radical Catholic movement in conflict with both the pope and the king of France.

Temple Sainte-Marie-de-la-Visitation (63)
1632–1634
17, rue Saint-Antoine / 4e
François Mansart

In 1610, Jeanne de Chantal founded the Order of the Visitation of Our Lady at Annecy on the initiative of Francis de Sales, bishop of Geneva. Henceforth, the Visitationist nuns operated schools and cared for the ill. Noël Brûlart de Sillery, Marie de' Medici's ambassador to Madrid, founded a first Visitationist convent in Paris in 1619. Despite its modest dimensions, the church – an early work by François Mansart – is a typical example of the monumentality of Classical buildings of the time (no. 84). The floor plan features an oval central space flanked by two elliptical chapels. The fine structure of the walls and the complex interaction of the various interior spaces already foreshadow the Val-de-Grâce (no. 67). The chief exterior features are the arched entrance and the dome supported by a drum with pilaster-like buttresses.

51

Chapelle de l'Hôpital Laennec (64)
(Hospice des Incurables)
1634–1640
42, rue de Sèvres / 7e
Christophe Gamard

Cardinal François de la Rochefoucauld founded a hospital for the incurably ill in 1634 at the edge of the city, along the road to Sèvres.

The chapel, consecrated in 1640, was placed at the intersection of the men's and the women's wings to permit separate access for the two sexes. The interior of the cruciform chapel is not decorated. In 1878, the medical complex was renamed after Doctor René Laënnec, inventor of the stethoscope.

Hôtel Lambert (65)
1640–1644
2, rue Saint-Louis-en-l'Île, Pont Sully / 4e
Louis Le Vau, Charles Lebrun,
Eustache Le Sueur

This city mansion was built to the east of Île Saint-Louis for Jean-Baptiste Lambert de Sucy et Thorigny, secretary of King Louis XIII. It was later expanded on the east side. The main features of the four-winged structure are the façades on the interior courtyard, which are structured by Doric and Ionic pilasters, and the staircase of the north wing, which becomes wider and lighter in the upper stories. The interior is lavishly decorated, as is evident in the Hercules Gallery, named for the ceiling fresco by Charles Lebrun which features the Triumph of Hercules. Eight windows in this long hall open onto the garden, while a semi-

circular front once offered a wonderful view of the Seine. The Rothschild family acquired the Hôtel Lambert in 1976.

Hôtel de Saint-Aignan / (66)
Hôtel d'Avaux
between 1642 and 1650
71, rue du Temple / 3e
Pierre Le Muet

Pierre Le Muet erected this stately three-winged building on behalf of Claude de Mesmes, Count of Avaux, a diplomat who represented the king of France at the 1648 Münster conference that put an end to the Thirty Years' War.

The plain façade facing the street contrasts with the splendid interior courtyard that is accessible through a monumental portal in the central axis of the main wing.

Colossal Corinthian pilasters structure the façades and unite the two stories. For the sake of symmetry, the architect used the same decorative elements and trompe-l'œil windows on the wall that borders the courtyard to the southwest.

Val-de-Grâce (67)
1645–1648, 1654–1669
277, rue Saint-Jacques,
place Alphonse Laveran / 5e
François Mansart, Jacques Lemercier,
Pierre Le Muet, Gabriel Le Duc

Louis XIII and Anne of Austria remained childless for the first twenty-three years of their marriage. The queen swore to build a new church for the Val de Grâce, a Benedictine abbey she had founded years before, if she bore an heir to the throne. She kept her vow after the birth of her son, the future Louis XIV, who personally laid the cornerstone of the church in 1645 as he was six. The building was originally designed by François Mansart. However, Mansart proved to be a perfectionist. When his successive alterations of the design became too expensive, Jacques Lemercier was commissioned to complete the work. The interior, which features a barrel vault supported by pillars, recalls that of the Church of the Gesù (cf. no. 57) in Rome, while the façade was inspired by another building in the Eternal City: Santa Susanna, built to plans by Carlo Maderno in 1603. Moreover, the dome supported by a drum with buttresses clearly evokes Saint Peter's Basilica, a work by Michelangelo. Such borrowings

from Roman Baroque architecture give surprising dynamism and plasticity to the Val-de-Grâce and make the church an untypical example of French 17th-century Classicism.

Saint-Sulpice (68)
1646 started, 1655,1660–1678,
1719–1736, 1733–1766, 1777–1780
place Saint-Sulpice, rue Saint-Sulpice,
rue Garancière / 6e
Christophe Gamard, Louis Le Vau,
Daniel Gittard, Giovanni Niccolò
Servandoni, Jean-François Chalgrin

Income from large rural estates secured the wealth of the Saint-Germain-des-Prés abbey (no. 5), which in the 12th century built a parish church for the peasants who worked its fields.

In 1646, queen regent Anne of Austria laid the cornerstone for a larger church to be built to plans by Christophe Gamard. Construction was completed only in 1780 after several interruptions, however. Like many other 17th-century sacred buildings, Saint-Sulpice has a floor plan similar to that of Notre Dame (no. 19). The flying buttresses that reinforce the choir also recall the cathedral that had been begun half a millennium earlier. But whereas Saint-Eustache (no. 37) revisited the early Gothic prototype using Renaissance elements, Saint-Sulpice already integrates Classical features, such

53

Jean-François de Guénégaud, who was appointed treasurer to the king, acquired a relatively small plot of land in 1647 and commissioned François Mansart to build a two-story, three-winged city mansion. A single-story structure with a terrace closes the inner courtyard on the street side. Although this mansion features a simple structure and decoration, it is an excellent example of the Mansart style, characterized by well-balanced proportions, charming details and exquisite stonework.

Extraordinarily high windows flood the interior with light. The garden side features two lateral pavilions and a slight central projection. The mansion was renovated between 1964 and 1966 and now houses the Paris Hunting and Nature Museum.

as the well-balanced proportions of the interior and the lunettes that complement the barrel vault. The main façade, whose construction began in 1732 to plans by Florentine backdrop designer Giovanni Niccolò Servandoni, features two towers framing a double portico. The succession of monumental Classical columns already announces the end of Rococo and its wealth of decorative detail.

Hôtel de Guénégaud (69)
1648–1655
60, rue des Archives,
rue des Quatre Fils / 3e
François Mansart

Hôtel d'Aumont (70)
1649–1650, 1655, 1703
7, rue de Jouy,
rue des Nonnains-d'Hyères / 4e
Michel Villedo, Louis Le Vau,
François Mansart (not verified),
Georges Maurissart

This city mansion near the Seine is the result of several building phases. Around 1650, Michel Scarron, the uncle of burlesque writer Paul Scarron, commissioned Michel Villedo to build a palace. Antoine d'Aumont, Scarron's son-in-law, inherited the mansion in 1656 and had Le Vau and Mansart remodel and enlarge it. Architect Georges Maurissart enlarged the complex again in 1703. The city of Paris acquired the mansion in 1957 and performed extensive renovation works. The Hôtel d'Aumont now houses the administrative court of Paris. A portal with lavish sculptural decoration provides access to the elegant interior courtyard, which is framed by a two-story corps de logis and two side wings that feature a similar façade composition. Draperies, masks and fruit garlands adorn the spaces between and above the high windows. On the garden side, two projections and no less than nineteen window axes structure the façade. Circular and rectangular dormer windows, the latter topped with pediments, enliven the roof.

Timber-framed house (71)
around 1650
3, rue Volta / 3e

Because the technology used to build this house, as well as the room disposition, reflect medieval tradition, experts long thought the structure dated from

the late 13th or early 14th century. However, documents found in 1979 show that "the oldest private house in Paris" was in fact built in the 17th century. Nonetheless, the building remains interesting as one of the rare half-timbered houses in the French capital.

Four half-timbered stories with vertical or cross braces surmount a ground floor of stone masonry. A steep staircase in the middle of the house gives access to four rooms on each level.

Saint-Roch (72)
1653–1740, 1754–1760
298, rue Saint-Honoré, rue Saint-Roch,
rue des Pyramides / 1er
Jacques Lemercier, Jules Hardouin-
Mansart, Robert de Cotte,
Étienne-Louis Boullée

In 1653, Louis XIV laid the cornerstone of this church dedicated to Saint Roch, the patron saint of the plague-stricken. Construction work began to plans by Jacques Lemercier, but was interrupted and could only be completed in 1701. In the meantime, the plans were altered – probably by Jules Hardouin-Mansart – to provide for the construction of a chapel to the Virgin Mary surrounded by an ambulatory to be built as an extension to the choir. Another round chapel was built to the east in 1711, and the construction of the vaults was completed in 1723. Robert de Cotte began to build the façade in 1736 and the church was dedicated in 1740. Later on, the sculptor Étienne-Maurice Falconet and the architect Étienne-Louis Boullée added a rectangular chapel to the east.

The floor plan of this building – a three-nave basilica with a short transept and an ambulatory with radial chapels – recalls that of the contemporary Saint-Sulpice church (no. 68). Moreover, both buildings revisit Notre Dame's (no. 19) early Gothic disposition. The façade, however, does without any borrowings from the Middle Ages. As at Saint-Gervais-Saint-Protais (no. 33), columns are the chief stylistic element. But while Saint-Gervais-Saint-Protais was the first French sacred building to use the three Classical orders to adorn its three stories, Saint-Roch does without the Ionic order and thus constitutes a Parisian interpretation of the Roman two-story Baroque churches.

Hôtel (de) Lauzun (73)
1656–1657
17, quai d'Anjou / 4e
Charles Chamois, Louis Le Vau (not verified)

This city mansion named after the Marquis de Lauzun, its second landlord, was built in 1656, probably to plans by Louis Le Vau, for Charles Gruyn des Bordes, commissioner general of the army. In the mid-19th century, the writer Théophile Gautier organized hashish-smoking parties here with other bohemians, including Charles Beaudelaire, still unknown at the time.

The Paris city council acquired the building in 1928, and uses it today for official receptions and to accommodate visiting heads of state. The Hôtel de Lauzun is one of the city's most beautiful private houses. The plain façade contrasts with the splendid interior decor.

Most of the rooms still feature the original grotesque gilt stucco and wall paneling. Among the ceiling paintings are works by Charles Lebrun and Eustache Lesueur.

Hôtel Salé/Aubert de Fontenay (74)
1656–1659
5, rue de Thorigny / 3e
Jean Bouiller de Bourges

This stately mansion was built for Pierre Aubert de Fontenay, whose wealth came from his function as collector of the salt tax. As the Parisians had the impression the palace had been built with their own money, and as the French word "salé" can refer not only to salt, but also to steep prices, the locals soon named the mansion "Hôtel Salé".

The building served successively as the residence of the Venetian ambassador, a boarding school and the home of the Paris School of Applied Arts. Since 1976 it has housed the collection of the Picasso Museum.

A rectangular portal recessed from the street provides access to a semi-circular inner courtyard where a single-story structure stands to the right. For the sake of symmetry, the wall to the left features blind windows opposite the real windows to the right. The three-story main wing, whose central projection is

Hôpital de la Salpêtrière (75)
1656 founded, 1670–1677
47, boulevard de l'Hôpital / 13e
Louis Le Vau, Pierre Le Muet, Charles
Duval, Libéral Bruant

In 1633, Louis XIII relocated gunpowder production from the Arsenal (no. 44) to an undeveloped area on the left bank. In 1656, the Sun King converted the factory into a homeless shelter but its name, referring to saltpeter, a main ingredient of gunpowder, remained. Later on, the facility run by a religious order was converted again to accommodate up to 20,000 of the homeless, prostitutes and mentally disabled who came here voluntarily or were kept by force. Hence the considerable length of the two-story building with an additional mezzanine level. The plain façade of La Salpêtrière recalls that of Hôtel des Invalides (no. 85), a contemporary structure. A chapel built by Libéral Bruant between 1670 and 1677 forms the center of the complex. This church has an unusual floor plan: an octagon complemented by a cross, with four octagonal chapels between the posts of the cross and arcades providing access from the chapels to the central space. Moreover, blind arcades are the sole decorative elements in the four rectangular rooms, so that the en-

crowned by a triangular pediment, has seven vertical axes.

A segmental pediment with rich sculptural decoration unites the three central axes at the level of the roof with its dormer windows.

Sculptures by Martin Desjardins adorn the staircase, which is of similar dimensions to stairways in contemporary royal palaces.

57

semble owes its unique atmosphere to the complicated and surprising perspectives inside the building.

Hôtel de Beauvais (76)
1658–1660
68, rue François-Miron, rue de Rivoli / 4e
Antoine Lepautre

58

Antoine Le Pautre built this mansion of exceptional historic and architectural importance in 1658 on behalf of Pierre de Beauvais and his wife Catherine-Henriette Bellier, lady-in-waiting to Anne of Austria. The building was inaugurated on August 26, 1660 – the day Louis XIV entered Paris together with Maria Theresia, the infanta whom he had married a few weeks before on the Spanish border. The queen mother and the court watched the bridal procession entering the capital from the balcony of the Hôtel de Beauvais. In 1763, the seven-year-old Mozart lived here with his father and sister. The small and irregularly shaped lot prompted Antoine Le Pautre to find original solutions for his design, and he succeeded in creating a harmonious, magnificent building. Due to the inner courtyard's semi-circular shape, the façades here feature a remarkable Baroque liveliness that once filled even architect and sculptor Gian Lorenzo Bernini with admiration. The round vesti-

bule and the staircase with sculptures by Martin Desjardins are particularly noteworthy. The broad street façade, however, makes a harsh impression since all its decorative elements and royal emblems were destroyed during the revolution.

Collège des Écossais (77)
1662–1672
65, rue du Cardinal-Lemoine / 5e

A college for Scottish scholars opened in Paris as early as 1326. The construction of the extant building began in 1662 to plans by an unknown architect. The Saint Andrew chapel was consecrated in 1672. The main façade features plain cornices and regular ashlar masonry. The unusual appearance of the central projection is the result of a lowering of the street level by several meters. As a consequence, the basement became the ground floor and the entrance portal a window over the present-day doorway. A hexagonal chapel with blind arcades on the walls is found in what is now the second floor.

Collège des Quatre-Nations (78)
1663–1691
23, quai de Conti / 6e
Louis Le Vau

Cardinal Mazarin founded a college for sixty gentlemen on March 6, 1661 – just three days before his death. The students were to come from Artois, Alsace, Roussillon and Pignerol in Piedmont, four provinces that had become French under the treaties of Münster (1648) and the Pyrenees (1659). Because the territories had formerly belonged to four different nations – Flanders, Germany, Spain and Italy – the building was named "Collège des Quatre-Nations". Construction to plans by Louis Le Vau began near the Seine in 1663. In 1684, the remains of Cardinal Mazarin were solemnly transferred to the college chapel completed ten years before. Construction works were completed in 1691 with the opening of the library. After the dissolution of the college in 1793, Napoleon installed the Institut de France in the buildings in 1805. The Collège des Quatre-Nations, which faces the Louvre (no. 49) across the river, is characterized by an imposing façade structure that makes it the dominant Baroque ensemble in the city. The curving main façade in particular, which ends in lateral pavilions near the Seine, features a vitality and virtuosity that place the ensemble on a par with the finest Italian Baroque buildings. Le Vau designed the cruciform chapel in the middle of the complex as an oval within a rectangle. The dome stands atop a high drum adorned with reliefs and paired pilasters that echo the paired columns of the portico.

who lived in the vicinity and built several city mansions on Île Saint-Louis, including the Hôtel de Lauzun (no. 73). After Le Vau's death in 1670, Gabriel Le Duc continued the works. Jacques Doucet completed the job with the construction of the naves and the transept between 1702 and 1725. Saint-Louis-en-l'Île is a three-nave, barrel-vaulted basilica with transept and ambulatory. The harmonious interior decoration is particularly noteworthy. The clear composition using Corinthian pilasters and a three-zone entablature reflects the design principles of Italian Renaissance. The façade merges perfectly with the street perspective.

Saint-Louis-en-l'Ile   (79)
1664–1670, 1679–1701, 1702–1725,
1765
19, rue Saint-Louis-en-l'Île / 4e
François oder Louis Le Vau, Gabriel Le
Duc, Jacques Doucet

This church, begun in 1664, replaced a chapel dedicated to the Virgin Mary that stood on the site. The initial building phase was directed by Louis Le Vau,

Champs-Élysées   (80)
1667, 1828
avenue des Champs-Élysées / 8e
André Le Nôtre

Luxury boutiques, international strollers, business headquarters, the home stretch of the Tour de France: the avenue that runs two kilometers between Place de la Concorde (no. 121) and Arc de

Triomphe (no. 121) is one of the world's most prestigious boulevards. "Oh, Champs-Élysées!" A forest bordered by fields and swamps existed here in the late 16th century. But André Le Nôtre, the leading French Classical landscape gardener, remodeled the area after he had designed the Tuileries garden (no. 41). He laid out a seventy-one-meter-wide boulevard lined with trees leading to the hill where a triumphal arch stands today. Those who climbed the hill could appreciate a wonderful view of the Tuileries garden. Systematic development of the area began after the city of Paris had acquired the avenue in 1828, and culminated under Napoleon III's Second Empire. In the 20th century, the area attracted the headquarters or branches of many national and international banks, airlines and automobile manufacturers. In the late 1990s, President Jacques Chirac initiated an extensive renovation and modernization program: pedestrian areas were paved with three different kinds of polished granite stones, modern benches were installed in the green spaces, new rows of plane trees were planted. The new exterior furniture of the Champs-Élysées was created among others by Wilmotte.

Observatoire   (81)
1667–1672
61, avenue de l'Observatoire,
rue Cassini / 14e
Claude Perrault

The physicist Adrien Auzout and the Controller General of Finances Jean-Baptiste Colbert initiated the construction of the first French observatory under the reign of Louis XIV. Claude Perrault, a physicist, naturalist and amateur architect who had already designed the east front of the Louvre (no. 49), began building the observatory outside the city in 1667. Two years later, the astronomer Giovanni Domenico Cassini had the original plans altered to accommodate a large hall in the second floor. Despite the delay, construction was completed in 1672. Perrault's design recalls Tycho Brahe's Uranienburg observatory, and the unusual floor plan perfectly matches the building's function: two pavilions flank the central cubic structure to the south; a rectangular tower topped with a triangular pediment stands in the middle of the three-story north façade. Perrault did without columns, using only cornices and arched windows to structure the façades. The resulting rationalist rigor perfectly embodies the basic principles of French Classicism, which are diametrically opposed to the Baroque style. The fact that Perrault illustrated his French translation of Vitruvius's De Architectura,

published in 1673, with a picture of the observatory exemplifies the building's function as a model for decades to come.The observatory's main façades are exactly aligned with the points of the compass, and its north-south axis was taken as the prime meridian until 1911 (it is 2°20'14" east of the present prime meridian, which runs through Greenwich Observatory). A clock located twenty-eight meters below the ground at a constant temperature of 11.86 °C still indicates the coordinated universal time.

Notre-Dame de l'Assomption (82)
1670–1676
263bis, rue Saint-Honoré, rue Cambon,
place M. Barrès / 1er
Charles Errard

The Augustinian nuns of the Assumption founded a convent in Paris on the initiative of Cardinal de La Rochefoucauld. A splendid church was built between 1670 and 1676, after plans by Charles Errard, director of the newly founded Académie de France in Rome, to replace the original convent chapel. The rotunda-shaped building with a dome and a portico – a quite unusual form in France – recalls Roman structures such as the Ancient Pantheon. Notre Dame de l'Assomption also shows similarities with Santa Maria dell'Assunzione, another church dedicated to the Virgin Mary that was erected in Arriccia between 1662 and 1664 by Gianlorenzo Bernini. Errard's work, however, has far less harmonious proportions, as the enormous dome and its high drum seem to overwhelm the lower levels. Hence contemporary critics ridiculed the architect and talked about "le sot dome" (French "sot" means "silly, foolish"). Notre Dame de l'Assomption has been the parish church of Polish Catholics living in Paris since 1850.

Hôtel de Lully (83)
1671
45, rue des Petits-Champs,
47, rue Sainte-Anne / 1er
Daniel Gittard

The city mansion built for composer Jean-Baptiste Lully (1632–1687) features a clearly structured design: above the ground floor with its rusticated masonry and large arched windows, colossal Corinthian pilasters frame the windows and unite the two main stories. A pair of such pilasters adorns the façade on Rue des Petits-Champs, while two more pairs face Rue Sainte-Anne. A relief featuring musical instruments complements the balcony and hints at the first landlord's profession.

61

Baroque – Classicism – neo-Classicism
Parisian architecture of the 17th and 18th century   (84)

During the middle of the 16th century, Protestant Reformation swept through large portions of Europe. The Roman Catholic Church felt that it forced to react to the previously underestimated movement with political means. Re-Catholization of Protestant areas was expected to succeed using diplomacy, mission and repression.

Sensually powerful art and architecture were quickly recognized as effective propaganda tools – the birth of Baroque had come. Architecture, stucco, sculpture and painting joined into a synthesis of art that created the context for incense-permeated, opulent liturgy. It is not by coincidence that the first examples of the new style were built by Il Gesù, the Jesuit order of the Roman Catholic Church, which was founded in 1534 in Paris and became the main proponent of Counter Reformation shortly thereafter. However, the dynamic, sculpted and spatially complex language of Baroque did not become the dominant form of expression in all areas of Europe. Countries that only marginally came under the influence of Counter Reformist movements or avoided them altogether displayed a Classicist, Palladian style in their buildings, as was the case in Anglican England and Calvinist Netherlands. It may be surprising that the architecture of Catholic France sometimes also had an "un-Baroque" appearance. This may be explained by the fact that the gradual re-Catholization was replaced here by the brutal persecution and execution of Huguenots. As the religious wars ceased with the coronation of Henry IV in 1589, Catholicism was established as the state religion. For this reason, Roman Baroque influences are only seldom so apparent as in the Jacques Lemercier's Val-de-Grâce monastery (no. 66) or Louis Le Vaus Collège des Quatres-Nations (no. 78). French architecture of the 17th and 18th century for the most part resisted Baroque's opulent decorative and dynamic tendencies, and instead created Classicist, monumentally influenced forms. At first, these buildings oriented themselves towards Italian structures from Antiquity and Renaissance (Palais de Luxembourg, no. 52), displaying increasing Palladian influence. This so-called Palladianism (in France "Classicisme") became the doctrinaire "state style," applied to all royal projects. The architectural-theoretical basis was delivered by Claude Perrault's treatise "L'ordonnance des espèces de colonnes selon la méthode des anciens" (1683) and even more so by François-Blondel's "Cours d'Architecture," that appeared eight years before. Telling is the rejection of Gian Lorenzo Bernini's design for Louvre's (no. 49) east facade, which was finally executed according to Claude Perrault's plan. Perrault's buildings, of which the Observatorium (no. 81) is the most exemplary, mark the most consistent renunciation of Baroque design principles.

Luis XIV's most ambitious architectural project is without question the expansion of the Versailles castle (no 98) conducted by Louis Le Vau and Jules Hardouin-Mansart. The garden façade with an almost monotonous sectioning creates a programmatic execution of the notion of neo-Classicism. With his innermost room of the castle chapel, regularly structured

using pillar and column rows, Hardouin-Mansart created one of the most important neo-Classicist religious buildings. The pronouncedly "un-Baroque" form vocabulary seen here is also apparent on the Grand-Trianon, which the architect built in 1687-1688 as a small park castle on the extensive garden grounds. The Dome Church of the Invalides (no. 89), started in 1671, is another important contribution to neo-Classical religious architecture by Hardouin-Mansart. Its design as a central volume crowned by a dome signals the architect's parting with the longitudinal structures in the medieval tradition with a basilica-like terraced nave and an ambulatory which were still being erected in the early years of the Sun King's reign. What is apparent is that the architectural legacy of Classicisme is so widely distributed over many top-notch architects and the whole country, that it can only be characterized in its entirety, as it is impossible to pinpoint it in individual biographies. The reception of Antiquity conveyed by the Renaissance and the grand monumentality of Classicisme predestined Parisian architecture to initiate the transition to actual neo-Classicism (Fr. Néoclassicisme) with Jacques-Ange Gabriel's buildings already in the middle of the 18th century, earlier than the rest of Europe.

Porte Saint-Denis (no. 86), relief

The Dome Church of the Invalides, façade

Église des Soldats (85)
Hôtel des Invalides
1671–1676, 1676–1678
esplanade des Invalides / 7e
Libéral Bruant, Jules Hardouin-Mansart

Louis XIV ordered the construction of this large complex devoted to caring for injured soldiers in 1670, and Libéral Bruant won the architecture competition held between 1671 and 1674. Construction works began in 1674 in the Grenelle plain. 1676, the State Secretary of War Louvois had commissioned Jules Hardouin-Mansart to modify Bruant's design by adding an oval choir and developing the Hôtel des Invalides to the south.

Bruant's design called for an extensive complex of 450 by 390 meters surrounded by a moat, with facilities grouped around 17 courts to accommodate up to six thousand injured veterans. Most of the façades, including that of the soldiers' church, are without ornament, which gives the complex a quite martial appearance.

The three-nave, nine-bay church with lateral galleries and a vaulted central nave is rooted in the tradition of the sacred buildings built for the Jesuits.

The oval choir flanked by circular sacristies, built to plans by Hardouin-Mansart, alleviates the austerity of the ensemble.

Porte Saint-Denis (86)
1672
24, boulevard Saint-Denis / 2e
François Blondel

Since the Middle Ages, the kings of France used to enter their capital city in a parade held on Rue Saint-Denis when returning from victorious campaigns in the North. Colbert had the Saint-Denis gate of the medieval city wall redesigned as a triumphal arch to celebrate the victories of Louis XIV in the Franco-Dutch war.

This building, which follows the theory formulated by Nicolas-François Blondel in his "Cours d'architecture", contributed to the definition of academic Classicism. The Saint-Denis gate is kind of a synthesis between Rome's Arch of Titus and the base decoration of Trajan's Column. It also integrates motifs taken from ancient obelisks and orators' tribunes.

Hôtel Mansart de Sagonne (87)
1674–1685
21–23, boulevard Beaumarchais,
28, rue des Tournelles / 4e
Jules Hardouin-Mansart

Louis Hardouin-Mansart, Count of Sagonne, the most productive French architect of the 17th century, built his

own city mansion in 1680. The main front was subsequently altered by the addition of a colonnade, but the garden side has kept its original appearance until today.

Its main characteristics are a balcony supported by ten Ionic columns that runs all along the façade on the ground floor, and smaller balconies on the second floor with French windows framed by rusticated ashlars and topped with triangular pediments.

Porte Saint-Martin (88)
1674
boulevard Saint-Martin,
rue Saint-Martin / 3e
Pierre Bullet

In 1674, the aldermen of Paris had this triumphal arch built in honor of Louis XIV, who had conquered the city of Besançon and the provinces of Limburg and Franche-Comté shortly before. With its three gateways, the Porte Saint-Martin

recalls the Roman triumphal arches of the imperial period, although without their pilasters and columns. The solid impression that emanates from the regular ashlars contrasts with the elegant reliefs that depict the victories of the Sun King. The massive attic story bears an inscription that commemorate the defeats of the German, Spanish and Dutch armies.

Église du Dôme des Invalides (89)
(Saint-Louis-des-Invalides)
1679–1708
esplanade des Invalides / 7e
Jules Hardouin-Mansart

François-Michel Le Tellier, Marquis de Louvois, Louis XIV's State Secretary of War, commissioned Hardouin-Mansart to extend the Église des Soldats (no. 85). Through its dimensions and its rich decoration which contrasts with the rest of the Invalides complex, the domed church can be considered something special. For this reason it was given a special name: Saint-Louis-des-Invalides and even Église Royale.

This structure, with a dome visible from afar, is a pendant to the Château de Versailles (no. 98) and is regarded as the most important Classical church ever built in France. It was probably intended to become the funeral monument of Louis XIV and the Bourbons, but it houses the mausoleum of another French ruler:

65

Napoleon, whose porphyry sarcophagus stands in a hall decorated by Louis Visconti since 1840

The building's floor plan forms a Greek cross composed of a rotunda inscribed in a square. It has rectangular and oval extensions on all four sides, and elliptical chapels with niches at the square's four corners. Narrow passageways adorned with pillars and columns offer access to the chapels from the rotunda. Jules Hardouin-Mansart took some inspiration from the burial chapel hat should have been built for the Bourbons at Saint-Denis Basilica (no. 11) to plans by his great-uncle François Mansart.

Hence the surmise that the Invalides was intended to be Louis XIV's mausoleum. Hardouin-Mansart succeeded in giving a unified façade to the square building topped with a high dome. The pairs of columns that adorn the drum and its buttresses echo the rhythmically arranged columns of the second floor and the portico.

The dome clearly shows similarities with that of Saint Peter's Basilica in Rome, although the attic story between the high drum and the cupola lends the Invalides more verticality.

The lantern and the finial, in the form of an obelisk, further emphasize the vertical dimension, thus giving the building a more vivid appearance than older domed churches such as Église de la Sorbonne (no. 58) and Val-de-Grâce (no. 67)

Chapelle du Séminaire (90)
des Missions Étrangères
1683–1689
128, rue du Bac / 7e
Jacques Lepas-Dubuisson

In 1663, the bishops of three Asian dioceses, China, North and South Vietnam, founded a society for training missionaries to be sent to foreign countries. Jacques Lepas-Dubuisson developed a single-nave church with a transept and a deep choir.

The two-story façade features Ionic and Corinthian pilasters supporting a triangular pediment. A flight of stairs

provides access to both the entrance and the crypt.

Saint-Thomas d'Aquin (91)
1683–1688, 1722, 1765–1770
place Saint-Thomas d'Aquin / 7e
Pierre Bullet

Saint Dominic founded a mendicant order of friars in Toulouse in 1215. Albertus Magnus and Thomas Aquinas, two Dominicans, taught and preached in the first Dominican convent in Paris, which was founded only three years later. Because the convent was located in Rue Saint-Jacques, the Paris Dominican friars were soon named "Jacobins". The radical revolutionaries lead by Robespierre later used the same name, as their political club met at the former convent. The original High Gothic structure had been demolished, however, as well as the second complex built here in 1612. The church and the cloister building that still stand today were erected after the convent had been refounded in 1632. The church built in just nine months in 1683, is a three-nave basilica with a transept that do not extend beyond the nave.

An opening in the semicircular apse connects the church with the square monks' choir added in 1722. The Saint-Roch parish church (no. 72) served as a model for both the addition and the two-story façade built in 1765–1770. The façade's Doric and Ionic columns bearing an entablature patterned after Ancient models prefigure the Classicism of the Louis Seize style.

Place des Victoires (92)
1685–1686, 1687–1690
place des Victoires / 1er, 2e
Jules Hardouin-Mansart,
Jean-Baptiste Predot

After the 1678 Treaty of Nimwegen had brought Louis XIV to the peak of his power, Marshall François d'Aubusson, Duke of La Feuillade, commissioned Martin Desjardins to create a statue of the king to be placed in the middle of a square that the marshall and the city of Paris jointly acquired in 1683. Beginning in 1685, Jules Hardouin-Mansart remodeled the U-shaped space, making it circular. The architect also designed an ensemble of buildings with a unified appearance based on rusticated masonry and arcades on the ground floor, colossal Ionic pilasters uniting the second and third floors, and roofs with dormer windows. Later alterations to the façades and the opening of several streets have considerably altered the original appearance of Place des Victoires, however.

In 1685, Hardouin-Mansart also designed Place Vendôme (no. 95), another square with an equestrian statue of the king in the middle and surrounded by buildings with palatial façades. Although the latter project was not completed until 1699, both monumental developments remained the epitome of a "royal square" until the 19th century.

Revolutionaries destroyed the statue of Louis XIV in 1792, and Napoleon replaced it with a figure of General Desaix. This in turn was replaced in 1822 by a new equestrian statue of the Sun King, a work by François Joseph Bosio.

Hôtel de Libéral Bruant (93)
1685
1, rue de la Perle / 3e
Libéral Bruant

The architect built a mansion for himself in 1685. This building of modest dimen-

67

sions features an outstanding façade using the same decorative elements on both stories: pilasters that support either arches or horizontal bands. Bruant thus revived a design favored by Palladio that was common in the late Renaissance and the Mannerist period. Rectangular and arched windows occupy the space under the arches and the bands. Four busts of Roman emperors adorn the circular niches above the small windows. The triangular pediment that crowns the entire façade contains a round window flanked by cherubs and cornucopias.

Notre-Dame-des-Blancs-Manteaux (94)
1685–1690, 1703, 1863
12, rue des Blancs-Manteaux,
53, rue des Francs-Bourgeois / 4e
Charles Duval, Jean-Sylvain Cartaud,
Victor Baltard

Over several centuries, various sacred buildings have stood on the site of the present church. In 1258, Augustinian friars founded a monastery that was taken over by the Hermits of Saint William in 1297. Between 1685 and 1690, Charles Duval remodeled the Gothic church and the associated cloister buildings. The ensemble had a provisional west façade for almost two centuries, however, as money was short. But in 1863,

elements from a Barnabite church built to plans by Sylvain Cartaud in 1703 and demolished at the behest of Napoleon III were used to improve the main façade of Notre-Dame-des-Blancs-Manteaux.

The two-story façade with Doric and Ionic pilasters is as plain as the interior. Toward the nave, the arches of the barrel-vaulted basilica feature Corinthian pilasters that support an entablature adorned with Christian symbols.

Place Vendôme (95)
1686–1691, 1699–1725
place Vendôme / 1er
Jules Hardouin-Mansart

Jules Hardouin-Mansart developed this square in 1685 together with Place des Victoires (no. 92) after Louis XIV had acquired the Hôtel Vendôme. The square, originally named "Place Louis-le-Grand", was to be flanked by the royal library and various academic buildings. When the project proved too expensive, the Sun King granted the site to the city of Paris in 1699 on the condition that it would develop buildings with unified façades as planned by Hardouin-Mansart. An equestrian statue of the king by François Girardon was unveiled in the course of the same year, but the urban development project could not be completed until 1725 due to financial constraints.

Today's Place Vendôme is considerably smaller than originally planned.

Moreover, the corners of the rectangular plot were cut off to increase the area of the individual lots sold to private investors. Money shortages also necessitated alterations in the design of the ground floor arcades that open on the square. The arches and the colossal Corinthian pilasters that unite the upper stories are similar to those on Place des Victoires. On the long sides of the rectangle, the central projections features semi-detached columns bearing triangular pediments.

After the destruction of the equestrian statue that portrayed Louis XIV as a Roman emperor in 1792, Napoleon commissioned Jacques Gondouin to create a victory column in 1810. This monument, patterned after Trajan's column and its winding frieze, commemorates the victorious 1805 campaign. Revolutionaries destroyed the original during the Paris Commune in 1871, however, and the monument was rebuilt two years later. In 1896 the house 15 at Place Vendôme was rebuilt into Hotel Ritz by Charles Mewès.

Amphithéâtre Anatomique (96)
(Université Paris 3,
Sorbonne Nouvelle)
1691–1695
5, rue de l'École-de-Médecine / 6e
Charles und Louis Joubert

In the Middle Ages, a church dedicated to Saint Cosmas and Saint Damian, two brothers who had become eminent for their medical skill in the Early Christian period, was the spiritual center of a confraternity of physicians. The association was to develop into a surgical school in the 17th century, and Louis XIV authorized his personal physicians to build an amphitheater for teaching anatomy. Charles and Louis Joubert designed a square building topped with an octagonal dome and a drum with vertical and horizontal oval openings. The dome was originally adorned with bands, obelisks and vases, but now features only high vertical windows. Two sculptures figuring genii adorn the main entrance. Louis XVI converted the amphitheater into an art school in 1777 as the building had become too small Auguste Rodin was among those who studied there. A language school has been using the structure as a lecture hall since 1933.

Hôtel de Brancas (97)
around 1700
6, rue de Tournon / 6e
Pierre Bullet

Jean-Baptiste Terrat, Marquis de Chantosme, had this stately U-shaped city mansion built. The two-story façades with a clear structure and plain decoration are typical of French Classicism, a style that propagates monumentality and dignity against the vigor and liveliness of the contemporary Baroque.

This is particularly evident in the cornices and pilaster strips that harmonize the horizontal and vertical lines. In the interior, the marble staircase is especially noteworthy. Since 1979, the Hôtel de Brancas has housed the French Institute of Architecture.

Palace in Versailles – the center of absolutist power (98)

Versailles and its gardens are among the most visited locations in Europe. Although Louis XIV (1643–1715) launched the greatest architecture programs in Paris, he did not like to reside in his capital city, preferring Versailles where he had a hunting lodge of his father's expanded into a prestigious palace. The royal court's move from the Louvre (no. 49) and the Tuileries palaces (no. 41) to Versailles in 1682 marked a break in French history, as the new, gigantic royal residence offered an ideal scenery for the Absolutist kings until the Revolution. Versailles thus became the setting for the unparalleled personality cult epitomized in Louis XIV's famous sentence: "L'État, c'est moi!". Arbitrarily distributed pensions, grandiose feasts and exquisite hunting parties made the nobility at court entirely dependent on the Sun King. Thousands of courtiers and noblemen lived at Versailles, some of them accommodated in small attic rooms due to the constant overcrowding of the palace. The aristocrats left their castles in the provinces en masse, and thus paved the way for the cultural and political central-ization of the country in the capital – a situation that persists today despite the decentralization measures undertaken since the 1960s. On special occasions, however, even the roturiers were allowed to enter the palace to receive charity or to satisfy their curiosity by watching the king dining, or even to see the birth of Marie-Antoinette's son.

Because not only Louis XIV, but also his successors Louis XV and Louis XVI lived at Versailles, the palace became a symbol of the French monarchy and was therefore destined to play a major role in the country's history. On May 5, 1789, on the eve of the Revolution, the king assembled the Estates-General in the great dining room. Versailles also played a part in the tumultuous history of Franco-German relations: King William I of Prussia was proclaimed German emperor in the Hall of Mirrors on January 18, 1871, as a result of his successful campaign in the Franco-German war. Remembering this profound humiliation, the French government purposely chose the same location for the signing of the treaty that ended World War I: Germany, now de-

The Sun King – relief on a pomp vase

View of the palace chapel

Mill in the Hameau of Marie-Antoinette

feated, was obliged to accept the burden of high reparations and to claim all guilt for the war. Today, however, Versailles has become a symbol of Franco-German reconciliation, and the 40th anniversary of the two countries' friendship agreement of January 22, 1963, was celebrated in the Gallery of Battles in 2003.

The Hall of Mirrors underwent restoration in 2007 as part of a program that will continue until 2017.

Versailles is the result of works by the best French architects over a period of more than one and a half centuries. Between 1631 and 1634, under the reign of Louis XIII, Philibert Le Roy designed the original hunting lodge on the site.

Louis XIV, who began to reign personally on coming of age in 1661, progressively expanded his father's three-winged palace into a gigantic complex around what is now the Marble Courtyard, and Versailles became a model for numerous princely palaces across Europe.

André Le Nôtre, the most outstanding landscape architect of the time, began to design the garden. He had already designed the gardens of Vaux-le-Vicomte between 1653 and 1660. This prototype of the Baroque French garden uses parterres with regular shapes, precisely cut hedges, small wooded areas and various basins to continue the château's symmetry and regularity in the landscape.

Beginning in 1668, Louis Le Vau quadrupled the volume of the palace by building a "great envelope" over the hunting lodge. Le Vau's façades facing the city replicate the brick-and-stone structure of the original building, while the three-story garden façade features a rusticated base and a regular succession of Ionic pilasters on the second floor that embody the strict monumentality of French Classicism. Projections with paired columns interrupt the somewhat monotonous succession of structuring elements here. The façade is recessed

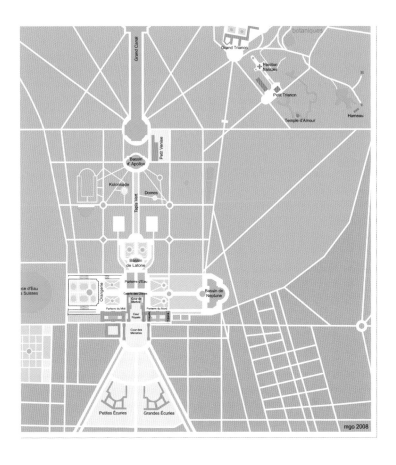

Masterplan

in the center, forming a terrace atop the rusticated base.

In 1678, Louis XIV finally decided to move to Versailles. In the next year, the Sun King commissioned Jules Hardouin-Mansart to expand the palace once more. The court architect began to build the seventy-three-meter long Hall of Mirrors between the two wings facing the garden. This extension has a façade that matches Le Vau's design, and the architect also added projections on both the south and north wings (1678-1681 and 1684-1689). Together with the east façade of the Louvre, completed a few years earlier to plans by Claude Perrault, Versailles's gigantic garden front is thus one of the major examples of secular Classical architecture. Between 1676 and 1684, Hardouin-Mansart in collaboration with the painter Charles Lebrun also developed the interior as an impressive total work of art including the decor of the Hall of Mirrors, the Queen's Guardroom, the Room of Plenty, the War Room, the Peace Room, and the Venus Room. Last but not least, Robert de Cotte decorated the Hercules Room in the late Louis Quatorze style between 1710 and 1736.

The construction of the royal chapel near the north wing began in 1689. The exterior's main characteristics are Corinthian pilasters, a cornice topped with a balustrade and statues, and scroll-shaped buttresses that flank the recessed upper story. The interior, designed as a two-lev-

The Temple of Love (Temple de l'Amour)

In 1687–1688, Hardouin-Mansart built the Grand Trianon in the park for the Marquise de Maintenon, the morganatic second wife of Louis XIV. This single-story building, where the Court used to gather for splendid parties, consists of two pavilions linked by an arcade and is the largest structure in Versailles's gardens.

Louis XV (1715–1774) launched another development program as he acceded to the throne at the death of his uncle. He first had the interiors remodeled, then commissioned Ange-Jacques Gabriel to build an opera with an oval ground plan in the Italian style near the north wing between 1763 and 1770. Gabriel also developed the Petit Trianon, a small château secluded in the park, and the Gabriel Wing, that Le Vau and Hardouin-Mansart had already designed as part of their "great envelop" project. The façade of this rectangular three-story building erected to the north of the Royal Courtyard is a typical example of the style developed by Gabriel, that already announces neo-Classicism with its monumental porticos copied from Antic temples. Moreover, the interior of the Golden Cabinet (also called "Royal Council Cabinet") is typical

el basilica, is the Classicist pendant of the late Gothic Sainte-Chapelle (no. 34) in Paris. The similarities between the two churches are not surprising, since Versailles's royal chapel is consecrated to Saint Louis, the king who had the Sainte-Chapelle built in the 13th century. The Corinthian columns of the gallery are typical elements of French Classicism.

74

French pavilion

of the intimate style developed under the reign of Louis XV. Louis XVI (1774–1792) mainly concentrated on the redesigning of the gardens, for which Richard Mique developed several small park buildings, including the Belvedere, the Temple of Love and the theater near the Petit Trianon. Mique's main work in the park, however, is the Petit Hameau de la Reine with its variety of pseudo-agricultural facilities. This ensemble, developed for Queen Marie-Antoinette, became the epitome of late Rococo sentimentality. The Revolution disrupted the continuity of both the French monarchy and the building activity in Versailles.

Garden façade of Versailles palace

Hôtel de Rohan-Soubise (99)
(Musée de l'Histoire de France)
1700–1709, 1732–1739
60, rue des Francs-Bourgeois; 58, rue
des Archives; rue des Quatre Fils / 3e
Pierre-Alexis Delamair, Germain Boffrand

François de Rohan, Prince de Soubise, acquired the medieval Hôtel de Clisson (no. 21) and the surrounding plot in 1700. In the nine years that followed, Pierre-Alexis Delamair remodeled the building and created a three-winged structure with a courtyard that forms a semi-circle on the street side. The two-story main wing features a central projection with a portico that extends through both stories. Pairs of Corinthian columns similar to those of the portico form a colonnade in front of the lateral wings.

Among the alterations performed by Germain Boffrand between 1732 and 1739, the two oval rooms in the elegant polygonal garden pavilion are particularly noteworthy. The complex is home to the National Archives and the French History Museum.

Hôtel de Tallard / (100)
Hôtel Amelot de Chaillou
1702–1704
78, rue des Archives; 10, rue Pastourelle,
3, rue de Beauce / 3e
Pierre Bullet

Jacques Amelot de Bisseuil acquired a mansion in 1658. Between 1702 and

1704, Pierre Bullet redesigned the building, creating an L-shaped complex complemented by two high walls enclosing a square courtyard. Unfortunately, the staircase on the garden side has lost most of its trompe-l'œil decoration.

Hôtel de Rohan-Strasbourg (101)
1705–1708, 1928–1938
87, rue Vieille-du-Temple,
rue des Quatre Fils / 3e
Pierre-Alexis Delamair, Robert Denis

Armand-Gaston de Rohan, Prince-Bishop and later Cardinal of Strasbourg, had a palace built for himself and his three brothers near the Hôtel de Clisson (no. 21), which his father had acquired in 1700. Pierre-Alexis Delamair, who already developed the Hôtel de Rohan-Soubise (no. 99) where de Rohan's mother was living, was commissioned to direct the building works.

He developed a complex whose single-story lateral wings contrast with the distinctly higher corps de logis. On the courtyard side, cornices and rusticated bands are the only decorative elements.

On the garden side, however, sculptures adorn the three-part portico of the central projection that features the three classical orders: Ionic and Doric columns in the two lower stories, and Corinthian pilasters in the attic story.

Apollo's Horses Drinking, a relief created by Robert Le Lorrain in 1735, adorns the door of the former stables. This work is among the major creations of French Baroque sculpture.

Hôtel Amelot de Gournay (102)
1712
1, rue Saint-Dominique / 7e
Germain Boffrand

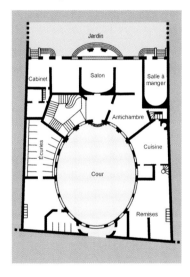

Germain Boffrand studied under Jules Hardouin-Mansart and later collaborated with the master. He was among the most successful architects of his time – and one of the richest, as he built and sold several city mansions, including the one acquired by the diplomat Michel Amelot de Gournay.

Rooms of various sizes and shapes are grouped around an oval courtyard. Colossal Corinthian pilasters between five groups of windows unite the two stories. On the garden side, the main wing has a slightly convex shape. This lively design recalls that of the courtyard of San Carlo alle Quattro Fontane in Rome, a work by Borromini.

Hôtel Clermont-Tonnerre (103)
1714
118–120, rue du Bac / 7e
Claude-Nicolas Lepas-Dubuisson

In 1714, Claude-Nicolas Lepas-Dubuisson erected this double palace on behalf of the bishop of the Foreign Missions near the church built to plans by his father (Chapelle du Séminaire des Missions Étrangères, no. 90).

Viscount François René de Chateaubriand, a political leader and writer, lived here from 1838 to his death in 1848. Both entrances feature rusticated stonework and understated sculptures evoking the remote countries to which missionaries used to be sent.

Maison Lepas-Dubuisson (104)
started in 1718
151bis, rue Saint-Jacques / 5e
Claude-Nicolas Lepas-Dubuisson

Claude-Nicolas Lepas-Dubuisson, the architect of the Hôtel de Clermont-Tonnerre (no. 103), richly adorned the façade of his own home. Corbels support the cornice, which becomes wider over the entrance

flanked by boutiques to form a balcony. An exquisite wrought iron balustrade underscores the balcony's elegant curved shape. Reliefs adorn both the French window on the balcony and the window above it. Pairs of columns flank the central window of the top story and support the eave cornice alongside volute-shaped corbels.

Palais de l'Élysée (105)
1718–1720, 1753–1755, 1773, 1787
55–57, rue de Faubourg Saint-Honoré / 8e
Claude Armand Mollet, Jean
Lassurance, Étienne-Louis Boullée,
Pierre-Adrien Paris

Louis Henri de La Tour d'Auvergne, Count of Évreux, had Claude Armand Mollet built the Palais de l'Élysée between 1718 and 1720. The three-winged, eleven-axis complex with lateral pavilions and a central projection follows the general scheme of Baroque palaces. The entrance, flanked by two pairs of Ionic columns on each side, is particularly noteworthy.

The palace has had a tumultuous history. Madame de Pompadour, the official mistress of Louis XV, lived here between 1753 and 1764. After her death, the king used the building to accommodate foreign visitors.

The Palais de l'Élysée subsequently housed a luxury brothel and a dance hall until it became the home of General Joachim Murat, who married a sister of Napoleon and was King of Naples for a time. Moreover, the Emperor signed his first abdication here in 1814. Louis Napoleon, his nephew, prepared a coup at the Palais de l'Élysée in 1849 but moved to the Palais des Tuileries (no. 41) after he finally seized power in 1851. The palace has been the official residence of the French President since 1873.

Hôtel de Gouffier de Thoix (106)
1719–1727
56, rue de Varenne / 7e

The site developer Baudouin built this intimate mansion between 1719 and 1727 on behalf of Henriette de Penancoët de Kéroual, Marquise de Thoix. The single-story wing along the street features a splendid entrance.

Its segmental tympanum is adorned with various types of shells typical of the Rococo style. Both door panels also feature similar "rocaille" motifs, as well as oval medallions portraying Mars and his consort Bellona. The halls and the dining rooms have retained their original decor.

Hôtel Chenizot (107)
1719–1732
51, rue Saint-Louis-en-l'Île / 4e
Pierre Vigné de Vigny

State Secretary Pierre de Verton had a city mansion composed of two parallel wings built here around 1620. The fiscal officer François Guyot de Chenizot acquired the ensemble in 1719. The splendid Rococo façade was completed in 1732.

The elegantly curved balcony over the entrance framed by rusticated ashlars rests on corbels adorned with exuberant foliage and lively dragons.

Hôtel Matignon (108)
1722–1723, 1724–1725
57, rue de Varenne / 7e
Jean Courtonne, Jacques de Matignon

This city mansion – one of the most beautiful in the Invalides neighborhood – has been home to the French Prime Minister since 1958. Jean de Courtonne began building the house in 1721 for Christian Louis de Montmorency. The prince, however, sold the estate before the construction works were completed. Jean de Matignon, the new landlord, had the job completed by Jean Antoine Mazin. A trapezoidal central projecting pavilion adorned with trophies extends over both stories of the main wing. Slender windows elegantly articulate the single-story lateral wings.

Hôtel de Noirmoutiers (109)
1722–1723
136, rue de Grenelle,
rue de Bourgogne / 7e
Jean Courtonne

Jean de Courtonne built this elegant city mansion between 1722 and 1723 on behalf of Antoine-François de la Trémoille, Duke of Noirmoutiers. The interior was remodeled and the short lateral wings built on after 1734.

On the main wing, the three central rows of windows feature rustication in the ground floor and pilasters topped with a triangular pediment in the upper floor. The central balcony rests on large corbels that are as richly adorned as also are the terminal quoins of the segmental windows. Ionic columns flank the monumental street entrance. They support a cornice that continues the segmental lines of the door. The Hôtel de Noirmoutiers has housed the Île-de-France regional agencies since 1970

Hôtel de Charost (110)
(British Embassy)
1722–1725
39, rue de Faubourg Saint-Honoré,
avenue Gabriel / 8e
Antoine Mazin

Jean Antoine Mazin, a military engineer born in Marseilles, built this stately city mansion for Paul-François de Charost, Duke of Béthune, between 1722 and 1725. On the street side, two-story lateral wings flank the concave entrance. Three projections structure the central façade on the courtyard side. Paolina Borghese, one of Napoleon's sisters, had the interior remodeled between 1803 and 1814. After the emperor's abdication, the British government acquired the palace that was henceforth used as an embassy by various countries.

Hôtel (de Loménie) de Brienne (111)
1724–1730
14–16, rue Saint-Dominique / 7e
François Debias-Aubry

Between 1724 and 1725, François Duret built the palace that today houses the French Ministry of Defense for the Marquise de Prie. The building is named after State Secretary of War Louis-Marie-Athanase de Loménie, Count of Brienne, who acquired the estate in 1776. Among the tenants in the centuries that followed are Letizia Bonaparte, mother of the emperor, and Charles de Gaulle (August 1944 to January 1946).

Rusticated quoins frame the two-story façade of the main wing. The three-axis central projection features Ionic and Doric pilasters supporting a triangular pediment. The sculptural decoration includes masks and shells above the first and second floor windows, and cherubs that bear the pediment medallion, inscribed with Lorraine cross that recalls General de Gaulle's stay here.

Hôtel de Roquelaure (112)
1695 started, 1724–1733
246, boulevard Saint-Germain / 7e
Jean Lassurance, Jean-Baptiste Leroux

Marshall Antoine Gaston de Roquelaure had a palace built in the late 17th century. Jean Lassurance remodeled and considerably enlarged the building starting in 1724.

Pavilion-like lateral wings complement the two-story corps de logis. Masks and shells adorn the keystones of the large windows. The original Rococo gilt panelling has been preserved in some rooms.

Hôtel Biron (Musée Rodin) (113)
1727–1732
77, rue de Varenne,
boulevard des Invalides / 7e
Jacques Gabriel, Jean Aubert

The royal counselor Abraham Peyrenc de Moras, who gained a considerable wealth through speculation, had a palace built by Jean Aubert to plans by Ange-Jacques Gabriel. The building is named after Antoine de Gontaut, Duke of Biron, however, who acquired the estate in the early 19th century.

Lateral pavilions and a central projection characterize the building. Rustication, delicate Rococo motifs over the ground floor windows, and exquisite reliefs on the pediment enliven the façade.

Various artists, including Isadora Duncan, Henri Matisse, Rainer Maria Rilke and Auguste Rodin lived here in the early 20th century.

In 1910, the French government granted Rodin leave to occupy the ground floor until his death.

In return, the sculptor bequeathed many of the works he created here to the state, and the building was converted into a Rodin museum after the artist's death in 1917.

Hôtel Portalis/Hôtel de Jaucourt (114)
1733
43, rue Croix-des-Petits-Champs,
2, rue La Vrillière / 1er
Pierre Desmaisons

This corner building – also known as "Hôtel Portalis" – features one of the most original Baroque façades in the city: turret – like oriels protrude on both sides of the corner. The attic story topped

with a terrace takes over the rounded form of the turrets only on the right side, whereas the left side is concave. The cornices are horizontal structure elements that follow and underscore the curves of the façade: like belts, they unite the oriels, the flat walls and the eaves. The partially non-functional wrought iron guard rail around the terrace is particularly worth a mention.

81

Chapelle du Collège des Irlandais
(Saint-Ephrem-des-Syriens) (115)
1738
15, rue des Carmes / 5e
Pierre Boscry

In 1677, Irish priests came to teach at a college that had been founded by Italians in 1333. In 1738, Pierre Boscry built a single-nave church with Ionic pilasters between the five bays.

The design of the oval porch is quite unusual: Corinthian pilasters support an arch and a semicircular frieze, while Ionic columns bear a semicircular entablature surmounted by two volutes that frame the coat of arms of the building's patron damaged during the Revolution.

The portal owes its energetic form unusual for Paris to the Rome sojourn of its architect. Among the high Baroque models there is mainly the façade completed in 1658 of Bernini's church Sant' Andrea al Quirinale to be named. Today the building is home to the Maronite parish of Saint-Ephrem-des-Syriens.

Hôtel d'Albret (117)
around 1640 started, 1740–1744
29bis–31, rue des Francs-Bourgeois / 4e
François Mansart (not verified),
Jean-Baptiste Vautrain

This palace, with four wings grouped around a courtyard, was built in 1640. Marshall César Phœbus d'Albret acquired the estate thirteen years later, and in 1740 Jean-Baptiste du Tillet purchased it and commissioned Jean-Baptiste Vautrin to remodel the façade on the street side. Its elegant arrangement and smooth design makes it one of the most beautiful examples of the Rococo style in Paris.

On the base, rustication frames the windows and forms an arcade. At its center, the façade features pilasters and a triangular pediment. The cornice gently

Fontaine des Quatre-Saisons (116)
1739–1747
57–59, rue de Grenelle / 7e
Edme Bouchardon

Edme Bouchardon designed this curved wall with doors on either side of the central fountain.

Above a rusticated base, pilasters divide the wall into various fields with coats of arms and allegories of the Four Seasons in niches.

The aedicule in the center contains the fountain proper. It features two pairs of Ionic columns that support a triangular pediment, as well as a sculptural group, an allegory of Paris between the Seine and Marne rivers.

The grace of this masterpiece of Parisian Rococo contrasts strongly with the strict neo-Classical form of the architecture. Voltaire was an early critic of the fountain's location in a narrow street that makes an overall view of the work impossible.

protudes here to form a balcony that rests on corbels at the top of the pilasters

École Militaire (118)
1751–1756, 1768–1782
1, place Joffre; 43, avenue de la Motte
Picquet, avenue Lowendal,
place de Fontenoy / 7e
Jacques-Ange Gabriel, Etienne-Louis
Boullée, Alexandre-Théodore Brongniart

With the help of Madame de Pompadour, Louis XV's mistress, the investor and supplier to the army Joseph Pâris-Duverney convinced the king to build a military academy for five hundred poor cadets. Ange-Jacques Gabriel began to built the complex in the Grenelle plain in 1751. The works were disrupted by the outbreak of the Seven Years' War in 1756, and resumed after a considerable simplification of the plans. The war academy closed and reopened several times after the death of the king in 1774, and Napoleon Bonaparte was among the cadets in 1784–1785.

With its clear, monumental design, the École Militaire is on the cusp between Classicism and neo-Classicism. Both façades of the elongated main wing feature a central projection with a Corinthian portico and a flat triangular pediment topped with a drum and a dome. The two-story lateral wings open with superposed Doric and Ionic colonnades on the southern courtyard side. The north side facing the parade grounds does without columns and features only plain rectangular windows. The main features of the interior are the majestic staircase and the Saint-Louis chapel.

Palais Royal (119)
1752–1770
place du Palais-Royal / 1er
Jacques Lemercier, Pierre Contant d'Ivry,
Pierre-Louis Moreau

The demolition of the city wall under Charles V provided Cardinal Richelieu, chief minister of Louis XIII, with an opportunity to build a palace for himself near the Louvre (no. 49). In 1629, Jacques Lemercier, the cardinal's favorite architect, began a three-winged complex, but Richelieu soon donated his palace to the royal family. Anne of Austria, the queen mother, and her son, the young Louis XIV, moved into it in 1643. But when they moved back to the Louvre, and later to Versailles (no. 98), the Palais Royal became the property of the Duke of Orléans, a brother of Louis XIII. Pierre Contant d'Ivry comprehensively remodeled the Palais-Royal between 1752 and 1770, so that the marine reliefs in the Galerie des Proues are the last remnants of the original interior decoration.

Moreover, the garden framed by a colonnade was redesigned in 1780. Between 1780 and 1790, during the erection of the Théâtre-Français (no. 144), Victor Louis expanded Palais Royal with three new wings, thereby reducing the size of the garden. A shopping and entertainment center came into being here as a result of

83

speculation – the buildings were sold in units of whole arcades to settle Philippe d'Orléans' debts. Today the Palais Royal houses the Council of State. An installation of black and white columns by Daniel Buren, which both art lovers and young skaters appreciate, has adorned the courtyard since 1986.

Temple de Pentemont (120)
1753–1756
104–106, rue de Grenelle / 7e
Pierre Contant d'Ivry

Bernardine nuns founded an abbey on a hillside (pentemont) near Beauvais in 1218. In 1671, the nuns moved to Paris and devoted themselves from then on to the education of noble young ladies. In 1753, the dauphin – son of Louis XV and father of Louis XVI – laid the cornerstone

of a chapel dedicated to Saint Clotilde. Pierre Contant d'Ivry later developed a cross-shaped building with a dome over the crossing.

Three doors open the street façade, the central door framed by Ionic columns and topped with a segmental pediment with two dolphins that recall the founder. The former abbey buildings, erected at the same time as the church, are grouped around a square courtyard to the north. Behind the choir stands a pavilion with a central projection topped with a triangular pediment.

Place de la Concorde (121)
1755 started, 1830–1846
place de la Concorde / 8e
Jacques-Ange Gabriel,
Jakob Ignaz (Jacques Ignace) Hittorff

In 1748, after the Treaty of Aix-la-Chapelle, the city of Paris decided to develop a large square near the Palais des Tuileries (no. 41) and to name it after King Louis XV. This square, measuring 360 by 210 meters, is the largest of Paris's three royal squares. It is located at the intersection of two important streets: the east-west axis that comes from Vincennes castle (no. 17), passes by the Louvre (no. 49) and continues as Avenue des Champs-Élysées (no. 80); and Rue Royale, which runs from the Église de la Madeleine (no. 125), crosses the river at the Pont de la Concorde (no. 121), and arrives at the Assemblée Nationale (no. 127), whose façade echoes that of the Madeleine. In 1755, Ange-Jacques Gabriel won the architecture competition for the development of the square. His designs called for the construction of buildings on three sides and for truncated corners as at Place Vendôme (no. 95), a project developed by Jules Hardouin-Mansart nearly fifty years

before. Originally, walls with a balustrade and sentry boxes had delimited the square. The buildings to the north, Hôtel Crillon and Hôtel de la Marine (no. 122), recall the colonnades of the Louvre (no. 49). Although Rue Royale, which runs between the two hotels, was only completed in the early 19th century, it was part of the original urban development design. The equestrian statue of the king, that was unveiled in 1763, was demolished during the Revolution. Among the thousands of people who died on the "Place de la Révolution" were Louis XVI and his queen, Marie-Antoinette, as well as the revolutionary leaders Danton and Robespierre. The square was renamed "Place de la Concorde" after the royalist riots in 1795 to underscore the wish for national unity and harmony. The Cologne-born architect Jacques Ignace Hittorff remodeled the square between 1836 and 1846. He added in particular a 220-ton ancient obelisk brought from Luxor, Egypt, and two fountains with allegorical sculptures.

Hôtel Crillon und   (122)
Hôtel de la Marine
1770–1775
10, place de la Concorde / 8e
Jacques-Ange Gabriel, Pierre-Adrien
Paris, Louis-François Trouard

The Place de la Concorde (no. 121) remains undeveloped on three sides: along the Tuileries Garden, the Champs-Élysées (no. 80) and the Seine. The buildings to the north form a kind of architectural backdrop, and originally housed the Royal Storehouse and private apartments. Today they are the Ministry of the Navy, a luxury hotel, and the headquarters of the French Automobile Association.

Ange-Jacques Gabriel designed a symmetrical ensemble inspired by the east façade of the Louvre (no. 49), a work developed by Claude Perrault some hundred years earlier. A rusticated base supports a monumental Corinthian colonnade that unites the two upper stories. Projections terminate the colonnade on either side and form grand pavilions on either side of Rue Royale. The street between them provides a wonderful vista on the Église de la Madeleine (no. 125), which also features a grand colonnade.

Sainte-Geneviève (Panthéon) – an ecclesiastical building for the national heroes (123)

The hill later named Mont Sainte-Geneviève was the cradle of Paris, and remains of the Roman forum of Lutetia still exist there. In 512, Saint Geneviève (born c. 422 in Nanterre; died 512 in Paris) was buried in the first Merovingian church built on the hill in the early 6th century. In her lifetime, she had contributed to the conversion of Clovis I to Catholicism and had a church built over the tombs of Saint Denis and Saint Eleutherus, where the Saint-Denis Basilica (no. 11) stands today. Because of her courageous intervention when the Huns besieged Paris in 451, and of her role in Clovis I's conversion to Catholicism, Geneviève became the patron saint both of Paris and of France, and was venerated in the church on Mont Sainte-Geneviève – the ideal location for a French Pantheon where the nation could celebrate its heroic sons and daughters. Of the church built around 1180, only the Clovis Tower has been preserved. Louis XV had a new church erected to fulfill a vow he had made in 1744 during a severe illness. After delays, the new building was completed in 1790, ten years after the death of its architect, Jacques-Germain Soufflot. The church evidences the growing importance of a new architectural style, replacing Baroque decorum and complex spatial concepts with simple forms that show a return to Classical sources and the influence of the English Palladian style. Christopher Wren's St. Paul's Cathedral (1675–1710) served as a model, and its drum surrounded by regularly spaced columns of is distinctly closer to that of Sainte-Geneviève's than the rhythmically projecting formulation of Michelangelo's Baroque resolution of the St. Peter's Basilica in Rome (Val-de-Grâce, no. 67). The colonnade around Sainte-Geneviève's stands so low on the main volume, that it makes it look almost like a free-standing monopteral. Easily recognizable building types from the Antiquity like the monopteral, a round temple surrounded by columns, were the ideals of neo-Clas-

sicism (La Madeleine, no. 125). Soufflot's enthusiasm for Classicism originated not only from his studies in Rome, but also from his travels throughout Italy together with the brother of Madame de Pompadour, Louis XV's official mistress, during which he discovered the "noble simplicity and quiet grandeur" of the ancient temples of Paestum. Rome's Pantheon also inspired Soufflot's design for the simple Corinthian portico of Sainte-Geneviève: the portico clearly defines the main viewing angle, thus integrating another neo-Classical concept, in contrast to the many possible perspectives for Baroque buildings. Moreover, the portico uses iron to reinforce the stone, thus transcending the ring beams already used in Gothic buildings. The ground plan of the Panthéon is shaped like a Greek cross. An elevated ambulatory surrounds the interior except for the entrance and the sanctuary.

Soufflot had envisioned a bright and spacious interior, but the interior is much darker than originally planned, as massive piers replaced the slender columns of the drum during construction, and 42 windows were walled up after the church was converted into a national mausoleum in 1791. The dome covers two smaller cupolas invisible from the outside. The innermost of these is lined with shallow coffers. An oculus affords a view of the intermediate dome that is adorned with a fresco of The Apotheosis of St. Geneviève. The parish church was secularized during the Revolution. Under Napoleon I, the building was used for religious services while retaining its function as a national mausoleum.

Louis-Philippe prohibited Catholic services and confirmed the use of the building as a French Pantheon. Napoleon III made it a church once more, but the sub-sequent Republic converted it into a Pantheon conclusively in 1885. Among the national heroes buried in the crypt are Voltaire, Jean-Jacques Rousseau, Victor Hugo, Émile Zola and Marie Curie.

View towards the Panthéon

Liberté, Égalité, Fraternité: Neo-Classicism and revolutionary architecture (124)

A sudden break in aesthetics took place during the reign of Louis XVI: revolutionary architecture featuring reduced basic stereometric forms and unadorned buildings (customs buildings no. 142, no. 145, no. 146) purges Ange-Jacques Gabriel's neo-Classicism of the last of its playful ornamentation. The buildings' bulky form retains few distinctly identifiable details. In addition to the influence of ancient Rome, Pompeii, Greek Paestum, Egypt and Etruria are now also accepted in art and architecture. Before this period, ancient Greece exerted almost no influence. Even the ruin-obsessed Giambattista Piranesi, an important source of inspiration for any reception of Antiquity, dismissed the Greek Dorian in favor of the Etruscan Tuscan order until he was finally persuaded of Paestum's greatness nearing the end of his life. Practically no architects knew Greek architecture from personal experience, mainly because Greece was considered a dangerous travel destination. In 1764 Jacques-Germain Soufflot published Suite de plans de trois temples à Péstum after visiting it in 1750 together with Marquis de Marigny, the brother of Madame de Pompadour who

later became the directeur des bâtiments (director of construction). Greece became a source for pared-down but massive design. While architecture sought the highest level of clarity, landscape design undertook a turn in the opposite direction. The strictly ornamental flower beds, trimmed-to-the-millimeter hedges and strict perspective axes of Baroque gardens gave way to landscape gardens that imitated natural growth. The new English garden with an asymmetrical structure and winding paths was scattered with subordinate buildings, often with a purely decorative character. Both trends displayed a search for the unspoiled, early archaic forms. In the garden this was achieved by the "design" of perfect "un-designed" nature; in art and architecture this entailed reverting to the antiquity that preceded imperial decadence. Rationalism and enlightenment in tune with nature (Jean-Jacques Rousseau's "noble savage") that underlie these ideas also have their philosophical origins in the French Revolution. On May 5, 1789 the first Estates-General since 1614 convened to address the country's social and economic crisis. If the First Estate (nobility), disem-

powered by Louie XIV, and the Third Estate (middle classes, artisans and farmers) had earlier stood together to oppose the King's absolute rule and pushed for the call to convene, but during the Estates-General they fought each other bitterly over the organization of the legislature. The quantitatively and economically stronger Third Estate no longer wished to be dominated by the nobility and clerics (Second Estate) and declared itself to be the only appropriately legalized Estate. Furthermore, the Third Estate proclaimed itself as the National Assembly and swore at the Tennis Court Oath (June 20) not to disband until they have drawn up a French constitution to replace the King's "l'etat c'est moi." The remaining two Estates were urged to take part in the process. The storm of Bastille (July 14, no. 20) was followed by the abolition of feudal rights and privileges (August 8), Declaration of the Rights of Man and of Citizen, and finally the adoption of the first written constitution that envisaged a constitutional monarchy (September 3, 1791). The National Assembly that produced the constitution was replaced by a legislative body within which political "clubs" (the leading Jacobists, moderate Girondists, radical Cordeliers and conservative Feullitants) competed to control its orientation. The abolition of the monarchy and the creation of the Republic followed on September 21, 1792. Louis XVI was executed on January 21, 1793. After the radicalization of the Revolution under Robespierres lasting until 1795 (the Reign of Terror), the Executive Directory was formed, which meant to prevent an atarchy with a five-member directorate. The series of coalition wars, fought at first to defend the Revolution from monarchical Europe, continued. Having risen to the rank of General in the course of these campaigns, Napoleon Bonaparte dissolved the Directory by a coup d'état and replaced it with the Consulate, making himself First Consul for life. This had, in effect, made him into a military dictator. In 1804 he crowned himself Emperor Napoleon I. The architectural influences mentioned earlier continued or even gained momentum (Egyptian expedition) in the course of this period, but neo-Classicism adapted to the government reform by becoming fittingly more Roman, or "imperial."

La Madeleine (125)
1763–1842
place de la Madeleine / 8e
Pierre Contant d'Ivry,
Guillaume-Martin Couture,
Pierre Vignon, Jean-Jacques-Marie Huvé

A church that had stood here since the Middle Ages had to give way to a more stately building after the construction of Rue Royale and the nearby Place de la Concorde (no. 121). Pierre Contant d'Ivry therefore designed a cross-shaped church with a dome, lateral towers and a peristyle. Louis XV laid the cornerstone, but d'Ivry's plans were soon abandoned. Étienne-Louis Boullée retained the idea of the peristyle and added a dome similar to that of the Panthéon (no. 123). The construction works were interrupted during the Revolution and the government considered new uses: should the building house the parliament, a stock exchange or a library? Anything was possible, since only the foundations and some pillars were in place after some thirty years of work.

Napoleon decided that the new building should be designed after the Athenian Acropolis and house a "temple to the glory of the Great Army". In 1806, Pierre-Alexandre Vignon, the favorite pupil of Claude-Nicolas Ledoux, won the architecture competition and began to build a Corinthian temple whose peristyle was to match that of the Palais Bourbon (now Assmblée Nationale, no. 127) across the Seine. After Napoleon's abdication and the Treaty of Paris in 1814, Louis XVIII decided that the building should be an expiatory church for the executed members of the royal family, and Vignon

modified his design accordingly. Nevertheless, his successor Louis-Philippe – the "Citizen King" who came to power after the revolution of 1830 – made the building a parish church consecrated to Saint Mary Magdalene. Jean-Jacques Marie Huvé completed the construction works in 1842. The Madeleine covers a rectangle of 108 by 43 meters. These considerable dimensions were necessary as the church was intended to close the vista along Rue Royale from the vast Place de la Concorde. Its design as an ancient temple is typical of the neo-Classical style. The peripteral building with twenty-meter-high Corinthian columns has a cella – the inner room of ancient temples – and no windows, so that the interior had to be lit from above. The architect therefore roofed the nave with three cupolas that rest on pendentives and Corinthian columns and recall the vertex opening of the Roman Pantheon.

Hôtel Alexandre (today part (126)
of Suez-Lyonnaise des Eaux)
1763–1766, 1998–2001
16, rue de la Ville-l'Evêque / 8e
Étienne-Louis Boullée, DTACC (Delage Tsaropoulos Architecture Carvunis Cholet, headquarters of Suez-Lyonnaise des Eaux, 1998–2001)

The city mansion built for the financier André-Claude-Nicolas Alexandre is one of the few works by Étienne-Louis Boullée that remain unaltered. The architect designed the building when he was only thirty-five years old. Like most of the contemporary city mansions, the Hôtel Alexandre has a courtyard and a garden side. The façade on the courtyard side features monumental half-columns, while the garden-side façade has pilasters only in the upper story. Despite the rich ornamentation, Boullée's use of basic geometric shapes presages the advent of the revolutionary style of architecture. The Hôtel Alexandre today forms the atrium of the headquarters of Suez-Lyonnaise des Eaux, built from 1998 to 2001 by DTACC (Delaage Tsaropoulos Architecture Carvunis Cholet).

Palais Bourbon / Hôtel de Lassay (today Assemblée Nationale)   (127)
1764–1765, 1795–1798, 1806,
1829–1832, 1843
126–128, rue de l'Université,
29–35, quai d'Orsay / 7e
Jacques-Germain Soufflot

The main façade of the Palais Bourbon, styled after a Greek temple, is part of one of Paris's most imposing vistas, as it forms the southern endpoint of a line leading across the Pont Royal, through the obelisk at the center of Place de la Concorde (no. 121), to the Église de la Madeleine (no. 125). In spite of its unified effect, however, the Palais Bourbon was built bit by bit over several decades of the 18th and 19th centuries.

What today is the seat of the French National Assembly was originally a small, single-story palace built from 1722 to 1728 to plans by Lorenzo Giardini for Louise-Françoise de Bourbon, the legitimized daughter of Louis XIV and his mistress Madame de Montespan. In 1756 Louis XV bought the palace, then sold it to Louis Joseph, Prince of Condé, for whom Jacques-Germain Soufflot directed an enlargement in 1765, add

ing an upper story and new wings, and joining the palace with the neighboring Hôtel de Lessay in a single complex. The revolutionary government confiscated the Palais Bourbon in 1792, and commissioned Guy de Gigors and Étienne Charles Lesconte to remodel it for French parliament.

The Classical portico with a triangular pediment above Corinthian columns, which impressively echoes the façade of the Église de la Madeleine, was added during the reign of Napoleon between 1803 and 1807. Jean-Pierre Cortot sculpted the attic relief, an allegory of France between Force and Justice (1839–1841). The French National Assembly has met here since 1827. The present semicircular chamber was developed between 1829 and 1832. Among other interiors, the Library with its ceiling paintings by Eugène Delacroix and his pupils (1838 to 1847) is especially noteworthy.

Wilmotte and Elizabeth de Portzamparc were among those behind the décor of the Assemblée National.

Hôtel de Tessé   (128)
1765–1768
1, quai Voltaire / 7e
Pierre-Noel Rousset, Louis le Tellier

The Count de Tessé had a city mansion built in the Louis Seize style even before Louis XVI acceded to the throne. Monumental Ionic pilasters unite the two upper stories and support a plain balustrade that conceals the roof. The first floor features horizontal joints as the only decoration. The original decoration of the Grand Salon is now exhibited in the Metropolitan Museum of Art in New York City.

Hôtel d'Hallwyl (129)
1766
28, rue Michel-le-Comte,
15 rue de Montmorency / 3e
Claude-Nicolas Ledoux

This mansion is the result of the alteration of a 17th-century building by Claude-Nicolas Ledoux. It was among the last houses to be erected for a nobleman in the Marais before craftsmen began settling in the borough during the Revolution. Moreover, the Hôtel d'Hallwyl is among the few mansions erected in the revolutionary style of architecture that have been preserved. Rustication dominates the façade of the entrance building on two stories. Doric columns, which enjoyed a revival during the neo-Classical period due to their plain appearance, frame the entrance and are complemented by Ionic columns inside. Two genii grouped around an urn adorn the tympanum. The main wing also features the simple design that characterizes the revolutionary style of architecture: balusters and pediments adorn only the three central windows of the main story. This reduction to an austere appearance is typical of the dignity aspired to in "revolutionary Classicism". The stately staircase in the left wing is the only remnant of the interior decoration by Ledoux, whose career began with the remodeling works commissioned here by Franz Joseph de Hallwyl, an officer of the Royal Swiss Guards.

Maison de Carré de Beaudouin (130)
1770–1771
119–121, rue de Ménilmontant / 20e
Pierre-Louis Moreau

The country house of Nicolas Carré de Beaudouin, built atop Ménilmontant Hill, remained outside the city limits of Paris until the middle of the 19th century. Unlike many pavilions built near the capital, it was preserved and now houses an orphanage. Pierre-Louis Moreau-Desproux's Italian-style design for this building clearly recalls Palladio's villas in Veneto.

Hôtel de la Monnaie de Paris (131)
(museum)
1771–1777
11, quai de Conti,
2–4, rue Guénégaud / 6e
Jacques-Denis Antoine

The royal mint was the first large building to abandon the Baroque and Rococo for the new Louis Seize style. Despite the building's importance and strategic location near the Seine, the ensemble has a plain decoration and does without a cour d'honneur. The main building is a plain parallelepiped. On the 177-meter façade, the decoration concentrates on the projection, where six monumental Ionic columns support an attic story with allegories of Intelligence, Abundance, Justice, Peace, Power, and Commerce – the guiding principles of any

plete the construction works. The building now houses the Hector Berlioz municipal conservatory.

Hôtel de Fleury (today École (133) **Nationale des Ponts et Chaussée)**
1772
28, rue des Saints-Pères / 7e
Jacques-Denis Antoine

This building is composed of three similar pavilions connected by two lower structures that were enlarged vertically when the Royal Engineering School moved here in 1831. Vestiges of the Tuileries Palace (no. 41) still exist on the site.

monetary policy even to this day. The ground floor is demarcated as a plinth by virtue of the joint outlines, and the upper side façades are accentuated solely by the rhythmic addition of balconies and triangular pediments. A half-story extends behind the plain top cornice. Personifications of Commerce and Agriculture made by Dupré flank the entrance. A peristyle with Doric columns and a courtyard with arcades and a dome provide access to the coinage workshops.

Hôtel Gouthière (132)
1772–1780
6, rue Pierre-Bullet / 10e
Joseph Métivier, Pérard de Montreuil (not verified)

This building, located behind the city hall of the 10th arrondissement, does without any vertical decorative elements. Horizontal joints and a cornice underscore the horizontal dimension, however. Two sphinxes flank the entrance. The first landlord, a goldsmith, lent a great deal of money to Madame du Barry, Louis XV's last mistress, and was left unable to com-

Théâtre de France / Théâtre (134) **de l'Odéon / Théâtre de la Nation**
1774–1789
1, place Odéon / 6e
Pierre-Louis Moreau, Marie Joseph Peyre, Charles de Wailly

Marie-Joseph Peyre and Charles de Wailly altered the original plans by Pierre-Louis Mareau during the construction works and the building, begun in 1774, was unveiled by Marie-Antoinette in 1782. This theater, originally topped with a pyramidal roof, shows that the revolutionary style of architecture already existed under the Ancien Régime. Horizontal and vertical joints

95

extend across the entire façade as the only decoration. The squat portico with Doric columns features a frieze whose metopes are only adorned with circles. Protruding keystones are the sole decorative elements of the arched doors, the rectangular and round windows, and the central lunette of the attic story.

Jean-François Chalgrin rebuilt the theater to the original design – except for the pyramidal roof – after it had burnt down in 1799. After a second fire, however, Pierre-Thomas Baraguey modified the building again in 1822, and did away with the two arches that had linked the building with the neighbor structures across the street. The ceiling painting is a 20th-century work by André Masson, and the semi-circular space in front of the theater is part of a modern urban development concept.

Saint-Philippe-du-Roule (135)
1774–1784
154, rue de Faubourg Saint-Honoré / 8e
Jean-François Chalgrin

Although this church one of the first sacred buildings ever erected in the neo-Classical style, it already shows variations from the new architectural canons.

Jean-François Chalgrin took his inspiration not only from Greek temples, as shown by the portico with four Doric columns, but also from Early Christian basilicas. Wooden barrel vaults supported by Ionic columns cover the nave and aisles. More columns form an ambulatory around the choir.

According to Chalgrin's design, the chapels in the prolongation of the aisles should have been the bases of two towers. Saint-Philippe-du-Roule, patterned after

Early Christian churches, was the first of a series of similar buildings erected during the Restoration. Étienne-Hippolyte Godde, who built several comparable churches, remodeled the apse between 1845 and 1852 and created a large choir with sacristies and a chapel of the Virgin Mary.

La Bagatelle (pavilion) (136)
1775
Bois de Boulogne
François-Joseph Bélanger

In 1720, Marshall Victor d'Estrées had a summer residence built to the south of the château de Madrid, a palace which had been built by Francis I in 1528 and adorned with ceramic tiles by Girolamo della Robbia, but which would be demolished after the French Revolution. Louis XV used d'Estrées's summer house for his amorous rendezvous. The Count d'Artois, a brother of Louis XVI, acquired the estate in 1775, although the small palace was in ruins. He wagered 100,000 pounds with his sister-in-law Marie-Antoinette that he could restore it within just sixty-four days.

To win the bet, he had to confiscate all building materials in and around Paris and employ nine hundred people around the clock. The works began on September 21 and were almost completed on November 26. The count won the bet – but at a cost of two million pounds.

The renovation of the garden and the interior decoration were completed by 1786, and courtiers used Bagatelle for many parties – the French word "baga-

telle" thus became a synonym for "sex affair". After the Revolution, when the count became King Charles X, he had the risqué murals painted over. François-Joseph Bélanger's design for Bagatelle transferred the rooms of the piano nobile to the first floor and provided bedrooms in the second floor. Alterations during the 19th century included the construction of an additional story topped with a cupola, and the redesigning of the park by the Scotsman Thomas Blaikie, who made it one of the first landscape gardens in France.

When the city of Paris acquired the estate in the early 20th century, Jean-Claude-Nicolas Forestier laid out a rose garden inspired by that of his friend Claude Monet in Giverny.

Université René-Descartes – (137)
Faculté de Médecine
1776–1786, 1878–1900
12, rue de l'Ecole-de-Médecine / 6e
Jacques Gondouin, Paul René Léon Ginain

Barbers and surgeons belonged to the same guild until the foundation of the royal surgery academy in 1748. A new building was erected on this occasion near the Amphithéâtre Anatomique (no. 96). On the street side, the three-winged complex in the Louis Seize style features a half-story with Ionic columns. Originally, a relief that portrayed Louis XVI handing over to Medicine the plans he received from Art – a work by Pierre-François Berruer – adorned the entrance, but an allegory of Charity replaced the king's portray in 1794. Columns surround the courtyard adorned with a statue of the physician Xavier Bichat - a work by David

d'Angers. An allegory of Theory extending her hand to Practice – another work by Pierre-François Berruer – adorns the portico of Corinthian columns that gives access to the amphitheater. The building houses also a museum devoted to the history of medicine. Between 1878 and 1900, Léon Ginain added other structures on three sides of the the original building.

Parc Monceau (138)
Folie de Chartres
1778–1861
boulevard de Courcelles / 8e
Bernard Poyet

GARDEN Philippe d'Orléans, Duke of Chartres, later nicknamed "Philippe-Égalité" for his revolutionary ideas, had a garden landscaped in the English style at the limits of the city. The landlord had a variety of ornamental buildings installed in his park to serve as enchanting backdrops for his guests as he strolled with

them across the landscape: Greek and Gothic ruins, a windmill, several tombs, an antique temple, a Chinese pagoda, a pyramid, an obelisk, a nymphaeum, and a naumachia whose columns were probably taken from the unfinished Valois chapel at Saint-Denis Basilica (no. 11). In 1788, Claude-Nicolas Ledoux built the Rotonde de Chartres at the edge of the park and Philippe d'Orléans used the upper story of this customs house as a belvedere. The park was neglected during the Revolution and annexed to the City of Paris in 1860. Baron Haussmann sold part of the garden and commissioned Adolphe Alphand to remodel the remaining nine hectares for the inhabitants of the newly developed districts nearby, now the 8th and 17th arrondissements. After the fire at the Hôtel de Ville (no. 208) during the Paris Commune in 1871, the remains of a Renaissance arcade by Domenico da Cortona "Boccador", were brought to the Parc Monceau. Among the many monuments to poets and musicians that adorn Parc Monceau, the monument to Chopin – a work by Jacques Froment-Meurice – is particularly noteworthy.

Saint-Louis-d'Antin (139)
(Convent des Capucins)
1780–1782
in the Lycée Condorcet:
65, rue Caumartin / 9e
Alexandre-Théodore Brongniart

The Chaussée d'Antin district, developed around 1720, had become fashionable by the end of the 18th century. However, it did not have its own church until a lady living there invited Capuchin friars to settle in the vicinity.

The church has a barrel-vaulted nave flanked by a single aisle to the south. The north entrance on the extremely simplified façade leads to the former monastery. Segmental pediments top the lateral entrance, while powerful Doric columns frame the main entrance and support a plain cornice with a semi-circular opening above it.

The portico between the church and the former monastery also includes strong Doric columns.

Jacques-Louis David adorned this part of the church with a painting of Brutus and His Sons.

In 1804, Napoleon converted the monastery into an upper secondary school, the "Lycée Bonaparte", which was enlarged by Viollet-le-Duc in 1865.

Hôtel d'Argenson (140)
1780
38, avenue Gabriel / 8e
Jean-Philippe Lemoine de Courzon

The widow of the Marquis d'Argenson had this neo-Classical palace developed near the Champs-Élysées in the late 18th century, as the district was becoming increasingly fashionable. Four mighty Ionic columns dominate and unite the lower stories and support an exceptionally protruding attic story.

Hôtel de Salm (141)
(Palais de la Légion d'honneur)
1782–1784
2, rue de la Légion d'honneur / 7e
Pierre Rousseau

Frederick III, sovereign prince of Salm-Kyrburg, abolished serfdom in his principality in the late 18th century, but this did not save him from being guillotined in Paris in 1793. Since 1804, his palace has been home to the Legion of Honor.

On the garden side facing the Seine, a rotunda covers the prominent central projection. On the street side, a triumphal arch provides access to the cour d'honneur with its Ionic peristyle and to the main entrance with its Corinthian portico. The three-story lateral wings are later additions.

Barrière d'Enfer (142)
(Mur des Fermiers Généraux)
1784–1787
place Denfert-Rochereau / 14e
Claude-Nicolas Ledoux

The two identical buildings at Place Denfert-Rochereau were once customs houses. Each of the cubic structures features three arches on the ground floor and several small windows on the upper stories. The stacked ashlars forming the ground floor are penetrated by columns that support the arches and the separated by deep, gaping joints; the protruding arch stones forming the arch underscore the semicircular shapes. The neo-Classical style found here is reduced to an interplay of geometric forms, imbuing the building with a martial atmosphere.

Building number 1 provides access to the Paris catacombs, which were filled with bones transferred from abandoned local graveyards between 1786 and 1814. The bronze lion that adorns the square is a smaller version of the monumental sculpture in Belfort by Frédéric Auguste Bartoldi. It commemorates the heroic resistance of Colonel Denfert-Rochereau in the besieged Alsatian city during the Franco-Prussian war of 1870.

Gloriette Buffon (pavilion) (143)
1786–1787
Jardin des Plantes; 57, rue Cuvier / 5e
Edme Verniquet

This small pavilion in the Jardin des Plantes is Paris's oldest iron structure. In 1626, Louis XIII had a garden planted with medicinal herbs. The Royal Cabinet of Natural History was also installed here. The Gloriette pavilion was built at the orders of Georges-Louis Leclerc, Count de Buffon, keeper of the royal botanical garden from 1739 on. Ten years later, Leclerc began to publish his monumental compendium of natural history (Histoire naturelle générale et particulière in 44 volumes). Edme Verniquet erected a grand amphitheater in the Louis Seize style in 1787–1788 near the Gloriette pavilion and Jacques Molinos enlarged the building in 1794.

Théâtre-Français / Comédie- (144)
Française / Théâtre de Duc d'Orléans
1786–1790, 1863
place Colette, place André-Malraux / 1er
Victor Louis, Prosper Chabrol

The structure built by Victor Louis in the 18th century, together with the Palais-Royal (no. 119), still stands behind the façade developed by Prosper Chabrol as Avenue de l'Opéra was laid out in 1863. Several theater groups merged in 1680 and were placed under the patronage of the king the following year. One of them was that directed by Molière. The statue of the playwright that stands here – a work by Jean-Antoine Houdon that was originally intended for the Academy – is among the best monuments to personalities erected in the late 18th century. It portrays Molière as a classical philosopher, and renders his humor as in a snapshot. Louis's works also include the arcades with boutiques in the garden of the Palais-Royal, which can be accessed via a passageway between the theater

and the lateral wing in the Cour de l'Horloge. The Théâtre Français became a state theater in 1812.

Rotonde de la Villette – (145)
Barrière de la Villette – Barrière
Saint-Martin (Mur des Fermiers
Généraux)
1786–1792
place de Stalingrad / 19e
Claude-Nicolas Ledoux

Only four of the fifty-five customs houses built by Claude-Nicolas Ledoux have been preserved. This one is the most archaic in appearance.

It is the central pavilion of an ensemble set at the parting of two roads, one leading towards Flanders and the other towards Germany (now Rue de Flandres and Rue Jean-Jaurès). The building is composed of a square single-story base with an open rotunda rising at its center. Low porticos face two sides of the square. Ledoux designed the building after having seen an English etching of the rotunda build by Palladio near Vicenza in 1591.

The base is characterized by horizontal mortar joints that compress the traditional window frames. Each portico is composed of eight pillars with tapered shafts and plain capitals supporting a simple cornice and a triangular pediment. A wider variety of forms can be found above: An endless circle of interlinked Palladian motives crowns the alternating round arches and cornices above pairs of columns, forming a walkway all around the circumference. Small square windows are the only interruptions in the

wall surface above the arches. The Doric cornice with a triglyph frieze dispenses altogether with corbels. The basin that extends in front of the building resulted from the digging of the Canal St-Martin, Canal St-Denis and Canal de l'Ourcq under Napoleon between 1806 and 1809. Bernard Huet designed the postmodern square between the basin and the rotunda in 1989.

Barrière du Trône   **(146)**
(Mur des Fermiers Généraux)
1787 started
avenue du Trône,
place de la Nation / 11e, 12e
Claude-Nicolas Ledoux

Among other temporary features, a throne stood here to welcome Louis XIV back to Paris after his coronation in Rheims on August 26, 1660. The Sun King's Minister of Finance, Jean-Baptiste Colbert, had wanted to erect a triumphal arch, a predecessor of the present-day Arc de Triomphe (no. 158), but the project was abandoned after the sovereign's death in 1715.

A customs house was to be built here after the "fermiers généraux", the general tax officers, had moved the tax boundaries. Because the land belonged to the crown and the king used to pass Place du Trône on his way to Vincennes Castle (no. 18), Claude-Nicolas Ledoux developed a stately gate similar to the Barrière

de l'Étoile which is no longer extant. He built two three-story buildings, each of which was to have had a twenty-five-meter column on a cube protruding from the roof. The design was altered, however, in favor of two thirty-meter Doric columns on separate structures placed between the two customs houses. Prominent voussoirs give a particular touch to the arched openings in the buildings.

In 1794, more than 1,300 people were guillotined within just six weeks on the square, which had been renamed "Place du Trône Renversé", i.e. "Toppled Throne Square". Bronze statues of Saint Louis and Philippe II by Dupont have stood atop the columns since 1843. The ornaments at the foot of the columns were also added under the reign of Louis-Philippe. The bronze statue that adorns the basin – a work by Dalou – is an 1899 addition that depicts the Triumph of the Republic.

Claude-Nicolas Ledoux
*1736 in Dormans-sur- Marne † 1806 in Paris (147)

The monumental forms of French Classicism became the official style of the absolutist state under Louis XIV. Under the reign of his successor Louis XV, a great-grandson of the Sun King, the intimate Rococo style with its profusion of detail reflected the decline of absolutism. And under Louis XVI, architects increasingly renounced ornamentation, leading gradually to the early neo-Classical style that could be described as "naked Rococo". The revolutionary style of architecture originated in France around 1770, and with time its "anti-Baroque" premises became increasingly uncompromising. The French architects of the late 18th century rejected all decorative and dividing elements, favoring plain volumes such as cubes, pyramids or even spheres. Étienne-Louis Boullée (1728–1799) and Claude-Nicolas Ledoux (1736–1806) were among the leading proponents of this style. They were rarely given an opportunity to realize their utopian designs, however, mainly because of their projects' oversized dimensions. For example, the mausoleum of Isaac Newton that Boullée planned was to have been a spherical planetarium with a diameter of no less than 150 meters. Smaller buildings that Boullée did build in Paris include the Hôtel Alexandre (no. 126) and the Hôtel Brunoy. Ledoux was more successful. A protégé of Madame du Barry, one of the official mistresses of Louis XV, he began his career with a design for her country home at Louveciennes. Ledoux became a fashionable aficionado of the Louis Seize style (Hôtel d'Hallwyl, no. 129, and Hôtel de Montmorency), and ultimately one of the major representatives of the Revolutionary style of architecture. The clear style of Ledoux's late works, influenced by Piranesi, is the result of a keen sensitivity to the interplay of elementary forms, and of his endeavor to create a "speaking architecture", that is, buildings with explicit characters and functions. For example, Ledoux designed the interior of the portico of the Royal Saltworks at Arc-et-Senans (1775–1779) as a grotto shaped by the local brine sources. The portico itself, composed of Ionic columns, became a model for Carl Gotthard Langhans when he designed the Brandenburg Gate in Berlin a few years later. Both buildings, like those of other architects who favored the revolutionary style's stately monumental proportions and clear geometric lines, show the inspiration of classical architecture, and of Doric temples in particular. This "Doric revival" would lead progressively to neo-Classicism, and in particular to the large triumphal arch that formed the entrance to the Hôtel de Thélusson, another work by Ledoux that is no longer extant. However, two of the customs houses built by Ledoux

The saline at Chaux

around Paris between 1785 and 1789 (Barrière d'Enfer, no. 142 and Rotonde de la Villette, no. 145) have been preserved. As surprising as it may seem at first glance, the French revolution did not advance the career of the foremost advocate of the revolutionary style of architecture.

On the contrary, Ledoux was even jailed for a year in 1793 as a former court architect and a potential supporter of the Ancien Régime. He barely escaped the guillotine, helped by his statement in a book that his Royal Saltworks were part of an ideal city conceived as a prototype of democratic architecture. In the last years of his life, Ledoux developed no noteworthy buildings and concentrated on his main written work, L'Architecture considérée sous le rapport de l'art, des mœurs et de la legislation, which was published shortly before his death in 1806. More than his buildings, this book was to remain a reference for architects until the postmodern period of the 20th century.

103

Design for the house of a landscape guard

Rotonde de Chartres –   (148)
Folie de Chartres
(Mur des Fermiers Généraux)
1788
im Parc Monceau / 8e
Claude-Nicolas Ledoux

Claude-Nicolas Ledoux patterned this rotunda – a former customs house at the edge of Parc Monceau (no. 138) – after the Tempietto Bramantes (San Pietro in Montorino) built in Rome in 1502 and after the Greek temples of Paestrum, which also feature a peristyle of Greek Doric columns without bases. The Duke of Chartres contributed to the construction, as the building stood on the boundary of his property, and used it as a belvedere. The original cupola was lower, however, which gave the building a more compact appearance, even if the basement was not deeply sunken in the ground as it is today.

Pont de la Concorde   (149)
1788–1791
Seine / 7e, 8e
Jean-Rudolphe Perronet

This bridge, which should have been named "Pont Louis XVI", was made using stones from the Bastille (no. 20).

Pierre-François Palloy, the entrepreneur who had demolished the fortress, said it was good that the people would tread upon this hated symbol of Absolutism.The director of the Royal Engineering School (École des Ponts et Chaussées, no. 133) developed here a novel solution: his filigree structure is not a succession of independent spans as the previous architects' bridges, but a static ensemble, which made the use of slender pillars possible.

Between 1929 and 1931, the width of the bridge connecting the Saint-Germain and Saint-Honoré boroughs was doubled.

Rue des Colonnes   (150)
1797
rue des Colonnes (from rue des Filles-Saint-Thomas to rue Feydeau) / 2e
Joseph Bérnard

This street lined with an arcade was the direct predecessor of Rue de Rivoli

(no. 154) laid out five years later north of the Louvre (no. 49).

Pillars with tapered shafts and columns without bases support the arches. Acanthus leaves above the Doric capitals at the base of the arches are the only ornaments.

Rue des Colonnes is the only street developed in the revolutionary style of architecture. It is crossed today by Rue de la Bourse.

Passage du Caire (151)
1798–1799
2, place du Caire; 44, rue du Caire,
33, rue d'Alexandre,
237, rue Saint-Denis / 2e
Philippe-Laurent Prétel

Several arcades were developed in the 18th century, but this one is now the oldest preserved in the city. With a total length of 370 meters, it is the longest as well. Most of the arcades in Paris were built during the Restoration. The entrance on Place du Caire, which features Egyptian motifs, was redesigned in the 1820s. Moreover, the original wood ceiling was replaced with a plain glass roof in the course of the 19th century.

Passage des Panoramas (152)
1800, 1834
11, boulevard Montmartre,
10, rue Saint-Marc / 2e
Jean-Louis-Victor Grisart

In the early 19th century, panoramas were popular attractions offering panoramic paintings of a city, a landscape or a battle from an elevated point and with real objects in the foreground. William Thayer, an American citizen, developed Paris's first two panoramas.

Passage des Panoramas, the city's second oldest arcade, was developed to link Thayer's panoramas. The arcade was equipped with gas lighting as early as 1816. It originally had a wooden ceiling, which was replaced with iron and glass probably during the extension works, and is attributed to Jean-Louis Grisart in 1834.

Pont des Arts (153)
1802–1804
Seine / 1er, 6e
Louis Alexandre de Cessart

This bridge linking the Louvre (no. 49) and the Institut de France is the oldest

105

iron bridge in the city. Stone remained the chief building material much longer in France than in England, where iron was cheap and abundant on the home market. The structural use of iron is still hesitant, and the execution imitates that of a wooden bridge. The steel copy that replaced the original bridge in 1981 has fewer and longer spans to accommodate shipping.

Apartments and office building (154)
1802–1804
place de Pyramides, rue de Rivoli, rue des Pyramides (Jean d'Arc) / 1er
Charles Percier,
Pierre-François-Léonard Fontaine

Napoleon commissioned the development of arcades, patterned after those in Rue des Colonnes (no. 150), on both sides of Place des Pyramides, where an equestrian statue of Joan of Arc was added in 1874 – a work by Emmanuel Frémiet. The original shed roofs were replaced with half-barrels, which afforded space for additional apartments and soon became typical of 19th-century residential architecture in Paris. Extension of the complex between

Place du Palais-Royal and Rue Saint-Antoine continued until 1850, but the portion west of Rue de l'Oratoire took on a slightly different appearance. The long, unified structure was to become the residential counterpart of the Louvre (no. 49). This modification of the traditional residential structure not only foreshadowed the remodeling of the French capital by Haussmann (no. 185) in the following decade, but also marked the transition to four-story buildings as the predominant type of construction in the city.

Cimetière de l'Est   (155)
(Cimetière du Père-Lachaise)
1804
boulevard de Ménilmontant / 20e
Alexandre-Théodore Brongniart

With an area of over forty-three hectares, this is the largest of all Paris cemeteries. It is famous not only for the graves of diverse celebrities, from Frédéric Chopin to Jim Morrison, but also for its mausoleums by many noted 19th-century architects and sculptors, such as Viollet-le-Duc, Félix Duban, Achille-François-René Leclerc, Léon Vaudoyer, and Hector Guimard. The cemetery was named after François de la Chaise d'Aix, Louis XIV's Jesuit confessor, who once owned the land. In 1804,

Alexandre-Théodore Brongniart laid out the cemetery on a hill planted with trees, thus creating kind of a park in the taste of the time. In 1823, Jean-Camille Godde built the chapel and designed the main entrance gate.

The sculptor Albert Bartholomé and the architect Jean-Camille Formigé created the monument that stands at the end of the main alley, titled Men Entering the Kingdom of Death. Jean-Camille Formigé also designed the neo-Byzantine crematorium (1886–1887) and columbarium (1894). In 1817, Alexandre Lenoir created a neo-Gothic mausoleum for the purported remains of Abélard and Héloïse, the most famous lovers of the Middle Ages, and integrated fragments of the Paraclet Abbey in Nogent-sur-Seine and of the Saint-Denis Abbey (no. 11) into his work. In 1804, Lenoir had already designed the sarcophagus for the transferred remains of La Fontaine and Molière. In 1871, during the Paris Commune, the last 147 defenders of the workers' district Belleville were shot along the southeast wall of the cemetery. A total of 1018 victims of the uprising were buried along the Communards' Wall (Mur des Fédérés). If you are having trouble finding your revered protagonists of 19th century Paris, you ought to have a look at the Cimetière de Montmartre or at the Cimetière du Montparnasse, both laid-out and built in1824.

Hôtel Beauharnais (156)
(Hôtel Torcy)
(1713–1715), 1804–1807, 1837–1838
78, rue de Lille / 7e
Germain Boffrand,
Jacques Ignace Hittorff

Germain Boffrand developed this palace (and the building on the neighboring lot)

between 1713 and 1715, before selling it to the Marquis de Torcy. Eugène de Beauharnais, who participated in the Egyptian campaign of his adoptive father Napoleon Bonaparte, acquired the estate in 1803. Beauharnais had the palace remodeled between 1804 and 1807: Laurent Edme Bataille created a portico in the Egyptian style and various craftsmen produced furniture in the Empire style. Frederick William III of Prussia acquired the palace in 1814 and installed the Prussian legation here. The building became the German embassy in 1874. Jacques Ignace Hittorff remodeled the palace again in 1837–1838.

La Fontaine de Mars (157)
1806
129–131, rue Saint-Dominique / 7e
Nicolas Bralle

Napoleon commissioned this fountain to ornament a military hospital that once stood here.

Above the fountain proper stands a structure with architectural elements including pilasters and a cornice. A relief portraying Mars, the Roman god of War, and Hygeia, the Greek goddess of Health, adorns the recessed space between the pilasters, which appear to represent three-dimensional architecture within the relief.

Arc de Triomphe de l'Étoile – the Napoleonic gate to the city (158)

The triumphal arch stands on an axis that also passes through the smaller Arc de Triomphe du Carrousel, the site of the Tuileries Palace (no. 41), and the Louvre (no. 49) to the east, and through the Great Arch of La Défense (no. 377) to the west. Construction began in 1806 to plans by Jean-François Chalgrin, and a full-scale model was built of wood and cardboard for the wedding of Napoleon and Marie Louise of Austria in 1810. Styled after triumphal arches of classical antiquity, as well as after the Porte Saint-Denis, the Arc de Triomphe at Place de l'Étoile embodies Napoleon's imperial ambitions. Consequently, the building works were stopped in 1814 after the emperor's abdication. In 1823, Louis XVIII rejected plans to finish the monument in the form of a fountain, preferring to complete the original arch as a monument to the victory of the house of Bourbon in Spain. However, Louis-Philippe decided to maintain the original function and the arch was completed as a monument to Napoleonic victories between 1832 and 1836. Several projects for today's Pace de l'Étoile were developed over the years. In 1758, during the reign of Louis XV, urban planers considered building a seven-story structure in the shape of an elephant with a fountain spouting from the trunk. Shortly before the end of the Ancien Régime, Claude-Nicolas Ledoux (no. 147) built a pair of customs houses here, since the square marked the city limits until 1860. Meanwhile, permanent triumphal arches were planned for Place de la Bastille and Place du Trône. After his victory at Austerlitz in 1805, Napoleon not only decided that the Église de la Madeleine was to become a temple to the glory of the Great Army upon completion, but he also considered building a monument to perpetuate his own glory at Place de l'Étoile. Therefore, the emperor commissioned the Triumph of Bonaparte, a sculpture by François Rude, to replace the traditional quadriga atop the arch. After Chalgrin's death, Louis-Robert Goust and Jean-Nicolas Huyot continued the building works and Guillaume Abel Blouet completed them in 1836. The dimensions of the arch (fifty meters high and forty-five meters wide) exceed that of all classical predecessors. Moreover, the Classical columns originally planned by Chalgrin and Raymond – who themselves disagreed on the issue – were omitted, and the resulting plain surfaces further reinforce the monument's massive appearance. Smaller transverse archways – another difference from classical triumphal arches – divide the structure into four piers, each as large as a house, and make the monument more suited to a location like Place de l'Étoile, at the center of a roundabout. High-reliefs placed above pedestals adorn the four piers and appear like free-standing works. Minister Adolphe Thiers chose their iconography in 1833. The best-known of them, on the right as viewed from Avenue des Champs-Élysées, is The Departure of the Volunteers in 1792, known colloquially as the Marseillaise – a work by François Rude that transports a scene from the Revolution into classical antiquity as it figures Vercingetorix and his Gaul warriors. The left pier bears The Triumph of Napoleon in 1810, a work by Jean-Pierre Cortot that portrays the emperor in Roman costume – a typical neo-Classical trope. Facing outward from the city center are The Resistance of 1814 and The Peace of 1815, works by Antoine Étex. Star-shaped street arrangements were a frequent urban planning motif in the Baroque period, and Place de l'Étoile – at the junction of twelve radially arranged streets – received its name early on. In the second half of the 19th century, however, Georges Eugène Haussmann redesigned the square around the triumphal arch as part of his extensive redevelopment of the French capital. Although Haussmann did not appreciate Jacques Ignace Hittorff's designs for the surrounding buildings, with their entrances facing away from the square on the farther concentric ring street, Place de l'Étoile belongs to the most outstanding urban developments of the 19th century. In 1921, the French government established the world's first "Tomb of the Unknown Soldier" under the arch.

View towards the Arc de Triomphe from north

Fontaine du Fellah (159)
1806–1808
42, rue de Sèvres / 7e
Nicolas Bralle

This fountain is the most important testimony to Egyptian architecture in the city. Its major feature is a copy of a Roman sculpture after an Egyptian work now exhibited in the Louvre (no. 49). It figures a fellah carrying two pitchers out of which water flows into the basin. The sculpture's niche is shaped like a pylon. The diagonally ascending course of the masonry is untypical of pure neo-Classicism, but quite common in architecture from the French Revolution.

Place du Châtelet (160)
1808, 1855–1858
place du Châtelet / 1er, 4e
Georges-Eugène Haussmann,
Gabriel Davioud

The "Grand Châtelet" that once stood here guarded access to the Pont au Change (formerly "Grand Pont") and the royal palace on the Île de la Cité (Conciergerie, no. 16).

The building was unpopular, having served as a courthouse, a torture chamber, a police station and a morgue. In 1802, Napoleon ordered its demolition and the construction of a fountain that was to combine Egyptian motifs, including a palm tree shaft with a palm-shaped capital and a commemorative column bearing the names of his military victories. The base of the monument with four sphinxes was added by Gabriel Davioud during the expansion and displacement of the square between 1851 and 1856.

Bourse de Paris (161)
1809–1813, 1821–1826
place de la Bourse / 2e
Alexandre-Théodore Brongniart,
Eloi de Labarre

The Paris stock exchange was founded in 1724. Alexandre-Théodore Brongniart erected a building for the stockbrokers a century later, as share trading was becoming ever more important. The "Palais Brongniart" was built on the site of the Saint Thomas Dominican monastery abandoned during the French Revolution. The construction of the stock exchange reinforced the second arrondissement's role as the financial center of Paris. The architect gave the building an imposing appearance to reflect the sovereignty of business. Fourteen colossal columns top a flight of stairs that extends along the entire façade. The building proper is hardly discernible behind the peristyle that supports a wide entablature. The stock exchange recalls antique temples, except that its main façade is on one of the long sides. The arcade on the first floor gives access to the stockbrokers' enclosure. The commercial court once held session on the second floor. The construction works were interrupted after the fall of Napoleon, then resumed in 1821, and completed in 1827 under the direction of Éloi Labarre. In 1902–1903, Jean-Baptiste Cavel built two additional wings.

Marché Saint-Germain (162)
1813–1818
rue Mabillon, rue Clément, rue Félbien, rue Lobinau / 6e
Jean Baptiste Blondel, Auguste Lusson

This building, an example of the late revolutionary style of architecture, was refurbished and reconstructed by Olivier-Clément Cacoub in the late 20th century. Another structure had stood here since 1511, housing in particular the Saint-Germain trade fair, but it was destroyed by fire in 1762. The present building contains modern boutiques.

Chapelle expiatoire (163)
1816–1826
place Louis XVI; 31, rue Pasquier, boulevard Haussmann / 8e
Pierre-François-Léonard Fontaine

After Louis XVIII had the remains of his brother and his sister-in-law Louis XVI and Marie-Antoinette brought to Saint-Denis Basilica (no. 11), he ordered the construction of an expiatory chapel near the place where the king, the queen and many other guillotined people had been buried during the French Revolution (Place de la Concorde, no. 121). The chapel stands in a garden where nearly one thousand people are buried. "Philippe Égalité", Duke of Chartres and Orléans, and Charlotte Corday, who assassinated the revolutionary leader Jean-Paul Marat, have individual tombs under the arches. A gate shaped like a sarcophagus and adorned with acroterions gives access to the plot. The chapel proper is a triconch with a portico. The sculptures of Louis XVI and Marie-Antoinette that stand in the lateral apses – works by Bosio and Cortot – portray them as martyrs, interpreting their political execution as a religious sacrifice.

Canal Saint-Martin (164)
with Morland bridges
1822–1825
Canal Saint-Martin / 4e, 10e, 11e, 12e
Charles-Edouard de Villiers, Tarbé (engineer), Brémontier (engineer)

The canal stretches four kilometers between the Basin de la Villette near Place de Stalingrad and the Arsenal Harbor near the Bastille, after disappearing underground near Rue du Faubourg du Temple.

Nine filigree footbridges cross the non-underground northern part of the canal, which was planned in 1802 but only materialized twenty years later.

Galerie Vivienne (165)
1823–1826
4, rue des Petits-Champs; 5, rue de la
Banque; 6, rue Vivienne / 2e
François-Jacques Delannoy

Numerous arcades were developed during the Restoration after Nicolas-Jacques-Antoine Vestier and François Debret had set new standards for such buildings: Passage Delorme (1808) was built with an iron-and-glass roof and Passage de l'Opéra (1822) was lit with gas.

François-Jacques Delannoy, the architect of Galerie Vivienne, set out to surpass his predecessors and indeed created one of Paris's most beautiful arcades. A pupil of Charles Percier, he used mosaics and numerous decorative elements of the Empire style. In 1826, Jean Billaud endeavored to create an even more magnificent interior decoration in the neighboring Galerie Colbert.

Notre-Dame de Lorette (166)
1823–1836
18bis, rue Châteaudun / 9e
Louis-Hippolyte Lebas

The exterior of this church is in the neo-Classical style, but the interior features Early Christian elements, like Saint-Philippe-du-Roule (no. 135) built nearly fifty years before.

Hippolyte Lebas designed Notre-Dame-de-Lorette after two churches in Rome: Santa Maria Maggiore (432–440) and San Crisogono (732–741 and 1123–1130). Jacques Ignace Hittorff interpreted the Roman models more freely in designing Saint-Vincent-de-Paul (no. 167) about the same time.

The portico is as high as the nave. The interior of the five-bay basilica with Ionic columns features a coffered ceiling in the style of the early Renaissance. The abundance of decorative elements, in particular the frescoes in the style of the early Renaissance painted under Lebas's supervision, borders on horror vacui.

Saint-Vincent-de-Paul (167)
1824–1831, 1831–1844
place Franz Liszt / 10e
Jean-Baptiste Lepère,
Jacques Ignace Hittorff

The church stands atop a monumental flight of stairs on a hillside and thus dominates the vista along Rue d'Hauteville. This disposition is similar to that of Rome's Santissima Trinità al Monte Pincio, best known for its location overlooking the Spanish Steps. In the early 19th century, Jean-Baptiste Lepère was commissioned to build a church for the highly populated Quartier Poissonnière on the spot where Saint Vincent de Paul had founded France's first state hospital during the Thirty Years' War (1618–1648). Jacques Ignace Hittorff, Lepère's son-in-law, took over the project, altered the plans and began building the church in 1833. Two towers frame a protruding portico with twelve Ionic columns. As at Saint-Sulpice (no. 68), an attic story with a balustrade and four statues connects the towers. Hittorff, who had found traces of paint on the temples of Selinunte, was among the first to believe that ancient Greek temples, now with unpainted surfaces, had originally a polychrome decoration. He therefore considered painting the church of Saint-Vincent-de-Paul, but he was not allowed to, as painting a sacred building was unconceivable in the neo-Classical period. However, the architect was able to realize his project on the Cirque d'hiver (no. 183), which still features polychrome decoration.

The five-nave interior recalls Rome's San Paolo Fuori le Mura, except for the outer aisles where grilles delimit side chapels. Ionic columns support galleries on both sides of the nave. The Corinthian columns of the galleries in turn support an architrave and a truss similar to that in two other Roman churches, San Lorenzo Fuori le Mura and Santa Agnese Fuori le Mura. Hittorff also designed the rich interior decoration that recalls the cathedral of Monreale and Sant'Apollinare Nuovo in Ravenna. Moreover, the frieze shows similarities with that of the Parthenon.

Passage du Grand-Cerf (168)
1825–1835
10, rue Dussoubs,
145, rue Saint-Denis / 2e

The boutiques in this arcade received new display windows in the mid-19th century, when the use of iron in architecture was growing increasingly common. The exceptional height of 11.8 meters allowed the construction of passageways in the third floor. The Passage du Bourg-l'Abbé, built in 1828 and adorned with entrance caryatids by Henri Blondel in 1863, was an extension of the Passage du Grand-Cerf. Its vaulted roof probably served as an example for the Galerie d'Orléans developed by Percier and Fontaine under the reign of Louis-Philippe. Once the most prestigious arcade in the city, this structure inspired Jean-Pierre Cluysenaar's designs for the Galeries Saint-Hubert in Brussels in 1847, and Giuseppe Mengoni's plans for the Galleria Vittorio Emanuele developed in Milan twelve years later. In 1933–1935, however, the dilapidated arcade was demolished.

Historical consciousness and romanticism: city expansion during the 19th century (169)

As civil engineering gradually progressed from hothouses to the Eiffel Tower (no. 218), France was oscillating between restorative, conservative tendencies and liberal, left-leaning governments. The restoration of the Bourbons, interrupted by the Hundred Days of Napoleon's return from Elba in 1815, retained some accomplishments of the Revolution but established a constitutional monarchy, beginning with Louis XVIII. The Chapelle expiatoire (no. 163) and the equestrian sculpture of Louis the XIV, destroyed during the Revolution and rebuilt on the Place des Victoires (no. 92), come from this period. Ultraconservatives began to assert themselves already during his rule, and as Carl X ascended the throne in 1824, his clerical and ultra loyalist politics led to the July Revolution in 1830. Although it was initially supported by the Paris working class, the revolution's real beneficiaries were the bourgeoisie. The crown was offered by Adolphe Thiers to the Duke of Orléans, who ruled as Louis-Philippe, King of the French. This period sees the completion of the Arc de Triomphe (no. 158) and the start of the restoration of Viollet le Ducs

and the construction of various passages. Between 1841 and 1845 a new fortified wall enclosing various suburbs is constructed around the city. Despite being leveled in 1920, it marks the city's border to this day. The working classes finally brought about the Revolution of February 1848, which led to the founding of the Second Republic. Louis-Napoléon Bonaparte, the cousin of Napoleon I who had already attempted two putsches during Louis-Philippe's rein, was elected its president. True to his name, he fashioned himself into Emperor Napoléon III by staging a coup d'état (1851) and founding the Second Empire. In 1848, Paris had one million inhabitants; as Napoléon III was forced to abdicate after the disastrous Franco-Prussian war in 1870, this number had doubled. The Louvre courtyard (Cour Napoléon, no. 49) was finally closed on its northern side during this period (1852–1870), shortly before the west wing, or the Tuileries Palace (no. 41), went up in smoke during the Paris Commune (1871). Napoléon III let Bois de Boulogne (Jean-Charles Adolphe Alphand) and Bois de Vincennes be turned into a public park after taking a liking to Hyde

park during his exile in London. These 20 or so years also saw the city's reorganization by prefect Haussmann. Narrow, medieval streets gave way to wide boulevards. Not only hygienic reasoning was behind these changes – small streets still remained between the large ones. Military thinking motivated planning, as barricading by native population could hardly be successful on streets of such a scale. The worst quarters were handed over to build representative structures of the authoritarian state (the Palace of Justice, military barracks). Half of the residential buildings in the city center were built between 1850 and 1914. The typical city house (5–6 levels with a mansard story and stretching balconies with metal grating) reflects the social structure of the city at the time: the bourgeoisie resided in the bel-etage and the social position went down with each higher story. After the final abolition of the Paris Commune, the Second Empire was followed by the Third Republic in 1875. Adolphe Theirs who, as the historian of liberal idealization of the French Revolution had certainly contributed to the stylization of Napoleon into a national hero, was its first

president from 1871 to 1873. The Republic's early days were marked by extreme instability, and 50 changes of government took place between 1875 and 1914. Historicism, the neo-styles, dominated the second half of the century. Neo-Baroque was the grandest of all, but all other historical architectural styles were represented. The fitting prototype was searched depending on the architectural task at hand and the desired effect. At first, regress was done in a mostly subjective way, but later became academically regimented or archeologically precise. It was not until the end of the century that creative freedom was let loose again, mixing stylistic elements from different epochs in the style of Eclecticism. Rue Réaumur shows Paris's typical turn-of-the-century structures. The Haussmannian standardization of the street disappears, shapes vary, but the general appearance remains quite similar. The wide historical repertoire of European style was additionally enriched using imported elements: the World Exhibitions during the second half of the 19th century (1855, 1867, 1878 and 1889) bestowed a vivd vocabulary from cultures around the world.

Galerie Véro-Dodat   **(170)**
1826
19, rue Jean-Jacques Rousseau,
2, rue du Bouloi / 1er

Most of the original interior decoration in this arcade has been preserved, including the wooden fronts of the boutiques and the mirrors intended to maximize the natural light. Mirrored walls were common in 19th-century arcades.

Saint-Denis-du-Saint-   **(171)**
Sacrement
1826–1835
68bis, rue de Turenne / 3e
Etienne-Hippolyte Godde

Étienne-Hippolyte Godde took his inspiration from Early Christian churches as he designed this extremely austere neo-Classical building. In the nave, a barrel vault rests directly on the entablature supported by Ionic columns. Only four windows light the interior. The aisles, porch and chapel are as austere as the exterior. The exterior of Saint-Pierre-du-Gros-Caillou (Rue Saint-Dominique 92, another work by Godde, 1822–1829) is even more austere – and almost modern – as it does without the

tympanum relief that figures allegories of Belief, Hope and Compassion (by Jean-Jacques Feuchères).

École Nationale Supérieure   **(172)**
des Beaux-Arts
1832–1872
14, rue Bonaparte,
11–17, quai Malaquais / 6e
Félix Duban, François Debret

This building complex was mainly developed in the 19th century, but also includes older buildings. The school of Fine Arts was part of the Royal Academy from the 18th century until 1863. As of 1816, it was located in the convent of the Austin Friars that Margaret of Valois had built in 1608-1617 along today's Rue Bonaparte. The convent was closed during the French Revolution, and then used as an art depot and a museum that exhibited fragments of buildings and sculptures destroyed in the Revolution (Musée des Monuments Français). Among the exhibits were the central projection from the Château d'Anet (Philibert Delorme, 1545-1550), façade elements from the Château de Gaillon (around 1508-1510, France's oldest Renaissance building), as well as Gothic exhibits and examples of north-Alpine Renaissance. Thus, the collection of the museum run by Alexandre-André Lenoir contrasted with the neo-Classicism favored by the Academy, that focused on Antiquity and the Italian Renaissance, and was a forerunner for the Eclecticism of the late 19th century. François Debret converted the old buildings and designed several extensions (Palais des Études and Bâtiment des Loges). Félix Duban, his brother-in-law, designed the entrance square and adorned it with exhibits from the Musée des Monuments Français. He also increased the height of the Palais des Études, covered the courtyard with a glass dome on iron supports, and redesigned the interior in the neo-Renaissance polychrome style (1863). The Bâtiment des Expositions (1858–1862), whose glass façade overlooking the Seine was unpopular at the time because of its industrial style, is another work by Duban. The Hôtel de Chimay (François Debias-Aubry, 1740–1756) became part of the school of Fine Arts in 1884. In 1945–1950, Auguste Perret developed a workshop building as the last extension to the complex.

building that strongly contrasts with the neighboring Bourse de Paris (no. 161). Its corner ashlars that replace the pilasters are among the elements that clearly show the decline of neo-Classicism and the rise of the neo-Renaissance style the mid-19th century. In 1891, Jules Lisch designed extensions in the courtyard and on Rue Notre-Dame-des-Victoires.

Apartments (174)
1835–1840
28, rue de Richelieu / 1er

Chambre de Commerce (173)
1833, 1891
21, rue Notre-Dame-des-Victoires / 2e
Félix Callet, Jules Lisch

In 1853, Paris's Chamber of Commerce moved into a former auction house – a

The façade of this residential building is typical of the 19th century: two entrances that provide access to the staircases flank the central gate leading to the courtyard. The two lateral entrances are adorned with Moorish arabesques. As this type of decoration element requires a hard material, the artist used a hard stone, although sculptors generally favored soft material at the time.

Jardin des Plantes und (175) Muséum d'Histoire naturelle (Galerie de Minéralogie)
1626 founded, 1836
57, rue Cavier, quai Saint-Bernard, rue Buffon, rue Geoffroy-Saint-Hilaire / 5e
Charles Rohault de Fleury

In 1805, Jacques Molinos built the glass-roofed Elephant Rotunda as a complement to the Gloriette Buffon (no. 143) and the Grand Amphitheater that already stood in Paris's botanic garden. Other alterations in the aftermath of the French Revolution included the transfer of the animals from the royal menagerie in Versailles, the opening of the garden

to the public, its partial redesigning in an English landscape garden, and the integration of the Hôtel de Magny into the complex (a work by Pierre Bullet, 1700). Hector Horeau built the greenhouses in 1833–1834 as an early example of structural engineering, and Charles Rohault de Fleury built the late neo-Classical, 187-meter-long Mineralogy Gallery with Doric vestibule in 1836. The main building, the Galerie de Zoologie (no. 215), followed in 1877.

Bibliothèque Sainte-Geneviève (176)
1840–1851
8–10, place du Panthéon / 5e
Henri Labrouste

This building not only qualified Labrouste for the construction of the Bibliothèque Nationale (no. 186), but also served as an example for the construction of Les Halles (no. 187) and the first railway stations in the city.

The neo-Renaissance façade in the style of the Cinquecento masks an iron frame spanning 85 by 21 meters. The vaults are made of gypsum raised on an iron mesh – effectively the precursor to reinforced concrete. The two-aisle hall recalls Gothic refectories, such as that of Saint-Martin-des-Champs (no. 7). The walls are glazed in the upper section above the bookshelves in the interior, and adorned with plates bearing the names of great authors in the exterior. Originally, Labrouste was supposed to restore the old building but could convince the authorities that a new building would be less expensive and could accommodate the growing number of users.

The original book collection had been rescued from the library of the Sainte-

Geneviève Church (today's Panthéon, no. 123) by Alexandre-Guy Pingré during the French Revolution.

Chapelle Notre-Dame-de-la-Compassion   (177)

1843
2, boulevard d'Aurelle-de-Paladines / 17e
Pierre-Bernard Lefranc,
Pierre-François-Léonard Fontaine

This chapel replaces a tavern where Ferdinand Philippe, Duke of Orléans, son of Louis Philippe and heir to the throne, died after a carriage accident. The unusual building was the first neo-Byzantine structure with a Greek-crossed floor plan ever built in Paris. It features stained-glass windows by Jean-Auguste-Dominique Ingres.

Mairie du 5ème Arrondissement   (178)

1844–1850, 1923–1932
21, place du Panthéon / 5e
(Jacques-Germain Soufflot),
Jacques Ignace Hittorff, François
Guenepin, Victor Calliat, extension:
René Patouillard-Demoriane

This city hall erected almost one hundred years after the Panthéon (no. 123) revis-

its Germain Soufflot's conceptions and integrates the longing for "archaeological correctness" that characterizes the 19th century. The basic differences on the main façade include the wall behind the Ionic columns and the clock on the pediment. The interior was remodeled in the Art Déco style after 1925 – the year of the Exposition Internationale des Arts Décoratifs. Soufflot himself began the construction of the Faculté de Droit, the pendant of the city hall located to the north of the square. This building was eventually extended down to Rue Saint-Jacques in 1876–1879.

Passage Jouffroy und Passage Verdeau   (179)

1845–1846, 1847
10–12, boulevard Montmartre,
6 & 9, rue de la Grange-Batelière,
31bis, rue du Faubourg Montmartre / 9e

These two arcades are extensions of the Passage des Panoramas (no. 152) that links Boulevard Montmartre and Rue du Faubourg Montmartre.

They are much more lavishly decorated than the Galerie d'Orléans and the Passage du Grand-Cerf built earlier, and were the first arcades in the city provided with floor heating.

Sainte-Clotilde-Sainte-Valère (180)
1846–1853, 1853–1857
23bis, rue las Cases / 7e
Franz Christian Gau, Théodore Ballu

The Cologne-born architect François-Christian Gau built Paris's first neo-Gothic church with a cathedral choir and using various 13th-century elements. However, unlike in England, the neo-Gothic never really caught on in France. After Gau's death, his assistant, Théodore Ballu, re-modeled the façade after Saint-Nicaise in Rheims.

façade bears plates with the names of numerous cities in the east of the country, and is topped with a figure that personifies the Alsatian capital. The building's iron frame is visible across the large, semi-circular bay that opens on the façade and recalls the city gates of the past. Until the 1920s, the glass roof covered only five tracks and was framed by facility buildings.

Infantry (182)
1852–1857
10–12, rue de la Banque / 2e
Jean-Louis-Victor Grisart

The barracks were built in the typical eclectic style of the late 19th century.

Gare de l'Est (181)
1847–1852
2, place du 11 Novembre 1918,
rue 8 Mai 1945 / 10e
François-Alexandre Duquesney, Pierre-Alexandre Cabanel de Sermet (engineer)

The terminus of the railway link between Paris and Strasbourg opened in 1849 and served as a model for stations in several French cities. Now the capital's oldest train station and a landmark of the city, the building faces Boulevard de Strasbourg that was developed by Georges Eugène Haussmann in 1852–1854. The

However, late-Renaissance brick-and-stone façades dominate, which is quite apt as military power characterized the period, and in particular the reign of Louis XIII.

Cirque d'Hiver – Cirque Napoléon (183)
1852
110, rue Amelot / 11e
Jacques Ignace Hittorff

The heated winter circus, originally called "Cirque Napoléon", was just one of many permanent circuses in 19th-century Paris. Jacques Ignace Hittorff, who had already built a summer circus on the Champs-Élysées in 1840, built it in the traditional theater district for the entertainment manager Louis Dejean in only seven months. The architect designed the Winter Circus for 4,000 spectators, but the authorities only authorized 2,000 seats for fire-safety reasons.

The 48-meter polygonal roof dispenses with central supports. As the circus is associated historically with horses and chariot races, equestrian statues of a warrior and an Amazon flank the entrance, while the frieze contains further equestrian reliefs. Part of Carol Reed's movie "Trapeze" starring Gina Lollobrigida, Burt Lancaster and Tony Curtis was filmed here in 1956.

Saint-Eugène (184)
1854–1855
6, rue Sainte-Cécile / 9e
Louis-Auguste Boileau,
Louis Adrien Lusson

Saint-Eugène, the first iron church ever built in France, is also among the oldest buildings of this type the world over. Lusson was commissioned first, but Boileau finally build the church – it is unknown who was responsible for which aspects. This five-aisle basilica is made of a slender iron frame wrapped in a stone shell. Tracery works, sexpartite vaults and slender columns recall the refectory of Saint-Martin-des-Champs (no. 7) and Gothic churches of the 12th and 13th centuries.

The statics are similar to that of medieval stone structures and do not really use the wrought and cast iron frame that, although the building dispenses with buttresses. The main reasons for using such a frame were the possible cost reduction and improved floor area. The interior painting was primarily meant to protect the metal from corrosion.

Baron Georges-Eugène Haussmann
*1809 in Paris, † 1891 in Paris (185)

At the dawn of the 19th century, the city center of Paris was still a mosaic of tiny buildings that had developed organically since the Middle Ages. Jumbled, mostly dilapidated structures of the 16th to 18th centuries lined a tangle of narrow lanes and small squares. The capital cities of other European powers appeared much more progressive by then: London and Berlin, for example, had already been modernized into the thoroughly planned metropolises of the industrial age. Napoleon III therefore contemplated a radical renewal of the French capital. Taking his

cue from the splendid ensembles developed under absolutist rulers (Place des Victoires, no. 92, Place Vendôme, no. 95, Place de la Concorde, no. 121, Champs-Élysées, no. 80, Versailles, no. 98, Louvre, no. 49), the emperor wanted to reorder the city's layout on a monumental scale, with thoroughfares and star-shaped squares, renovating entire neighborhoods and connecting them to a modern, hygienic sewer system. However, to implement the ambitious plans he had conceived during his imprisonment at Ham Fortress after a failed coup in 1840, the emperor required a man of action with both relevant experience and the necessary determination.

Georges-Eugène Haussmann, who was born in Paris in 1809 to a protestant family of German origins, was that man. He had entered the civil service after graduating in law, and gained experience in developing street networks and water supply infrastructures as a sub-prefect of various provincial cities.

His achievements in Bordeaux and the Yonne départment came to the attention of Napoleon III, who appointed him prefect of the Seine département in 1853 and entrusted him with the renovation of the French capital.

Over the next seventeen years, Haussmann radically changed the face of the city. Armed with the emperor's unrestricted authority, he condemned whole neighborhoods. Tradesmen living in the city center were mercilessly expropriated and workers displaced en bloc to the suburbs. Only paintings, drawings, and some of the earliest photographs still convey an impression of "pre-Haussmann" Paris. Straight boulevards with a total length of 150 kilometers, often radiating from star-shaped squares (Place de l'Étoile, no. 158), were laid out for aesthetic, logistical and riot-control reasons. Haussmann's boulevards thus offer impressive vistas of important buildings such as Notre Dame (no. 19), Arc de Triomphe (no. 158), and Opéra Garnier (no. 198). Haussmann also ordered the installation of 3,200 gaslights along the sumptuous grands boulevards, and the construction of palatial residences, elegant boutiques, exquisite restaurants and the first department stores along the new avenues.

Most of the buildings developed during this period, including those by Jacques Ignace Hittorff, Victor Baltard, Charles Garnier and Antoine Bailly, are examples of the late neo-Classical and neo-Renaissance styles that the French Academy of Fine Arts favored at the time. Moreover, the late-19th century architects did not dare to use iron-and-glass construction for façades, and hid such light frameworks behind eclectic fronts, such as those of Gare du Nord (no. 196) and Halles centrales (no. 187).

Haussmann's modernization plans for the French capital also included 800 kilometers of water mains and 500 kilometers of sewers, as well as the construction of an enormous covered market in the heart of the city (Les Halles, no. 187), which would remain practically unaltered until his destruction in the 1970s. Moreover, the prefect initiated the annexation of villages that had been outside the city limits, and the administrative division of the municipal territory into twenty arrondissements.

The World's Fairs organized by Haussmann in 1855 and 1867 not only documented Paris's new status as the cultural and artistic center of Europe, but were also occasions to shower the leading urban planner of the 19th century with countless honors and distinctions under the eyes of the international political, financial and cultural elite of the time.

Haussmann's activity in Paris ended with the fall of his imperial patron during the Franco-German war. After his dismissal as prefect in 1870, he retired at first to Cestas, near Bordeaux, where his wife had inherited a mansion. Ismail Pasha then summoned Haussmann to Constantinople and commissioned him to rebuild a part of the city destroyed by fire. Haussmann later worked on the modernization of Cairo as well.

After shuttling between Paris and Cestas during the last years of his life, Haussmann died in 1891.

125

"La Place de l'Europe, temps de pluie", ainting from Gustave Caillebotte, 1877 (detail)

**Salle de Travail des Imprimés (186)
of Bibliothèque nationale**
1854–1875
58, rue de Richelieu / 2e
Henri Labrouste

This building is another work by Labrouste (Bibliothèque Sainte-Geneviève, no. 176), who was able to pursue his ideas here. In the reading room, sixteen slender columns support domes covered with terracotta tiles. At the center of the exedra, caryatids flank the entrance of the passageway to the depository.

The complex of the old National Library ("Site Richelieu") also includes the Hôtel Tubeuf (1635, Jean Thiriot), a gallery section (1645, François Mansart; parts of the interior decoration by Grimaldi and Giovanni Francesco Romanelli), the courtyard (1731, Robert de Cotte) and the

Royal Study (also Robert de Cotte, with paintings by François Boucher).

Halles centrales – 'Les Halles' (187)
1854–1857, 1860–1866
rue Rambuteau / 4e
hall no. 8 displaced as pavilion Baltard: 12, avenue Victor Hugo in Nogent-sur-Marne
Victor Baltard, Félix Emmanuel Callet

The construction of a central market made of stone and iron began in 1851. However, neither Napoleon III nor Haussmann was satisfied with the building. The baron, who usually favored stately projects, declared iron-frame pavilions would be sufficient in this case, and Victor Baltard was commissioned with the development of a new central market. Baltard's design was to be reused for market halls throughout the country in the following decades.

Paris's central market was an extensive complex of twelve identical, prefabricated, and systematically assembled pavilions. It extended over nine hectares in two groups of six buildings from the present-day Forum des Halles to the Bourse du Commerce (no. 213). Streets covered with similar structures ran between the individual pavilions. Only the plinths and foundations were made of brick, while the rest of the buildings consisted of cast iron and glass built on a six-by-six-meter grid. Slender columns that also functioned as gutter pipes were as subtly decorated as the open-work pendentives between them. A scheduled subterranean train service to Gare de l'Est (no. 181) did not come to fruition, however.

The central market was torn down after construction of new facilities at Rungis, in the suburb, in 1969. However, two pavilions were preserved: one stands in Yokohama, the other in the outskirts of the city where it now houses a television studio.

Pont des Invalides (188)
Seine / 7e, 8e
1855
Paul-Martin Gallocher de La Galisserie,
Jules Savarin

Savarin and La Galisserie built the bridge in 1854 for the World's Fair held the following year.

In 1821, a first bridge was constructed in the axis of Hôtel des Invalides (no. 89) near today's Pont Alexandre III (no. 223) to plans by Claude Navier, but it had to be demolished before completion due to structural problems.

The second bridge was built further west to avoid obstructing the view of the church of the Invalides.

The imagery on the sparingly decorated bridges is by Victor Vilain and shows two allegories: Victory on Land and Victory at Sea. The piers on the shore are decorated with military trophies by the sculptor Astyanax-Scévola Bosio.

Hôtel de la Païva (189)
1856–1866
25–27, avenue des Champs-Élysées / 8e
Pierre Manguin

One of the few private houses on today's Champs-Élysées (no. 80), this stately building once belonged to Thérèse Lachmann, who was born in a Jewish ghetto in Poland and by gradually climbing the social ladder through favorable

marriages became Marquise de la Païva, then mistress of Count Henkel von Donnersmark, who finally married her.

The exterior blends elements of the Italian and French Renaissance, and the splendor of the luxurious interior made under the oversight of Henri Manguin can only be compared to the Opéra Garnier (no. 198).

Mairie du 1er Arrondissement (190)
1858–1860
4, place du Louvre / 1er
Jacques Ignace Hittorff

In 1860, the City of Paris incorporated various villages from the surrounding area, which led to the administrative sub-division that exists to this day (twenty arrondissements instead of twelve), and to the construction of several new city halls in the style of historicism. That of the central district had to look impressive to contend with the former royal palace (Louvre, no. 49) and church (Saint-Germain-l'Auxerrois, no. 12).

The façade of the city hall by Jacques Ignace Hittorff recalls that of the former royal church: the porch features three high gateways flanked by two lower, narrower ones; a gallery extends between

tween the two unaligned structures. The tower built by Théodore Ballu between the church and the city hall can be regarded either as the steeple of a sacred building, or as a belfry in the tradition of Flemish city halls.

Fontaine Saint-Michel   (192)
1858–1860
place Saint-Michel, pont Saint-Michel / 6e
Gabriel Davioud

This fountain adorned with a monumental sculpture of the Archangel Michael subduing the devil stands in the prolongation of the bridge that leads to the Sainte Chapelle (no. 33). A triumphal arch frames the figure group (a work by Francisque-Joseph Duret. Twenty years later, Gabriel Davioud was commissioned to create the eccentric Palais du Trocadéro with stylistic elements taken from Spanish-Moorish and Byzantine architecture for the 1878 World's Fair. This was eventually demolished to make way for the Palais de Chaillot (no. 304) of the 1937 exhibition.

Passage des Princes   (193)
1859–1860
5, boulevard des Italiens,
97–99, rue de Richelieu / 2e

The last of the grand Parisian arcades no longer has its original façade, and its colored glass dome added in the 1930s

---

pillars above the windows; a tracery window and a pediment adorned with reliefs top the ensemble. However, the city hall differs from the church building in its wealth of late-Gothic and Renaissance detailing added to the latter by Hittorff.

Beffroi du Louvre   (191)
(belfry)
1858–1862
place du Louvre / 1er
Théodore Ballu

The belfry to the rear of the Louvre (no. 49) formed a vertical axis between the Mairie du Ier arrondissement (no. 190) and Saint-Germain-l'Auxerrois (no. 12) since the remodeling of Place du Louvre by Georges Eugène Haussmann in the late 19th century. In his purpose of modernizing the square, Haussmann originally intended to demolish the church to make space for a boulevard that was to lead to the Hôtel de Ville (no. 208). Ultimately, he commissioned Jacques Ignace Hittorff to develop the city hall as a pendant to the sacred building, and Théodore Ballu to erect the belfry as an optical link be-

originally covered a hotel. The interior of this small arcade was reconstructed in 1990–1995, however, so that Passage des Princes now conveys an impression of the original appearance.

Saint-Alexandre-Nevski (194)
(russian-orthodox cathedral)
1859–1861
12, rue de Daru / 8e
Roman Ivanovich Kuzmin (Kouzmine),
J. B. Strohm

Russians living in France financed the construction of Paris's orthodox cathedral. Roman Ivanovich Kuzmin, the court architect of the tsar, designed the building and sent his plans to Jean-Baptiste Strohm, who carried out the construction. The building, with a Greek-cross floor plan, reflects the Russian Gothic style and includes five towers topped with polygonal spires such as those common in Russia on 17th-century churches. The central steeple is forty-eight meters high. A mosaic that figures Christ – a replica from a 6th-century original in Sant'Appollinare Nuovo in Ravenna – adorns the main portal. The interior likewise conforms more to a Byzantine than to a Russian model. Windows in the tambour under the central spire light the gilt paintings of the interior, in particular that figuring the Blessing Christ. In accordance with orthodox tradition, an iconostasis separates the sanctuary from the nave. The red columns of the arcades are reminiscent of the porphyry posts of Hagia Sophia in Istanbul.

Saint-Augustin (195)
1860–1871
46, boulevard Malesherbes,
place Saint-Augustin / 8e
Victor Baltard

The church allegedly should have been the mausoleum of Napoleon III. After the construction of Boulevard Malesherbes, the surroundings of Saint-Augustin evolved from a seedy area to one of the most fashionable districts in the city. Victor Baltard suggested that the church be constructed using an iron frame, as such this solution makes a system of flying buttresses superfluous, saving space on narrow building sites. The sacred building located in the city center was fitted with a stone shell to preserve its prestige. The main façade arbitrarily mixes Gothic and Renaissance elements. Above the three portals is a "gallery of the kings" that portrays several French sovereigns, monarchs by divine right. These Gothic elements are flanked by pilasters that support a broken triangular pediment with a rose window – two Renaissance elements. The façade of Saint-Augustin is thus kind of a merging between an Antique triumph arch and a Gothic cathedral. Renaissance motifs mingle with Baroque elements on the sides of the building, while the choir draws on both Romanesque tower installations (triconch, choir flanking towers) and on pivotal French buildings (Les Invalides, no. 89). Besides the delicate metallic lantern, the cast and wrought iron frame is visible only inside the church. Slender columns adorned with iron angels and girders decorated with tendrils structure the nave and the two lateral aisles that broaden progressively up to the choir as the exterior walls follow the irregular shape of the plot.

Gare du Nord (196)
1861–1865
place Napoléon III / 10e
Jacques Ignace Hittorff

In 1861, Jacques Ignace Hittorff altered a design probably drafted by Lejeune and Ohnet in 1857.

As at Gare de l'Est (no. 181), the temple and gate-like façade is opened with a bay that lights the interior. The female sculptures atop the building and on the façade personify northern French and European cities. The large semicircular bay revisits antique thermae windows over columns.

A modern canopy impairs its original appearance, however. Behind the façade, the self-contained, thirty-eight-meter-high hall that rests on cast iron pillars has lost its original polychrome decoration. Modern alterations of the station include the VIP lounge for passengers of the Eurostar bullet train to London – a work by Philippe Starck – and an extension developed to the east in 1999–2001 that reproduces the original pitched roof with an even more delicate design – a work by Jean-Marie Duthilleul and Étienne Tricaud for Agence des Gares SNCF. This part of the station extends on three underground levels.

Saint-Trinité (197)
1861–1867
place d'Estienne-d'Orves / 9e
Théodore Ballu

Theodore Ballu, a near collaborator of Georges Eugène Haussmann, designed this church that stands on Place d'Estienne-d'Orves as the crowning achievement of Rue de la Chaussée d'Antin, a street developed by the baron. The ensemble with a sixty-meter-high central tower includes elements of the Italian and French Renaissance. With its single-tower façade, the building recalls rather a Flemish town hall than a German sacred building. The interior is also oversized for a parish church, with a length of ninety meters and a crown height of thirty meters.

Like Saint-Augustin (no. 195), the Trinity Church is an iron-and-stone structure, but this remains invisible on the façades and in the interior. It features a neo-Renaissance nave, while its choir imitates an earlier Gothic building.

Théâtre National de l'Opéra   (198)
(Opéra Garnier)
1861–1875
8, rue Scribe, rue Auber, place de
l'Opéra, place Diaghilev / 9e
Charles Garnier

This building - the most prestigious example of bourgeois architecture from the Belle Époque - served as a catalyst for the pompous neo-Baroque style. Construction of a new opera house had already been decided on before the provisional theater erected in 1821 in Rue Le Pelletier was destroyed by fire in 1873. The "new opera" - actually the old one since the construction of Opéra Bastille (no. 366) in the 1980s - was built after Garnier had won an architecture competition in 1863. When asked what kind of style the new structure was supposed to be, the architect reportedly answered: "Napoleon III". Indeed, the Garnier Opera is the most imposing building erected under the reign of the second French emperor.

In contrast to contemporary theaters, Opéra Garnier is a palace of bourgeois recreation and societal contact in an architecturally opulent framework. Approximately half of the building is made up of spaces which do not directly have to do with performances: loggias and balconies, as well as indoor and outdoor foyers complement the grand staircase with colossal red columns. The variety of forms, materials and decorative elements that characterizes the Baroque style dominates the staircase which also functions as a multi-storied foyer. Victor Louis developed a similar solution for Bordeaux's Grand Theater. In the auditorium, designed to afford a good view not only of the stage, but also of the other members of the audience, paintings by Marc Chagall rather inauspiciously cover the original frescos.

The grand dome over the auditorium and the statue of Apollo of Millet that crowns the backstage tower are among the elements that evidence the prestige function of the building visible from several streets. The ground floor opens with arcades similar to those in the buildings by Ange-Jacques Gabriel on the north side of the Place de la Concorde (no. 121), while pairs of Corinthian columns dominate the main floor, like on the gallery of the Louvre (no. 49).

A wealth of relief elements - busts, festoons, cherubs, theater masks and portrait medallions - as well as rich materials and a great variety of colors contribute to the overall impression of grandeur. Numerous allegoric representations compose an extensive iconographic program. Among the rich statuary on the façade, the "Dance" - a work by Carpeaux - is particularly noteworthy for it unconstrained composition and great naturalness. Other statues are more classical, while Carpeaux takes the opportunity of this subject to a much relaxed composition and greater naturalness. The cande-

labra – also by Garnier – are composed of several elements, including the ship from Paris's coat of arms.

The extension in Rue Auber was developed as a pavilion for the exclusive use of Napoleon III. After the fall of the Empire, however, the structure was remodeled to house an opera museum in 1878–1881. Jean-Loup Roubert modernized and refurbished the theater in 1992.

Carreau du Temple / Marché (199) du Temple

1863–1865
rue Eugène Spuller, rue Dupetit-Thouars,
rue de Picardie, rue Perrée / 3e
Jules de Mérindol, Ernest Legrand

During the Middle Ages, a market was already held near a fortress hold by the Knights Templar.

A wooden structure was later built to house the shops of ragmen. The tower of the old fortress, where Louis XVI was jailed until his execution, was razed under Napoleon III. Jules de Mérindol, who also designed a pavilion in the former slaughterhouse (Grande Halle aux Bœufs, in today's Parc de la Villette, no. 404), built the market hall as it stands today in the manner of Baltard's pavilions in Les Halles (no. 187).

Parc des Buttes-Chaumont (200)

1864–1867
rue Manin, place Armand Carrel,
rue Botzaris, rue de Crimée / 19e
Gabriel Davioud, Adolphe Alphand
(engineer)

GARDEN Since the Middle Ages, a gallows had stood on a hill northeast of Paris. The site gradually developed into a garbage dump and a limestone quarry, so that it was no longer suitable for building due to the many tunnels and differences in height.

Napoleon III, who discovered landscaped gardens during his exile in England, commissioned Georges Eugène Haussmann, engineer Adolphe Alphand and the Municipal Garden Authority to transform the area in such a park after annexation of the land by the City of Paris in 1860.

Alphand modified the site using dynamite, built grottos and pumped water from the Saint Martin canal into an artificial lake. The Buttes-Chaumont – one of the first parks in the French capital to be developed for the working population – opened on the occasion of the 1867 World's Fair.

On an islet in the lake stands a replica of the Vesta Temple in Tivoli – a work by Gabriel Davioud – that provides a panoramic view over the city. A thirty-two-meter high waterfall runs down the slopes of the islet. Davioud also built an English cottage and a Swiss chalet that house cafés, while Gustave Alexandre Eiffel built a large suspension bridge in the park.

A footbridge and various fences appear at first glance to be made of wood, but are actually made of iron with a concrete coating that imitates knotholes and branches with a wealth of details and a great variety.

Marché Saint-Quentin (201)
1866
85, boulevard de Magenta / 10e
refurbished by architect Rabourdin and
sculptor Bernard Lassus

This covered market inspired by Baltard's pavilions in Les Halles (no. 187) and restored in the 1980s is among the last market halls that kept their original appearance and still function in Paris. The main features are the large bay windows and the stonework in the "Beaux-Arts" style made up of red and yellow bricks. This simple surface ornament was widespread in the late 19th century as it was printed in a variety of pattern books used by architects.

Synagoge rue de la Victoire (202)
1867–1876
44, rue de la Victoire / 9e
Alfred Philibert Aldrophe, Théodore Ballu

In 1791, the revolutionary government passed a law that gave full citizenship to French Jews. In the middle of the 19th century, however, the Jewish sacred buildings became more conspicuous and as richly adorned as the Christian churches. Alfred-Philibert Aldrophe, a Jewish architect noted for his buildings for the 1855 and 1862 World's Fairs, designed the synagogue in Rue de la Victoire to seat one thousand, as the Jewish community considerably increased in the 19th century. The sacred building revisits Christian architectural patterns in a rather exotic manner. The round pediment, for example, is common in Italian Renaissance architecture and in Byzantine buildings, such as today's Kalenderhane Camii in Istanbul – a structure built as a church in the 12th century. It is also found on the Saint Ferdinand Chapel developed by Lefranc and Fontaine in 1843 in Neuilly-sur-Seine near Paris. Neo-Romanesque elements prevail in the interior. This style – quite rare in Paris, but particularly suitable for a sacred building pertaining to the Old Testament – was preferred to the Moorish style that is common in other European countries on 19th-century synagogues, but already used in the French capital for bathhouses and places of amusement. Moreover, the elongated floor plan is uncommon for a synagogue.

Parc de Montsouris (203)
1867–1878
22–28, boulevard Jourdan / 14e
Adolphe Alphand (engineer)

133

GARDEN Like Parc des Buttes-Chaumont (no. 200), its pendant in the northeast of the city, this English garden was developed on a former quarry and also includes several hills, a cascade and a lake. The Moorish pavilion built on the occasion of the 1867 World's Fair is a replica of the Bardo, the summer residence of the Beys of Tunis.

Musée Jacquemart-André   (204)
1869–1875
158, boulevard Haussmann / 8e
Henri Parent

This museum is worth visiting not only for its artwork collections that include works by Rembrandt and Mantegna, but also because it offers visitors an opportunity to discover a complete bourgeois interior of the second half of the 19th century: that of Nélie Jacquemart and Édouard André.

After the fall of the Second Empire, the scion of a banking family and his wife – herself a society painter – devoted their lives to building a considerable artwork collection. The works are exhibited in their private house that resembles a Louis Seize château and was built in a neighborhood recently developed by Baron Haussmann.

Apartments and   (205)
office building
1869
19, rue des Halles / 1er
P. Lobrot

This building combines commercial (ground floor) and residential (top floors) uses, and is exemplary of the type of house that was new for the time, but which had come to characterize the second half of the 19th century in its endless variations using changing façade arrangements and

stylistic elements. The severe caryatids created by Charles Gauthier support a rather light balcony, and are an unusual aspect of the façade .

Magasins du Bon-Marché   (206)
1869–1872, 1872–1874, 1879–1887,
1920–1923
22–36, rue de Sèvres / 7e
Alexandre Laplanche, Louis-Charles
Boileau, Gustave Eiffel,
Louis-Hippolyte Boileau

This department store that opened in 1852 is the oldest example of the commercial structures developed in Paris in the second half of the 19th century to replace the traditional arcades. The oldest part of the building – a work by Alexandre Laplanche – still features a conservative architecture style, while the stone-encased iron extension built by Louis-Auguste Boileau and his son Louis-Charles (Saint-Eugène, no. 184), realized in part by the Gustave Eiffel Company, features two glass-covered atriums that characterize the spaciousness of this building type. The extension has kept its original appearance, except for the neo-Baroque staircase that was replaced by elevators. Louis-Charles Boileau, the grandson of Louis-Auguste, built an additional extension in the Art Déco style on the left bank in Rue du Bac ("Nouveau Magasin"). Le Bon Marché is likely to have inspired Émile Zola's novel The Ladies' Delight.

Apartments and office buildings (207)
1873
38–40 & 47–49, avenue de l'Opéra / 2e
Henri Blondel

ENSEMBLE These two buildings stand on both sides of the avenue that begins at Paris's oldest opera house (Opéra Garnier, no. 198). They are typical of the new developments initiated by Georges Eugène Haussmann as they blend into the neighboring structures instead of emphasizing their own personality. Lines of balconies in the second and fifth floors dominate the horizontality, while order elements that extend up to the roof underscore the vertical dimension. The two rounded corner buildings that take over the design structure of the façade along the street direct the observer's eye along the axis that leads to the Louvre (no. 49).

Hôtel de Ville (208)
1873–1882
place de l'Hôtel-de-Ville / 4e
Théodore Ballu
Pierre Joseph Eduard Deperthes

The city hall built by Pierre Chambiges according to plans by Domenico da Cortona, nicknamed "Boccador", and expanded in the 1830s by Étienne-Hippolyte Godde and Jean-Baptiste Lesueur was destroyed by fire in 1871 during the Paris Commune. The government of the Third Republic organized an architectural contest to rebuild the structure.

Today's Historistic west façade is a copy of the original developed by Boccador and extended in the early 19th century. The ensemble of 136 sculptures featuring noted artists and statesmen is, however, an addition. The exterior Renaissance adaptation integrates Flemish-Gothic elements and is juxtaposed against an interior typical of the Third Republic, developed starting in 1885 and featuring a wealth of ornaments, colors, materials and motifs. Particularly noteworthy are the paintings by Puvis de Chavannes. The Salle Saint Jean was refitted by dZ° architecture

Sacré-Cœur (Basilica) (209)
1875–1884, 1884–1886, 1886–1891,
1891–1904, 1904–1923
place du Parvis-du-Sacré-Cœur / 18e
Paul Abadie, Honoré Daumet, Charles
Laisné, Henri Rauline, Lucien Magne,
Louis-Jean Houlot

During the Roman times, a temple likely dedicated to Mercury stood on the hill overlooking Paris to the north of the city. In the Middle Ages, the prominence was

135

named after Saint Denis who had been martyred here in the third century. According to the legend, the beheaded saint picked up his head and walked to the place where Saint-Denis Abbey (no. 11) stands today (French "Montmartre" means "Mount of the Martyrdom").

In 1870, Catholics subscribed to building a church "in witness of repentance and as a symbol of hope" following the defeat in the Franco-German war. The idea of dedicating the new church to the Sacred Heart originated in the fact that the nuns of Saint-Pierre-de-Montmartre venerated it. The Sacré-Cœur was built on a knoll to be seen from afar, in a district that still had a rural character in the late 19th century. The church's neo-Byzantine design recalls Roman domed churches in Aquitaine refurbished by Paul Abadie (Saint-Front in Périgueux, for example). One dome and four cupolas rise above the building inscribed within a square ground plan. A tower above the summiting chapel joins a Roman choir ambulatory with radiating chapels that faces away from the city. Particularly noteworthy in the grand interior is the mosaic that adorns the vault of the apse – a work by L. O. Merson. Pilgrims from the north and east of the country still use the sacred building to stop off on their way to Lourdes.

Siège Crédit Lyonnais (210) (headquarters)
1876–1883, 1905–1913
17–23, boulevard des Italiens,
16–18, rue du Quatre-Septembre / 2e
William Bouwens van der Boijen,
Victor Laloux, André-Felix Narjoux

In the last quarter of the 19th century, banks competed with one another in building ever more magnificent company headquarters. The Dutch-born architect and his Frensh partners built this structure with an eye on the Louvre (no. 49), and expanded it in several phases between 1905 and 1913, so that the complex now covers an entire block along one of Paris's most prestigious boulevards. He also developed a bank building in a neighboring lot (6, rue Ménars).

Comptoir National d'Escompte (211) de Paris (today Banque National de Paris BNP)
1878–1882
14–20, rue Bergère / 9e
Edouard-Jules Corroyer

This building stands in a street running parallel to Boulevard Saint-Martin – one of the "Grands Boulevards" – in Paris's bank district. The projection is shifted from the center of the façade so that it is visible from the street that comes from the boulevard. Statues that represent Industry, Trade and Reason adorn the loggia above the three arches forming the entrance. Just as Charles Garnier Édouard Corroyer used a variety of forms and colors in designing this bourgeois palace with a magnificent façade and a glass-roofed galleried hall of impressing dimensions. Constant Bernard expanded the building in 1903.

invention of elevators, the annex built on the other side of the street is a six-story structure. The concept developed by Paul Sédille influenced a variety of department stores in Paris and other cities. René Binet, the architect who had renovated Au Printemps, also constructed a modernized copy of the original edifice. Its Art Nouveau glass cupola still exists, while other parts of the building were destroyed by fire during further extension works in 1921. Le Déli-cieux was designed by Noé Duchaufour Lawrence.

Au Printemps   (212)
1881–1885, 1907–1910, 1921–1924
64–70, boulevard Haussmann; 2, rue du Havre; 115–117, rue de Provence / 9e
Paul Sédille, René Binet, Georges Wybo

This department store was built in 1865, destroyed by fire and reconstructed in 1881. In the late 19th century, iron frames were favored for building warehouses as they permitted to reduce the thickness of the walls and thus to enlarge the usable floor space. Although Au Printemps was the first department store to be fully provided with electric lighting, the building features open façades and a three-story central atrium topped with a stained glass cupola. In the 1960s, however, the atrium was demolished as another story was added to the building. Thanks to the

Bourse de Commerce   (213)
1885–1889
2, rue de Viarmes / 1er
Henri Blondel

In 1575, Catherine de' Medici had Jean Bullant build the Hôtel de Soissons on this plot. In 1767, Le Camus de Mézières replaced the building with a circular structure housing the corn exchange. A wooden dome was added over the courtyard in 1783. It was destroyed by fire in 1802, and replaced by an iron-framed dome spanning forty meters in 1811 (a work by François-Joseph Bélanger).

Today's building maintains the interior structure and the external rotunda shape, although the original roof covering was partially replaced with glass. Four massive Corinthian pillars flank the entrance and support a pediment adorned by personifications of Trade and Wealth. These figures frame a statue that represents the city of Paris. The buildings along the circular Rue de Viarmes were developed at the same time as the rotunda.

One tower containing a stairwell of the old Hôtel de Soissons still stands at the back of the former exchange. This oversized, thirty-one-meter Doric column with a Tuscan capital that forms a platform was probably built to serve astrological purposes.

Rue d'Uzès   (214)
1885–1886, 1887
13 & 15–27, rue d'Uzès / 2e
Gustave Raulin & Etienne Soty

The buildings in this narrow street originally housed printing works and textile workshops. In order to maximize natural lighting, they were built using iron frames holding large glass plates and only a few bricks. Marc Mimram restored house number 5 in the Rue Uzes in 2005.

Galerie de Zoologie   (215)
Galerie d'Évolution
1886–1889, 1987–1994
inside Jardin des Plantes,
rue Geoffroy-Saint-Hilaire / 5e
Louis Jules André, Paul Chemetov &
Borja Huidobro

Jules André built the main structure in the Jardin des Plantes (no. 175) complex in 1877. It associates an iron frame and late 19th century stone façades that recall the style of the 17th century. Three-story galleries surround the main hall that is topped with a glass roof and houses a rich collection of stuffed animals. The great size of the exhibition rooms makes them suitable for a collection of dinosaurs.

The building had to be closed in the 1960s due to the lack of maintenance, and it was not reopened until 1994. By that time, Paul Chemetov and Borja Huidobro had built underground exhibition rooms. Together with the designer René Allio, the architects designed them to present an exhibition dedicated to Evolution.

Ferdinand Dutert built the Paleontology Gallery in 1894-1896. This hall recalls the Machine Gallery - an iron-frame structure with brick-and-stone façades that spans 107 meters, the second attraction at the 1889 Universal Exposition beside the Eiffel Tower. Orangutan Strangling a Native of Borneo, a marble by Emmanuel Frémiet that caused a sensation at the 1895 Salon, is exhibited here. The tropical greenhouse (René Berger, 1934–1937) is a 20th-century addition to the complex.

Distribution d'Air Comprimé   (216)
1890–1891
3–13, quai Panhard-et-Levassor / 13e
Joseph Leclaire (engineer)

This building, only partially preserved, was built in the late 19th century as energy consumption began to increase drastically. It housed air compressors that powered pneumatic lifts, clocks on buildings, and other machinery.

Frédéric Borel is currently converting the industrial building into an architecture school as part of the "ZAC Rive Gauche" (no. 452) urban development project.

Saint-Jean-de-Montmartre   (217)
(l'Évangéliste)
1894–1898, 1902–1904
19–21, rue des Abesses / 18e
Paul Cottancin, Anatole de Baudot

Anatole de Baudot, a pupil of Viollet-le-Duc, designed this church for the rural borough of Montmartre, which had been annexed by the city of Paris in 1860 and then developed until the end of the 19th century. Saint-Jean-de-Montmartre is the first contemporary expression of Gothic

ideals using reinforced concrete. The St.-Jean-l'Evangéliste church in Montmartre makes use of the new possibilities offered by the material for artistic expression. Influenced by the Gothic Revival style of his tutor, de Baudot created a design that modified Gothic decorative forms and especially the tracery into a form that corresponded to the new materials. The exterior is covered to a large extent with brickwork, with areas of exposed concrete used as a support for structural ceramics. Concrete remains visible in the slender load-bearing elements of the interior. Glazed openings in the vault prove that a concrete skeleton is sufficient to carry the load of the ensemble. The municipal building authorities, however, did not believe that the pillars – only fifty centimeters in diameter in spite of their twenty-five-meter height – would be able to support the seven-centimeter vault, and thought that the ensemble would collapse. The building works were therefore disrupted in 1899 and not resumed until 1902, after tests had proved that the vault could withstand a load of 800 kilos per square meter and the pillars up to 1,500 kilos.

The church uses the Cottancin technique, in which pillars are made of hollow bricks stacked on metal rods.

139

The Eiffel Tower – "Tour de 300 mètres" (218)

Paris's best-known landmark was inaugurated in 1889 at the World's Fair organized by the French Republic for the Centennial of the Revolution. The engineer Gustave Eiffel supervised the construction of the graceful tower, completing it in just sixteen months. In spite of its considerable height of 300 meters (without the twenty-meter broadcasting antenna added later), the structure weighs just 7,000 tons. This makes the Eiffel Tower surprisingly light: a thirty-centimeter iron model of the building would weigh only seven grams. Moreover, if it were melted down to an area of its base, it would form a plate just ten centimeters thick. In the course of the 19th century, various 1,000-foot (304.80 m) buildings had been designed, but none were realized. In 1884, Eiffel and two engineers, Émile Nouguier and Maurice Koechlin, designed a structure made of four merging pillars. In May, 1886, the organizers of the World's Fair announced an architecture competition for a 300-meter iron tower with a 125-square-meter base area. Eiffel gave the architect Stephen Sauvestre the task of designing the crown and the four arches at the base of the tower, as well as the first-level galleries that were removed in 1937. These decorative, non-load-bearing elements helped to make the structure's appearance less technical and more contemporary. In spite of these concessions to the taste of the times, various artists including Charles Garnier (Opéra Garnier, no. 198), Guy de Maupassant and Émile Zola protested against "Eiffel's tower" as construction began in 1887. Moreover, the great engineering achievement rapidly lost its sensational appeal, and during the 1900 World's Fair, the Tower received only a million visitors – half as many as during the year of its inauguration. Although the original building permit allowed the structure to stand for twenty years, the local authorities considered dismantling it earlier. But new functions secured the tower's future: it became a radio station after a first signal broadcast to the Panthéon over a distance of four kilometers in 1898, and a television transmitter in 1925. The new generation's enthusiasm for progress and technology, as expressed in Robert Delaunay's painting of the Eiffel Tower around 1910, was another factor that ensured the building's preservation. Of his work on the structure, Eiffel wrote, "In a way, the tower was shaped by the wind," explaining that resistance to the force of the wind had been the most important engineering challenge. The tower stands on four concrete blocks that reach fourteen meters into the ground. Like the bridges that the Eiffel company built in various countries since 1867 (including the Maria Pia Bridge over the Douro River, Portugal, 1877–1878), the tower is composed of a wind-permeable latticework of three-dimensional iron beams held together by some 2.5 million rivets. Struts connect the four fifteen-meter-wide pillars below the first platform at a height of fifty-seven meters, where the tower's cross-section covers an area of 4,010 square meters. The pillars here are tilted at 54 degrees. The great arches served as a symbolic gateway to the World's Fair. Between the first and second platforms, the pillars taper to 10.4 meters in width, while their slope increases to 80 degrees. The second platform, 115 meters high, has a cross-section of 1,300 square meters. The distance between the pillars is now similar to their own width. As the tower continues to rise from this point on, the 3-by-3 trusses on each side do not become thinner at the same rate, but instead the corner braces displace the truss girded from the inside in a step by step, petering out to a point. Half way to the third floor, the middle truss is eliminated. The highest platform with a panoramic terrace 276 meters above the ground has a cross-section of 270 square meters. The Eiffel Tower was an innovation not only in its design, but also in the systematic use of prefabricated elements. All its parts were manufactured from commercial wrought iron at Levallois-Perret near Paris, and assembled by some two hundred workers.

View of the Eiffel Tower over the Mars Field, La Défense appears in the background

Théâtre de l'Opéra Comique (219) (Salle Favart)
1894–1898
place Boieldieu / 2e
Stanislas Louis Bernier

The interior of this theater, also called the "Salle Favart" after its first director, Charles Favart, is almost as lavishly decorated as the Opéra Garnier (no. 198). It exemplifies the bourgeois taste for neo-Baroque profusion that remained fashionable for public buildings until the early 20th century.

The exterior, however, is much simpler than the façade of the Grand Opéra, partially because of the lot's smaller dimensions.

La Pagode (220)
1895
57bis, rue de Babylone / 7e
Alexandre Marcel

A Japanese building with its typical upswept eaves stands right in the middle of the French capital. François-Émile Morin, director of the Magasins du Bon Marché, had it built for his wife.

Japan was fashionable at this time, in particular among the Impressionist painters, whose art was influenced by Japaneese graphic. The property behind high perimeter walls includes a small Japanese garden. The building was converted into a cinema and cultural center in the 1930s.

École de Sacré-Cœur (221)
1895
9–16, avenue de la Frillière / 16e
Hector Guimard

This school, built to plans by Hector Guimard, applies an idea formulated by Viollet-le-Duc in a drawing in 1855: On the ground floor, V-shaped pillars support a horizontal beam on which the second floor rests.

Other iron beams are visible above the windows of the second floor. A succession of small segmental arches provides a visual transition from the long beam

of the first floor to the brickwork of the upper stories.

The use of various building materials in different colors bear witness to Guimard's interest in the Art Nouveau principles that he discovered in 1894 during his stay in Brussels, the city of Victor Horta. Two other buildings by Guimard, Villa Jassedé (Rue Chardon-Lagache 34) and Maison Roszé (Rue Boileau 3), show the architect's preference for the Eclectic style before his Brussels sojourn.

Gare de Lyon   (222)
1895–1902
20, boulevard Diderot / 12e
Marius Toudoire

Marius Toudoire developed this station on the occasion of the 1900 World's Fair, but it was not completed until 1902.

The iron hall of this civil engineering achievement covers the tracks behind the station, while the façades, unlike those of Gare du Nord (no. 196) and Gare de l'Est (no. 181), do not immediately reveal the building's function. Both inside and out, the station integrates a variety of styles in typical Eclectic fashion. In 1903, Toudoire also designed the neo-Baroque interior of the Le Train Bleu restaurant.

Pont Alexandre III   (223)
1896–1900
Seine / 7e, 8e
Jean Résal, Amédée Alby (engineer),
Joseph Cassien-Bernard, Gaston Cousin

This bridge, also called "Pont de l'Exposition" because it was built on the occasion of the 1900 World's Fair, stands in the prolongation of the avenue that runs between the Petit Palais (no. 224) and the Grand Palais (no. 225), and crosses the Seine with a single span 107 meters long. The arch has an exceptionally large radius in order to keep the roadway low and prevent it from impairing the vista to the Champs-Élysées (no. 80) in one direction and the Invalides (no. 89) in the other (Pont des Invalides). Nicholas II, the last Russian tsar, laid the foundation stone of the bridge named after his father. Pairs of seventeen-meter-high columns at either end of the bridge add to its rigidity. Each column is crowned with a gilt bronze group featuring the winged Pegasus together with various figures of glory. On the left bank, glorifications of Commerce (by P. Garnet) and Industry (by C. Steiner) stand above bas-reliefs portraying The Resurgence of France (by J. Coutan) and France under Louis XIV (by L. Marqueste). On the right bank, glorifications of Science and

the Arts (by E. Frémiet) surmount bas-re-liefs portraying Contemporary France (by G. Michel) and France under Charlemagne (by A. Lenoir).

Cartouches in the middle of each parapet are flanked by nymphs: Paris and the Seine on one side, Russia and the Neva on the other (works by Récipon). Gauquic designed the lampposts; Morice and Massoule created the fishes and water genii at their feet.

Petit Palais (Musée des (224) Beaux-Arts de la Ville de Paris)
1896–1900
avenue Winston-Churchill / 8e
Charles-Louis Girault

Together with the Grand Palais (no. 225) on the other side of the street and the Pont Alexandre III (no. 223) at the end of Avenue Winston-Churchill, the Petit Palais composes an architectural en-

semble developed on the occasion of the 1900 World's Fair. The two palaces are the result of an architecture competition held in 1896 to replace the pavilion of the city of Paris that had stood here since the 1878 World's Fair.

Ionic colonnades extend on either side of the central projection, whose great arch stands in front of a dome over the entrance hall reminiscent of the cupola on the Invalides (no. 89). The Petit Palais, a neo-Baroque building to plans by Charles Girault, integrates early Art Nouveau elements – in particular in its statuary –, the result being a structure in the "Beaux-Arts" style typical of the turn of the century. The building impressed King Leopold II of Belgium so much that he appointed Girault his court architect.

Chaix & Morel et associés refurbished the structure in 2005. While the Grand Palais is a venue for temporary exhibitions, the Petit Palais now houses the municipal art museum. Its collections are fascinating, but remain overshadowed by those of the Louvre (no. 49).

Grand Palais (225)
1897–1900, 2000–2005
avenue Winston-Churchill / 8e
Charles-Louis Girault, Henri Deglane,
Albert Thomas, Albert Louvet,
Agence Alain-Charles Perrot,
Jean-Loup Roubert

Although this building, erected together with the Petit Palais (no. 224) on the occasion of the 1900 World's Fair, incorporates Art Nouveau elements, it is still dominated by the monumentality and solemnity of the neo-Baroque style, and has little to do with Guimard's intimate Metro (no. 232) entrances that also made their appearance

at that time. Whereas the buildings erected for the 1889 World's Fair dramatized the potential of civil engineering (Eiffel Tower, no. 218), those developed at the turn of the century celebrated the importance of the arts. Therefore, the Grand Palais was designed as a vast glass hall with natural stone walls. With a mass of 340 tons, the Grand Palais is the largest glass building in the world. Paris also hosted the Olympic Games in 1900, and the Grand Palais was used for the riding competitions. Charles Girault, who built the Petit Palais, had to harmonize the plans of the three winners of the architecture competition for the Grand Palais: Degalne had designed the main building, Thomas the parallel extension, and Louvet the wing connecting the two. The Grand Palais is another academic neo-Baroque building with Art Nouveau elements. The quadrigae at the corners of the gigantic glass roof are by Georges Récipon.

The agency of Alain-Charles Perrot and Jean-Loup Roubert restored and modernized the Grand Palais between 2002 and 2005.

Gare d'Orsay (Musée d'Orsay) (226)
1898–1900, 1983–1986
quai Anatole-France / 7e
Victor Laloux, Renaud Bardon,
Pierre Colboc, Jean-Paul Philippon,
Gae Aulenti, ACT architecture

This station on the left bank of the Seine is another building in the neo-Baroque style erected on the occasion of the 1900 World's Fair.

It originally included a hotel – a combination that already existed in London and at Paris's Gare Saint-Lazare, built in 1889.

The building decayed after rail traffic was shifted to Gare Montparnasse in the 1950s, and President Giscard d'Estaing decided to convert the station into a museum for 19th-century painting. ACT Architecture refurbished the building as of 1979 and performed the conversion works in collaboration with Gae Aulenti between 1980 and 1986, creating 43,000 square meters of exhibition space for the Musée d'Orsay inside the long station hall and in new rooms.

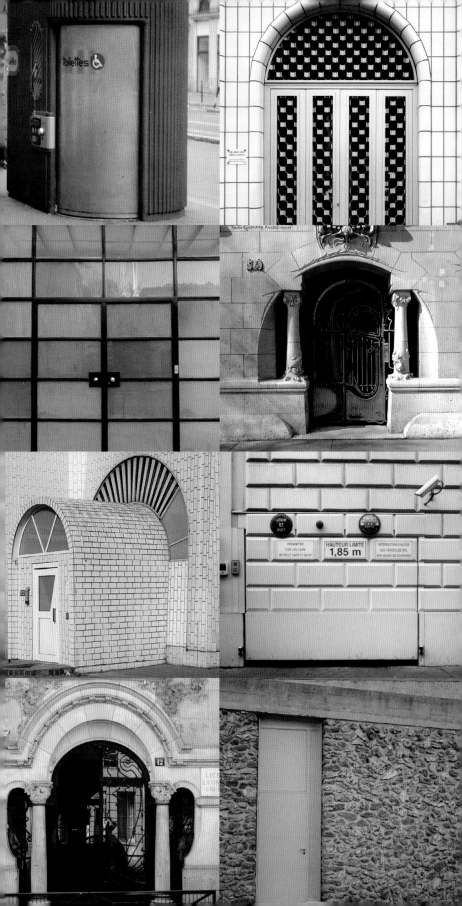

Fin de siècle: Anti-rationalism at the turn of the century (227)

Around the turn of the century increasingly more heavy industry settled in the city's suburbs. At the same time, the newly rich moved to the outskirts of Paris. This moneyed clientele continued to build in Historicist or Eclecticist styles, but soon the arrival of a Belgian artist would introduce a change in the city's appearance. Henry Clemens van de Velde (1863–1957) studied painting in Brussels and Paris, and was exposed to impressionism, pointillism and symbolism, but later converted to Jugendstil. He was active as an architect and craftsman in the tradition of the English Arts and Crafts movement, and built his own house Bloemenwerf in Uccle near Brussels in the corresponding fashion in 1894-1896. Around almost the same time, Victor Horta built Hôtel Tassel (1893-1897) in Brussels, which was the first building that replaced traditional decorative forms with floral motifs.

The line work of curving plant stalks figured especially prominently in his vocabulary. Van der Velde brought these forms to Paris, where he used them to decorate four rooms of Samuel Bing's gallery in 1896. The name of the gallery, "L'Art Nouveau" was later transferred to the style. His furniture enjoyed success at the 1897 Dresden Decorative Arts Exposition, but failed to impress Parisians. The following year van der Velde founded a decorative arts workshop in Brussels.

The same year, he executed the interior design of Julius Meier-Graefe's Parisian art gallery, Maison Moderne. In the years 1906–1914 he directed the School of Arts and Crafts in Weimar, the predecessor to the Bauhaus school. There, he not only established ties to the industry which would serve as an example for the Werkbund, but also reformed how the subject was taught.

His only remaining building in Paris was completed during this time. Under great influence of the Viennese geometric Jugendstil, he planned the Théatre des Champs-Elysées (no. 256) in 1911, which was built with some changes by Auguste Perret. Art Nouveau's breakthrough came with Castel Béranger (no. 228) by Victor Guimard, whose name is now synonymous with the style.

World exhibition 1900

In just a short time the "Style Guimard" gained an enormous presence in the city with countless metro stations on the six new lines constructed for the 1900 World Exposition. But as it was, the time had definitely come for shoots, twines and whip-lashes – Guimard built numerous buildings ranging from villas to multi-storied residential houses in the affluent 16th arrondissement.

No other style has made itself more popular in such a short space of time. Cheerful interplay of colors and lines was taken up even in warehouse architecture, which established itself already in the 19th century.

At the turn of the century, buildings everywhere used the vocabulary or at least assimilated it in neo-Renaissance or neo-Baroque.

Neo-Baroque style lingered in the official architecture around 1900 and sometimes, as with Grande and Petit Palais (no. 225, no. 224), it ventured into the picturesque in spite of the ornamentation's monumentality.

Behind the façade of the larger World Exposition palace is an enormous glass roof. The advantages of constructive engineering increasingly influenced traditional building types, as in the case of the open load-bearing framework of the Notre-Dame-du-Travail (no. 231). At the end of the century Francois Hennebique built the first house of reinforced concrete on Rue Danton (no. 229). Auguste Perret's house on Rue Franklin 25 (no. 240) was the first to use a reinforced concrete frame as a façade design element. Perret's houses display a renewed draw toward a reformed, modern neo-Classicism. This new austerity without any monumentalism characterizes the buildings, which present themselves as being in the service of public health, like the terraced apartment buildings by Henri Frédéric Sauvage or Auguste Labussière's Rue de Saïda (no. 259).

The Office public d'habitations à bon marché pour la ville de Paris (OPHBM.VP, since 1987 Office public d'aménagement et de construction de Paris OPAC) was founded in 1914 with the purpose of improving residential conditions, but could begin to pursue its purpose only after World War I in 1919.

149

Castel Béranger   (228)
1895–1898
14, rue La Fontaine / 16e
Hector Guimard

This complex of thirty-six apartments developed by Hector Guimard – known primarily for his Paris Metro entrances – is both the architect's masterpiece and Paris's first Art Nouveau building. The landlord gave Guimard a free hand within the allocated budget.

Upon completion of his studies at the School of Fine Arts, Guimard traveled to England in 1895, then to the Netherlands and finally to Belgium, where he discovered Victor Horta's floral style of architecture. Back in France, he carefully implemented the new style in his designs for Castel Béranger. Elements of Eclecticism are still to be found as borrowed from Viollet-le-Duc's Rationalism, but the pure new artistic vocabulary of Art Nouveau dominates the building. The entrance concentrates a number of Art Nouveau elements, such as the columns which have been whittled down to functional shafts and the asymmetrical grille with the typical whiplash bars. Evidently, the

time had come for such a new, original style, as is evidenced by Castel Béranger's being awarded a prize for the beauty of its façade in 1898. This success led to other commissions, including that for the metro entrances (no. 232) that Guimard created in the following year.

Immeuble Hennebique   (229)
1898–1900
1, rue Danton / 6e
François Hennebique, Edouard Arnaud

In 1892, François Hennebique patented ferroconcrete. He built this house to popularize the new material in Paris and became famous for his invention during the 1900 World's Fair. But the patent was declared invalid three years later, as Joseph Monier had already obtained a similar one in 1878. Nonetheless, the Immeuble Hennebique still shows the engineer's expertise.

Unlike the somewhat unconventional Maison Hennebique in Bourg-la-Reine near Paris that aimed at evidencing the potential of ferroconcrete, this building primarily intended to demonstrate that the new building material could replace brick and natural stone in traditional designs. The Immeuble Hennebique includes but few Art Nouveau elements, but a wealth of conventional features such as

corbels, columns and pilasters. Such elements, which are often more decorative than functional even on stone buildings, look perfectly superfluous on a ferroconcrete structure.

Apartment (230)
1898–1899
95, rue Montmartre / 2e
Sylvain Périssé

The building asserts itself against the neighboring buildings using its open structure and iron framework. While the sides are walled-in, the structure can be traced by following the two middle axes. The scaffolding is filled to a large extent with glass and only a narrow lower area displays a clinker façade in Beaux Arts masonry style. The third axis juts out from the other two as a bay, additionally underscoring the modular structure at the core of the building.

Notre-Dame-du-Travail (231)
1899–1902
59, rue Vercingétorix / 14e
Jules Astruc

This church, consecrated to Our Lady of Labor, was built in a working-class district. The façade of brick and natural stone conceals an exceptionally light iron frame, which is made from recycled material from the Palace of Industry built for the 1855 World's Fair. The unadorned interior with no added forms is composed of a nave and four aisles, and creates an industrial aesthetic that remained unparalleled up until the construction of the Centre Pompidou (no. 334). At the time, construction of such a building was possible only in a working-class neighborhood.

Late 19th-century architects found that the Gothic style had particular affinities with industrialized buildings, and this building reflects this taste. Notre-Dame-du-Travail eliminates Romanesque vaulting, with a gable roof resting directly on the wall arches. Only the passage to the choir is marked with a Palladian motif – a large round arch opening flanked by two smaller ones with a straight lintel.

Parisian metro station entrances – street furniture for World exhibition (232)

In 1897, in preparation for the 1900 World's Fair, the city of Paris and the French government agreed to build six underground rail lines with a total length of sixty-five kilometers – an idea that had been under discussion for almost thirty years. Work began in 1898 on Line 1, from Porte de Vincennes to Porte Maillot.

The World's Fair opened in April 1900, but the line was not finished until July. Nonetheless, it carried four million passengers during its first six months of operation.

As tunneling technology was little developed in the early 20th century, the oldest metro lines were built above ground or using the cut-and-cover technique along the boulevards laid out by Haussmann.

On the surface lines 2 and 6, construction of several bridges – including Pont de Bir-Hakeim, Viaduc de Passy (1903–1905, architect Jean-Camille Formigé and engineer Louis Biette) and Viaduc d'Austerlitz (1903-1904, Louis Biette) – was required to cross the Seine. Yet the greatest interest of the metro from an architectural standpoint remains the entrances to the underground stations, designed by Hector Guimard.

Charles Garnier (Opéra Garnier, no. 198) had declared that the people of Paris would accept the metro only as a work of art, not as a functional installation. After a competition had failed to produce satisfactory designs for the stations and their entrances, the authorities commissioned Guimard directly due to the success of his Art Nouveau Castel Béranger (no. 228).

This task perfectly matched the architect's profile. Faced with the task of giving the modern, functional structures a contemporary yet artistic appearance, Guimard merged Viollet-le-Duc's rationalism with Victor Horta's botanical elements to create his famous Art Nouveau cast-iron gateways and entrance pavilions.

Their generically organic forms admit all kinds of associations: buds, nodes, bones, or other amorphous shapes.

Moreover, Guimard combined high aesthetic standards with the low costs of serial production, since many of the elements could be prefabricated and pre-assembled.

Only a few of the entrance pavilions have been preserved, however, including those at the stations Châtelet (1901), Porte Dauphine and Abbesses (formerly at Hôtel de Ville, both 1900).

The pavilion at Étoile was lost to remodeling in 1925, and one of those at Bastille, dismantled in 1962, is now on exhibit at MoMA in New York.

By 1914, the metro network included ten lines with a total of 141 pavilions and unroofed entrances designed by Guimard.

In spite of many changes over the years, about eighty of the unroofed entrances have survived.

In 1975, the European Architectural Heritage Year led to a rediscovery of the Art Nouveau style, and hence to a new appreciation of Guimard's works for the Paris metro. Their restoration did not begin until the 1990s, however. Today, specimens of the famous "Métro style" developed by Guimard can be found not only in New York, but also in Lisbon, Mexico City, Montreal, Moscow and São Paolo.

Post card of the period showing the former metro station Place de la Bastille

153

Gristle and buds in flowing forms became first possible with the fabrication from cast-iron

Lycée Italien Léonard-da-Vinci (233)
1899
12, rue Sédillot / 7e
Jules Lavirotte

Just a year after the construction of the Castel Béranger (no. 228), Art Nouveau style became highly fashionable in Paris: Hector Guimard designed his famous Metro entrances (no. 232) on the occasion of the 1900 World's Fair, while Jules Lavirotte developed buildings with an even greater profusion of vegetal and dynamic forms. Compared with later works by Lavirotte such as Avenue Rapp 29 (no. 239), the Léonard-de-Vinci secondary school appears hesitant to copy Guimard, so that the style of the first Parisian Art Nouveau building is found mainly on the entrance. The roof windows feature sinuous ornamental lines, but the façade maintains a strict vertical structure despite of an asymmetrical main axis.

Italien Léonard-de-Vinci (no. 233), the façade here is much more exuberant: it integrates a wealth of ornaments, and even neo-Mannerist banded rustication on the first floor. Not only the decorative elements are asymmetric, but the entire façade, with the entrance to the left and a corbelled turret to the right. Lavirotte also designed the wrought iron gate that borders the lot in the cul-de-sac where the building stands.

Apartments   (235)
1899
16, rue d'Abbeville / 10e
Georges Massa, Alexandre Dupuy
(sculptor)

Except for some contemporary elements on the corner, the decoration of this building is mainly composed of neo-Mannerist ornaments. The two oversized female figures that support an escutcheon above the entrance (works by Daniel Dupuis) have a sinuous pose common to both the Art Nouveau and Mannerist styles. Above them, the truncated axis is resolved completely using glass.

A similar axis can be found on the long façade of the building at Rue d'Abbeville 14 (no. 238) built three years later by Alexandre Autant and his son Édouard.

Apartments   (234)
1899-1900
3, place Rapp / 7e
Jules Lavirotte

Although Jules Lavirotte erected this building in the same year as the Lycée

The coming together of Mannerism and Art Nouveau appeared natural to the building's contemporaries, who found this combination consistent.

Designed by Georges Massa, house number 16 was at first falsely attributed to Jules Lavirotte.

Entrepôt du Métropolitain (236)
around 1900
29, rue Le-Brun / 13e
Hennebique, Firma

This unornamented functional hall developed by the Companie Générale des Omnibus marks the origins of a taste that endured for decades. The 13th arrondissement was an industrial district in the early 20th century, and concrete was then considered particularly suitable for industrial buildings.

Iron pillars and concrete form a framework closed by a gate, translucent panes or cobblestones, according to the desired function.

La Ruche (237)
(ateliers d'artistes – the beehive)
1900–1902
2, passage de Dantzig / 15e
Gustave Eiffel

The sculptor Alfred Boucher acquired the Wine Pavilion from the 1900 World's Fair, and had it moved here and converted into eighty artists' studios and apartments for up to forty-six artists. In the decades that followed, noted artists worked at La Ruche, including Alexander Archipenko, Marc Chagall, Fernand Léger, Amedeo Modigliani, Chaïm Soutine and Ossip Zadkine. The complex, which housed a theater until the 1930s, has been occupied by artists once again since extensive refurbishment in the 1990s.

Apartments (238)
1900–1901
14, rue d'Abbeville / 10e
Alexandre & Edouard Autant

While the building at Rue d'Abbeville 16 (no. 235) mixes several styles, this structure shows similar elements designed exclusively in the Art Nouveau style. Alexandre Bigot designed the exuberant floral ornaments of both the corbels and the window frames, which only appear Mannerist in their free treatment of architectural details without adapting the style's forms. The brick façade is also more in keeping with the taste of the time that the natural stone of the neighboring building.

Apartments (239)
1900–1901
29, avenue Rapp / 7e
Jules Lavirotte

This major example of the Art Nouveau style features still more reliefs and ceramic ornaments than the neighboring build-

ing at Square Rapp 3 (no. 234). The ceramist Alexandre Bigot (1862–1927) who was also the owner of the building, used the façade as an oversized advertisement for his work. He also created the façade statuary of Saint-Jean-de-l'Evangéliste (no. 217), Castel Béranger (no. 228), Rue Franklin 25 bis (no. 240) and Les Grands Magasins La Samaritaine (no. 247) in Paris, as well as that of several buildings outside Paris, including Villa Majorelle in Nancy (Henri Sauvage, 1902) and the outer shell of the dome of the Russian Orthodox Cathedral in Nice. The first and second floors form the base of this six-story building. The profusion of blossom shapes on the gable recalls other buildings in Nancy, the cradle of Art Nouveau. The entrance, with its wealth of floral and figurative ornaments, underscores the asymmetry of the façade.

Apartments (240)
1903–1904
25bis, rue Benjamin Franklin / 16e
Auguste & Gustave Perret

This residential building designed by Auguste Perret integrates a number of novelties visible at first glance. The reinforced concrete frame is discernible at a glance behind the Art Nouveau ceramic tiles (by Alexandre Bigot, Avenue Rapp 29, no. 239) intended to protect the façade from moisture. Another novelty is the replacement of the interior walls with concrete pillars, which permits large modular rooms.

Perret abandoned his studies at the École des Beaux-Arts and took over his father's building enterprise, implementing new technologies. He preferably referred to the Gothic style as also did Viollet-le-Duc, considering that medieval architects also left the structural frame visible underneath the ornamentation. As the neighbors refused windows on the rear, Perret oriented all rooms towards the street and encased the rear staircase in glass blocks, another innovation. In 1905, Perret developed an even more radically modern garage in Rue de Ponthieu, but unfortunately that building has not been preserved.

Apartments (241)
1903
7, rue Trétaigne / 18e
Henri Sauvage, Charles Sarazin,
Frantz Jourdain

This trend-setting building with a visible concrete frame similar to that of
Rue Franklin 25 bis (no. 240) was developed on behalf of the Hygienic Low-rent
Housing Company. Frantz Jourdain, who
was one of the founders of the development company and who later designed

the La Samaritaine 1 department store
(no. 247), promoted modern design.

The building includes community
rooms such as a restaurant and a library – a trend typical of the early 20th
century.

Armenian church / (242)
Notre-Dame-de-la-Consolation
1903
15, rue Jean-Goujon / 8e
Albert-Désiré Guilbert

Resisting the modern rationalism of
construction that employed reinforced
concrete and playful aesthetics of Art
Nouveau, stately buildings in the style
of Historicism continued to be erected
in Paris at the end of the 19th century.
The church was built on the site of a fire
that destroyed a wooden bitumin-covered
bazaar, taking 135 lives. The memorial
serves the Armenian congregation to
this day.

In contrast to Église Arménienne's
neo-Romanesque style, unusual for Paris,
Notre-Dame-de-la-Consolation, built by
the same architect down the street at
number 23 in 1900 to commemorate the
same occasion, is a more conventional
neo-Baroque building.

157

L'art pour l'art
Art for art's sake – culture of aesthetics at the turn of the century (243)

In the biographies of most artists, Art Nouveau features only as an intermediate period or, as in the case of Héctor Guimard, it looses its power of innovation to become a degenerate, commercial ornamentation. Already around the end of the 19th century anti-rationalist undercurrents intensified to result in an aestheticism that escaped all sense and purpose. L'art pour l'art (art for art's sake) is a catchphrase coined by Victor Cousin und Théophile Gautier to describe art that is self-sufficient and developed solely around the ideal of beauty.

In literature, sounds and rhythm of words and sentences, even their typography, became more meaningful as the correspondence of their content to the real world.

The representatives of the Surrealist literary scene create a sensual world filled with unbridled, hallucinatory fantasy which in its decadence implied the idea of decay and demise that became commonplace around the turn of the century.

During this period, architecture and visual arts coalesce into a unified work of art which encompasses all details and connects to the design tendencies of Baroque in its pursuit of sensual vividness.

In their connection to architecture, furniture and artisan crafts, painting and drawing avow to two-dimensionality, relinquishing hundreds of years' of perspective illusion tradition.

Jugendstil (Henri de Toulouse-Lautrec, Jules Chéret, Alfons Mucha) as well as the parallel post-Impressionism currents (Paul Gauguin, Paul Cézanne) transpose the three-dimensional reality into a stylized world of consciously organized surface. The artist becomes the creator, not just the imitator of the creation. "Art is a harmony parallel to nature" formulated Paul Cézanne.

In the search for abstract linear clarity and surface ornamentation, interesting connections to medieval art come about. But if medieval art aspired to represent the spiritual world freed of earthly perspective, color and anatomical laws, the reordering of reality in Art Nouveau took place according to solely aesthetic considerations.

In architecture, precise surface effects and polychrome abundance play a deciding role. The existing hierarchy of building materials is dissolved. In renunciation of predominating Historicisms, especially Belgian (Victor Horta, Henry van de Velde) and French (Guimard, Henri Sauvage, Jules Lavirotte) Jugendstil schools seek their inspiration not in the traditional architectural and visual arts repertoire, but directly in nature.

The world of plants fails to deliver concrete prototypes; more often, a formal language is developed using swinging lines and dynamic contours of the botanical world, and geometrical and symmetrical biomorphous structures and organic processes are generalized.

The association of a hair blowing in the wind, rising smoke or lashing whips are rarely made concrete.

This "botanization" of architecture and furniture design in Paris or Nancy goes considerably further than in other centers of European Jugendstil, whose repertoire in Glasgow, Vienna or Darmstadt is primarily derived from abstract geometrical forms.

The biomorphic character of the "Style Guimard" becomes especially obvious in artisan crafts. Glass and enamel pieces by René Lalique or ceramic works by Edmond Lachenal often display more specific floral and animal motifs.

It is this concretization of natural form that often places artisan creations of École de Nancy or Parisian Art Nouveau in the eyes of a modern viewer near the category of kitsch, which defines itself exactly by this discrepancy of content and form.

Thus, the design of a desk lamp as a glowing rose or a vase as a swan is just as functionally ungrounded as a flower arrangement or an ossuary transformed into a Metro station entrance (no. 232).

The common disagreement between form and function is quite possibly the reason for the dead-end character of this style epoch, whose brevity was unprecedented.

The late Historicist abundance of structure and decoration was simply replaced by a new repertoire of forms. Modernity will come only with its abstraction and reduction. But other European art metropolises will still witness a forward-looking objectification of Jugendstil. The way into the 20th century for Parisian Art Nouveau, however, lies first in the embedding of its ornamental repertoire into the pre-Modernist structural engineering of Auguste Perret (no. 240).

above: former brasserie Equivoque, contemporary photography Eugène Atget (detail)
left: Entrance Castel Béranger (no. 228)

Les Chardons   (244)
1903
9, rue Claude-Chahu,
2, rue Eugène-Manuel / 16e
Charles Klein

The lavish thistle decoration that gives "Les Chardons" its name makes it difficult to identify the building as a concrete construction developed using the Hennebique technique. In 1903, the façade was awarded a prize as one of the year's best. The Émile Müller company manufactured its ocher and green tiles after works by the Swiss-born Art Nouveau painter Eugène Grasset. Despite these Art Nouveau elements, however, the building with its columns and corbels is still clearly rooted in Historicism.

Immeuble Félix Potin   (245)
1904
140bis, rue de Rennes,
10–12, rue Blaise-Desgoffe / 6e
Paul Auscher

An unusual corner tower dominates the former headquarters of the Félix Potin grocery chain. On the fifth floor, oversized corbels support the corners of the tower shaped as pillars. At the top, these merge like Art Nouveau blossoms, reminiscent of medieval pinnacles.

Cartouches with mosaics advertise the store's specialties from Pontin's assortment. The architecture of the Magasin Félix-Potin (no. 252) built in 1910 is even more fanciful. The grocery chain operated until 1996.

Ceramic Hôtel   (246)
1904
34, avenue de Wagram / 8e
Jules Lavirotte

This reinforced concrete building owes its name to the ceramic tiles of the façade, a work by Alexandre Bigot that was awarded a prize in 1905 as the most beautiful in the city. The composition of the Ceramic Hôtel's façade is quite unusual,

resembling two three-story buildings one on top of the other rather than a six-story structure. The entrance to the right of the ground floor and the bow windows to the left of the second and third floors provide the asymmetric touch typical of Art Nouveau architecture. The second part of the façade begins above the fourth floor balcony, and from there up the bow windows are located to the right.

La Samaritaine (247)
1904–1910, 1912, 1926–1928,
1930–1933
17–19, rue de la Monnaie; 34, rue de
l'Arbre Sec; 1, rue du Pont-Neuf,
rue Baillet, rue Boucher / 1er
Frantz Jourdain, Henri Sauvage

This Art Nouveau department store built on the site of a pump house adorned with a relief depicting Jesus and the Samaritan woman at Jacob's well has a long history. One of Frantz Jourdain's first commissions as an architect was to unite the various buildings that housed the Samaritaine department store – and he worked on the structure many times throughout his carrier. In a second development phase, Jourdain remodeled the building under the

influence of the Art Nouveau style and Viollet-le-Duc's rationalism. Remnants of this phase are still visible on Rue de la Monnaie. In 1912, the architect also remodeled the interior and the façade on Rue de Rivoli in the Art Nouveau style. Portions of this building phase are also retained to this day. His structural, colorful design did not suit the taste of the time, however, and the public was Argus-eyed at the extension of the store that he built along the Seine.

Office building (248)
1904–1905
124, rue Réaumur / 2e
Georges Chédanne

Standing on a street characterized by Eclectic and Historicist structures, this commercial building is unique for Paris. The iron-structured façade reveals neither concrete nor building stone nor ceramic tiles, but only metal and glass. Moreover, the metal elements are devoid of ornament. The only minor concessions to the Art Nouveau fashion of the time are the S-curves of the entrance arches and the oriels. The elevation likewise features an unusually austere appearance:

three vertical strips composed of wide windows flanked by smaller openings that prefigure the sides of the oriels alternate with four strips of small windows framing the projecting bay windows. Steel is such a dominant element on the façade that the brick masonry on the upper story is barely noticeable.

In view of the architect's otherwise academic or overly decorated work, its remains uncertain if the building's design is really a by Georges Chedanne.

Apartments (249)
1905
2, rue Dorian; 1, rue Picpus / 12e
Jean Fal

Crenelation and a corner tower give this residential building a castle-like appearance. The decoration includes arabesques and whiplash lines (two stylistic elements of Art Nouveau) as well as a variety of figurative ornaments such as cats, rats and wisteria that evoke a fairy tail word from the Middle Ages, and female figures inspired by Botticelli and the Pre-Raphaelites (a movement that considered Raphael the first Renaissance painter). The architectural structuring elements merge smoothly into the main building volume; a frieze adorns the entrance hall.

Galeries Lafayette (250)
1906–1908, 1910–1912, 1926–1936, 1958
38–46, boulevard Haussmann / 9e
Georges Chédanne, Ferdinand Chanut, Pierre Patout, Louis Majorelle

Unlike its nearby competitor Au Printemps (no. 212), this department store developed by Georges Chedanne in 1906–1908 has a façade typical of the "Grands Boulevards" laid out by Baron Haussmann. But the building's most interesting feature is probably the circular four-story ferroconcrete atrium covered with an exquisite polychrome glass dome and adorned with Art Nouveau reliefs by Édouard Schneck. In 1932, Pierre Patout remodeled part of the façade on Rue de la Chaussée d'Antin in the Art Déco style.

Office building (251)
1908
6, rue du Hanovre / 2e
Adolphe Bocage

The commercial building by Adolphe Bocage clearly recalls the structure at Rue Franklin 25 bis (no. 240), a work by Auguste Perret which was built three years earlier and which also features protective tiles by Alexandre Bigot. However, the third story with a balcony at the front features even larger openings than Perret's building. The façade's general appearance, dominated by equally large windows and similarly reduced street-

The first large store of the Félix Potin (no. 245) grocery chain dominates the junction of Rue Réaumur and Boulevard de Sébastopol.

With its squat appearance characterized by a dome and Palladian motifs on the first floor, this rotunda-like structure is clearly apart from other corner buildings developed during the same period. The decorative elements, which include bees as a symbol of business and wealth, are rooted in the neo-Baroque style despite the presence of Art Nouveau elements.

Hôtel Guimard (253)
1910–1913
122, avenue Mozart / 16e
Hector Guimard

parallel balconies each with three regular oriels extending over two stories, remains more conventional. The three uppermost stories are recessed from the street. Like Perret, Bocage studied at the School of Fine Arts under Julien Guadet.

Magasin Félix Potin (252)
(today Monoprix)
1910
51, rue Réaumur / 2e
Charles Henri Camille le Maresquier

163

The façades of the corner building that Hector Guimard developed for himself catalogs most of the Art Nouveau forms and features that the architect favored: asymmetry, curves, whiplash lines, bow windows, wrought iron and a variety of materials merge in a synthesis of the "Guimard style". The interior designs also incorporate the "Guimard style". Guimard had his office on the first floor and lived on the second floor. His wife, the painter Adeline Oppenheim, worked in a pentagonal atelier on the third floor. The neighboring building at Avenue Mozart 120 shows the influence of the Art Déco style on Guimard after World War I.

Hôtel Paul Mezzara (254)
1910–1911
60, rue La Fontaine / 16e
Hector Guimard

The construction of the Castel Béranger (no. 228) was a great success for Hector Guimard and secured him several commissions in the wealthy 16th arrondissement, including the development of the La Rue Moderne complex that includes detached houses and multiple family dwellings (1912, Rue Gros 43/Rue La Fontaine 17–21/Rue Agar 8). In 1911, Guimard also developed the Hôtel Paul Mezzara for a wealthy entrepreneur. Both the façade and major elements of the interior decoration are now under a preservation order. Other works developed in the 16th arrondissement by the star architect of the French Art Nouveau include Avenue de Versailles 142 (1903–1905), Villa de la Réunion 8 (1908), Rue François-Millet 5 (1909), Rue Erlanger 25 (1906), Square Jasmin 3 (1921), Rue Henri-Heine 18 (1926) and Rue Chardon-Lagache 41 (1912).

Sous Station Bastille (255)
1911
31, boulevard Bourdon; 5, rue de la Cerisaie; 18, rue de l'Arsenal / 4e
Paul Friesé

Paul Friesé built several transformer stations whose façades conceal their function while intimating that there is something special behind them. The Clichy power plant (Rue des Dames 51–53, 1890, one of the oldest in the city) already features pillars that frame large glassed areas, but later industrial buildings by the architect, have an even more filigree structure. The brick façade of the Bastille substation is much more massive, however.

Théâtre des Champs-Élysées (256)
1911–1913, 1986–1987, 1989–1990
13–15, avenue Montaigne / 8e
Henry van de Velde,
Auguste & Gustave Perret, Jantzen &
Marrast-Guillaumont, Brigitte de Kosmi

The theater shows more similarities with Jugendstil than any other building in Paris, even after Auguste Perret, who directed the concrete works, replaced van de Velde's smooth forms with the angular neo-Classical lines that he considered more suitable for a concrete structure. The style of the ensemble remains quite simple and flat compared with 19th-century neo-Classical structures, without the monumentality that has its roots in this type of building and went on to characterize mid-20th-century architecture. The theater is thus the first example of both the geometric Jugendstil reception and

the monumental style in Paris. Émile-Antoine Bourdelle created the reliefs that adorn the façades.

In 1991, Brigit de Kosmi developed the roof pavilion that affords a panoramic view of the city from Montmartre to the Eiffel Tower. Imaad Rahmouni designed the restaurant.

Immeuble Louis Majorelle (257)
(today Parexel International France)
1911–1913
126, rue de Provence / 8e
Henri Sauvage, Charles Sarazin

Henri Sauvage designed this commercial building fifteen years after he had built one of the masterworks of Art Nouveau as a private villa for the same developer, the furniture manufacturer Louis Majorelle of Nancy. This Paris ferroconcrete building, however, has no floral ornamentation and recalls the austerity of the house at Rue Vavin 26 (no. 260), another work that Sauvage designed in collaboration with Charles Sarazin. The plain façade differentiates the stories according to their functions: showrooms in the lower stories, then offices and manufacturing halls in the upper stories.

Central téléphonique (258)
1911–1914
17, rue de Faubourg Poissonnière,
2, rue Bergère / 9e
François Le Coeur

The building's plain façade was a provocation to critics in the early 20th century, although similar brick structures had already been developed in city-center locations, such as Hendrik Petrus Berlage's commodities exchange in Amsterdam (1896–1903). In both cases, however, ornamental elements are not totally absent, but concentrated at special spots: the curved zone below the cornice features rich mosaics, while the clock and the window grids include elaborate wrought iron works. Last but not least, the oval canopy with glass bricks over the main entrance is quite unusual.

Social housing (259)
1912–1919
5, rue de la Saïda / 15e
Auguste Labussière

The low development costs of this modern council housing estate built using modern technology are visible at a glance. A regular concrete frame filled with con-

165

trasting bricks structures the façades. The sole decorative elements are the red strips near the eaves that correspond to traditional cornices. The complex consists of several volumes, providing the interiors with plenty of light and air. The open staircase and the flat but still overhanging roofs are forerunners of the modern style of architecture.

In fact, the residential building displays the same rationalism as the industrial estates developed at the turn of the century using a reinforced concrete framework. From 1914 on, Le Corbusier would systematize this "domino technique" in developing villas and residential estates.

Apartments (260)
1912–1914
26, rue Vavin / 6e
Henri Sauvage, Charles Sarazin

With its novel aesthetics and philosophy, as well as the functional and humanist principles that predetermined its design, this building by Henri Sauvage was a forerunner of the "white modern" style of architecture. Geometric forms inspired by both Charles Rennie Mackintosch and the Austrian Jugendstil dominate the façade and contrast with the floral ornaments of Art Nouveau. Sparse blue tiles form geometric patterns on a background of "hygienic" white tiles similar

to those found in many metro stations. Sauvage was among the founders of both the Terraced Façade Building Company (the landlord of Rue Vavin 26) and the Hygienic Low-rent Housing Company. Since sanatoriums with terraced façades had been developed for the treatment of tuberculosis, Sauvage thought that this form, providing the lower stories with much light and fresh air, was the wave of the future for urban development, and he patented plans for terraced houses that included vertical gardens – a novelty in France. His goal was to develop healthy residential buildings for workers but for financial reasons he first developed the building at Rue Vavin for middle-class occupants. For a time Sauvage himself lived in the building, which includes community rooms and various types of apartments, including several artists' studios.

Synagogue rue Pavée (261)
1913–1914
10, rue Pavée / 4e
Hector Guimard

This house of worship shows that even Guimard was influenced by the monumental style.

The façade recalls neo-Classical buildings, while the juxtaposition of small openings on three levels at the center also recalls Gothic tracery.

Moreover, the curvature of the front, the roof and the entrance is rooted likewise in Rococo and Art Nouveau, the style for which Hector Guimard became famous.

raries. A pupil of Anatole de Baudot, Henri Deneux designed the basic plans of Saint-Jean-de-Montmartre (no. 217), a concrete structure with a protective skin. He copied the straight lines of that classical modern building in designing his own house. The sharp edge and the main façade featuring almost entirely glazed strips at intervals that cannot be logically explained from the outside are modern design elements. Moreover, the terrace on the flat roof was to become a standard for later modern buildings. The only features rooted in the style of the early 20th century are the mosaic at the entrance and the ceramic tiles of the façade.

Magasins de la Samaritaine (263)
de Luxe
1914–1917
25–29, boulevard des Capucines,
18–24, rue Daunou / 2e
Frantz Jourdain

Maison Deneux (262)
1913
185, rue Belliard / 18e
Henri Deneux

Except for the façade covering, this unusual wedge-shaped building with a flat roof was almost a decade ahead of its contempo-

After having developed La Samaritaine 1 (no. 247), Frantz Jourdain built this subsidiary for the department store's wealthier customers.

The central part of the façade, flanked by more or less traditional lateral axes, is dominated by a glass surface spanning three axes and three floors. The thin ironwork with slender columns and the rich floral façade decoration has been preserved. The grand staircase – a must in department stores of the time –included a lift from the beginning.

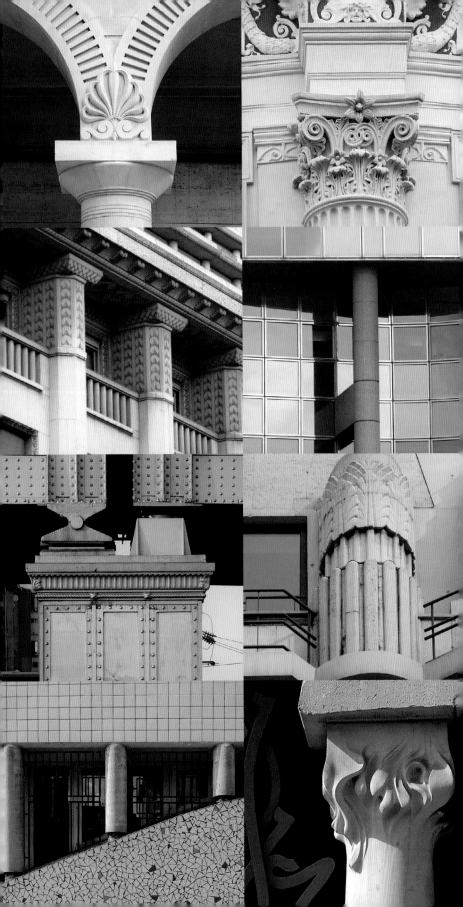

Forward, backward, sideward: controversy between the styles in Classical Modernism (264)

Although the political situation improved at the end of World War I, many economic (reparation payments, worldwide economic crisis) and social problems remained. The city's expansion was placed on the political agenda already before the war. Finally, in 1919 a competition for expansion plans was held, followed in 1920 by the demolition of the Thiers fortification to make room for social residential units and, eventually, Boulevard Périphérique. In the decades that followed, the petite couronne of suburban districts to the other side of the ring grew to double the size of the inner city's area without any urban plan. Since 1928 it was understood that the problems of the city could only be conquered in the "région parisienne." Otherwise, the same questions were awaiting a solution here as in the rest of Europe: closed block construction was opened up and finally replaced by row buildings; garden cities and skyscraper construction were discussed, although both were only marginally realized; adequate air and light in apartments was seen as the cure for tuberculosis, and architecture was expected to contribute to

hygiene. Louis Bonnier, an Art Nouveau architect of whose built work almost no trace survives save for the La Butte-aux-Cailles swimming pool (1920-1923, 13e), had a lot of influence on the theoretical end of these developments. In light of the collapse of the old Europe, Art Nouveau and Historicism had definitely outlasted it. The tradition of border-spanning enlightenment was to be carried on by a league of nations beyond the 19th-century nationalism, and a moderate, unassuming neo-Classicism as seen in the works of August Perret was to predominate.

Both of these qualities are manifested in Paris in the Cité International de l'Université (no. 308). The arrival of a young generation completely turned against the tradition was to give the technical achievements of the 19th century a new form of expression. Charles-Edouard Jeanneret, a student of Perret's, worked to accelerate these developments in France: known as Le Courbusier (no. 293) he announced his wish to tear down the majority of the buildings in the old city, with the exception of historical monuments, and build hi-rises separated by large dis-

Citroën-Garage Marbeuf, 1927–1929 by Albert Laprade and Léon Émile Bazin. The showroom was destroyed in 1954.

tances from each other. The International Style, Classical Modernism in white, arrives in Paris. The concept is defined by the art historian Henry Russel-Hitchcock and the museum director (and later, architect) Philip Johnson with the help of three criteria set out in "The International Style. Architecture since 1922," published on the occasion of the "Modern Architecture: International Exhibition" (Museum of Modern Art, New York, 1932). These are as follows: individual volumes, not mass defines the architecture; clean lines are achieved through (modular) ordering, not using predominant axial symmetry; and no haphazard decoration is to be added to the design. In contrast to the New Objectivity and Functionalism movements that arrived at a later date, the International Style had a deep-reaching consistent aesthetic, which nonetheless wasn't theoretically laid down. The rectilinear buildings were to lose their material quality thanks to the white plaster and glass, or at least appear to be lighter; in France, they additionally aspired to fulfill Le Corbusieres "Five Points." Although the New Objectivists built many

projects in the 1930s, these were mostly limited to villas or interiors (Maison Jean Badovici on Rue Chateaubriand by Eileen Gray, 1930-1931). Art Déco was just as unsuccessful in establishing itself, even though for a time it significantly influenced the city's image. The "International Exposition of Decorative Arts and Modern Industries" (1925) helped spread the countermovement to the International Style, which took on its clear lines and form, but followed Jugendstil in its stylistic form and emphasis on the materials. Less conspicuous than the International Style and Art Déco, neo-Classicism outlived these decades and developed into a monumental neo-Classicism. Like the Modernists, the monumental Classicists also found their inspiration in Perret and Tony Garnier, who at the time was the city planner for Lyon.

Monumental Classicism dominated the 1937 World Exhibition – it is here that the Palais de Chaillot (no. 304), the Palais de Tokio (no. 302) and Perret's Musée des Traveaux Publics (no. 306) clearly revealed their similarity to the pavilions of dictatorial Germany and Soviet Union.

Social housing with (265)
swimming pool
1921–1927, 1930
13, rue des Amiraux,
4, rue Hermann-Lachapelle / 18e
Henri Sauvage

After completion of the building at Rue Vavin 26 (no. 260), Henri Sauvage was finally able to build a terraced house for workers when the City of Paris commissioned him to develop an eight-story structure with seventy-eight living units.

The terraces of the building covering almost an entire block allowed Sauvage to provide the structure with vertical gardens. Other vertical elements, such as loggias, staircases and bow windows at the corner of the building, alleviate the overall impression of a ziggurat.

Sauvage had planned a cinema in the basement, but the city authorities preferred a swimming pool which they considered more hygienic and was built in 1930.

Cinéma le Louxor, former (266)
1921
170, boulevard de Magenta,
boulevard de la Chapelle / 10e
H. Ripey

Even before the official birth of the Art Déco style, this cinema theater used a wealth of Egyptian decorative motifs, such as papyrus, lotus flowers and irises, in the tradition of the oriental style favored in the late 18th and early 19th centuries.

Tibéri created the mosaics that adorn "Paris's most beautiful cinema". The original seats, also in Egyptian style, were removed during renovation works in the 1970s.

After a last screening in 1979, demolition was averted in the 1980s, but the building is now in poor condition, proving that a preservation order is not sufficient in France to guarantee the future of a historic monument.

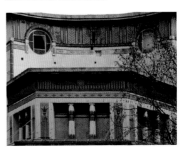

Grande Mosquée de Paris (267)
(mosque)
1922–1926
1, place du Puits-de-l'Ermite,
39–47, rue Geoffroy-Saint-Hilaire,
2, rue Daubenton,
2bis, rue des Quatrefages,
10, rue Georges-Desplas / 5e
Tranchant de Lunel, Robert Fournez,
Maurice Mantout, Charles Heubès

The French government built this mosque with its thirty-three-meter minaret as a tribute to the 100,000 Muslims who died serving under the French colors during World War I. But because a 1905 law mandated the separation of church and state, the authorities developed the sacred building as part of an "Islamic institute".

North-African workers built the mosque to plans by Maurice Tranchant de Lunel, head of the Colonial Department of Fine Arts in Morocco. The complex integrates several influences: the mosque recalls the grand mosque of Fez, while the inner court recalls that of Granada's Alhambra.

Maison et atelier Ozenfant (269)
1923
53, avenue Reille,
place de Montsouris / 14e
Le Corbusier, Pierre Jeanneret

Ensemble HBM (268)
1922–1926
140, rue de Ménilmontant / 20e
Louis Bonnier

In 1889, the government therefore passed a law to promote low-rent housing. Most of the "habitations à bon marché", characterized by red brick façades, were not developed until the 1920s and 1930s, however. Compared with similar housing estates in other European capitals, such as Vienna's expressionistic "red fortresses" or Amsterdam's ensembles arranged along streets with a fanciful design, the French "HBMs" look unobtrusive and conventional, despite the introduction of quite modern elements such as building parts extending across streets. Another example of early 20th-century council housing in an even more backward style is at the corner of Rue Brillat-Savarin 16–24) and Rue de la Fontaine-à-Mulard 1–19.

The 1924 building is a work by André Arfvidson, Joseph Bassompierre and Paul de Rutte.

In the first years after he moved to Paris in 1917, Charles-Édouard Jeanneret (alias Le Corbusier, no. 293) had very few architectural commissions. He therefore collaborated intensively with the painter Amédée Ozenfant, who was a regular contributor to the journal L'Esprit Nouveau, which appeared from 1920 to 1925. During that year, Ozenfant also exhibited works at the Exposition Internationale des Arts Décora-

173

tifs and, after coming into an inheritance, commissioned Le Corbusier to build a corner house with an atelier on the third floor. This was one of the first Parisian buildings that Le Corbusier built according to the principles formulated in his book Towards a New Architecture published in 1923. The atelier's fully glazed walls dominate the façade with an unconstraint design. To this "free façade" corresponds a "free ground plan". However, the horizontal window bands are disrupted at the corner of the building as this part of the structure is a load-bearing element. A terrace was added in 1946, replacing the original double shed roof.

Maison Planeix   (270)
1924–1928
24bis, boulevard Masséna / 13e
Le Corbusier, Pierre Jeanneret

This building, erected for Antonin Planeix, a sculptor of funeral monuments, recalls the Maison Tristan-Tzara (no. 276). On the street façade, the only break in the symmetry is the window to the right on the fourth story. Another difference is the presence of a piano nobile. The garden side features a more relaxed design, with bridges and staircases as metaphors of ships – a particularity of the "white modern" style of architecture.

Villa La Roche und Villa Jeanneret-Raaf (Fondation Le Corbusier) (271)
1924–1925
8–10, place du Docteur-Blanche / 16e
Le Corbusier, Pierre Jeanneret

ENSEMBLE Le Corbusier began this double villa in the same year as the Maison et

atelier Ozenfant (no. 269). The landlord, the Swiss banker Raoul La Roche, lived and exhibited his collection of Cubist paintings in one half of the villa, while Le Corbusier's brother Albert Jeanneret lived with his wife Lotti Raaf in the other half. The building integrates all the elements that Le Corbusier lists in his work Towards a New Architecture: free ground plan, horizontal window bands, unconstrained façade with pillars on the first floor, volumes of different heights, and roof gardens.

Today the villa houses the Le Corbusier Foundation and Museum.

Villa Seurat   (272)
1924–1926
101, rue de la Tombe-Issoire; 1, 3, 4, 5, 7bis, 8, 9, 11, Villa Seurat / 14e
André Lurçat, Auguste & Gustave Perret

ENSEMBLE Between 1924 and 1926, André Lurçat designed eight artists' workshops in the "white modern" style to be developed along a new street called "Villa Seurat". With their extensive glazed surfaces, his works recall the Villa La Roche/Jeanneret-Raaf (no. 271) that le Corbusier designed shortly before. At Villa Seurat, Lurçat built No.1 for the writer Frank Townshend, No.3 for the painters Édouard Georg and Marcel Gromaire, No. 4 for the painter Jean Lurçat (the architect's brother), No. 5 for the painter Pierre Bertrand, No. 8 for Mademoiselle Quillé, No. 9 for Madame Veuve Bertrand, and No. 11 for the sculptor Arnold Huggler. Auguste and Gustave Perret designed the house at No. 7 bis for the sculptor Chana Orloff. The modern glazed surfaces leave the load-bearing elements visible and deprive the buildings of the immaterial appearance that characterizes the white-fronted Villa La Roche/Jeanneret. The artists' estate inspired the American writer Henry Miller when he wrote Tropic of Cancer in 1934. Miller also published La Revue Officielle de la Villa Seurat, together with Anaïs Nin, while living at No. 18.

Arcades des Champs-Élysées (273)
Arcades du Lido
1925–1926, 1928
76–78, avenue des Champs-Élysées / 8e
Charles Lefebvre, Marcel Julien,
Louis Duhayon, René Berger

This shopping arcade, developed by the investor Léonard Rosenthal, copies the pattern of 19th-century covered walkways.

Its width of fifteen meters is unusual, however, and provides an interesting extension of the prestigious address Avenue des Champs-Élysées.

The luxurious decoration that combines Historicism and Art Déco integrates marble columns from an earlier building on this site, designed by Gustave Rives in 1905. René Gobert created the grille and other metal art elements, while René Lalique designed the glasswork, which is only partially preserved. The Lido, one of Paris's most luxurious casinos, opened here in 1929. René Berger designed the underground theater and swimming pool. The Lido moved to Avenue des Champs-Élysées 116 bis (no. 285) in 1977.

Institut d'Art et d'Archéologie (274)
de l'Université de Paris
1925–1928
3, rue Michelet / 6e
Paul Bigot

175

The design for the Art History Institute was selected in the course of a competition organized by Sorbonne. The building is unusual in that its Historicist ornamentation was completed after Modernism had conclusively asserted itself, and follows the structure's function. The basic box-shaped concrete form is thoroughly modern. This form is, however, ornamented not only using clinker, but also with layers and layers of decorations from various art historical styles and cultures. Much of it is Babylonian and sub-Saharan African, sources untapped by the 19th-century Historicism, and is enriched with Moorish, Sienese and Florentine details. The terracotta frieze that encircles the building at the level of the ground floor quotes from major sculptural works of other epochs ranging from Greek Antiquity to Renaissance.

La Samaritaine extension (275)
1926–1928, 1930–1933
17–19, rue de la Monnaie / 1er
Henri Sauvage, Frantz Jourdain

During the expansion of the La Samaritaine complex built along the Seine close to the Louvre in 1928 , the opinion of the Commission d'esthétique de la Ville de Paris carried a lot of weight. Jourdain, the author of the original modernist building, who supported the Perret successor building on rue Trétaigne, 7 (no. 241) and would rebuild the Magazins de la Samaritaine de Luxe (no. 263) more to his taste, had to be convinced to build something more stately to the east of the La Samaritaine, 1.

Because his design for the original department store had caused a long-lasting controversy, Jourdain collaborated from the beginning with Henri Sauvage, who had already developed well-accepted

buildings and had a good knowledge of prefabricated construction.

The architects thus developed two extensions, La Samaritaine 2 (east of La Samaritaine 1) and La Samaritaine 3 (now free standing) using prefab iron elements with natural stone façades that favor the angular shapes typical of the Art Déco style. A part of the department store has been housing the flagship sales premises of the Kenzo group since 2003, but the rest of the building is currently undergoing restoration.

Maison Tristan Tzara (276)
1926
15, avenue Junot / 18e
Adolf Loos

This is the only house built by the Austrian architect Adolf Loos, during his sojourn in the French capital between 1924 and 1928. The landlord was the Romanian-born poet Tristan Tzara, the inventor of the "spontaneous poem", who had founded the Dada movement together with Jean Arp and Hugo Ball in Zurich in 1916, and joined with André Breton in Paris in 1919 to found another group from which the Surrealist movement would originate.

A statement by Tzara such as "Morality infuses chocolate into every man's veins" illustrates the aim of Dadaism: to

introduce chance, chaos, playfulness and absurdity into the process of artistic creation. The result may appear pointless at first glance, but has a cryptic second-level signification.

Likewise, Tzara's home is not an absurdity, but the result of rational considerations. The natural stone of the two lower floors matches the style of the surrounding buildings in a borough that kept its rural flair until the early 20th century. The plastered and orthogonal upper stories, however, are clearly rooted in the modern style of architecture. This combination of various building materials also characterizes the Art Déco style and the buildings designed by Ludwig Mies van der Rohe, as Loos wrote the "Ornament and Crime" (1908), a title that was often misinterpreted as "Ornament as Crime". Yet the symmetry of the façade is evidence that the Tzara House does not claim to belong to the avant-garde of the 1930s. The left door leads to the garage, the right to an apartment on the second floor and to the poet's apartment on the upper levels. The interior implements Loos's "spatial plan theory" with rooms that are located within the building according to their respective purposes. Although this building enabled Loos to

multiply his contacts with potential clients, no project came to fruition.

Josephine Baker for example had him design a house decorated with black and white marble stripes in 1927-1928, but the "black Venus" did not commission him to build it, and he left Paris in 1928.

Théâtre des Folies-Bergère (277)
(1868), 1926–1927
32, rue Richer / 9e
Piollenc, Morice, Maurice Pico

The theater where Josephine Baker performed in her famous banana skirt in two revues produced by Louis Lemarchand in 1926-1927 is a typical example of the Art Déco style. The original theater, developed in 1868, was remodeled in the 1920 to match the modern character of the revues.

The façade, visible from afar along a perpendicular street, is adorned with a large relief by Maurice Pico that portrays the dancer Anita Barka.

Rue Mallet-Stevens (278)
1926–1927
2, 4, 6, 7, 12, rue Mallet-Stevens,
9, rue Docteur-Blanche / 16e
Robert Mallet-Stevens

ENSEMBLE The six buildings developed by Robert Mallet-Stevens along this private street compose a unique ensemble that integrates almost all the characteristic features of the "white modern" style: garages, filigree railings, protruding elements, terraces with open screening walls, overhanging corners without corbels, asymmetric façades, cubic volumes with a few circular shapes, round openings and horizontal windows with thin frames, white plaster that conceals all load-bearing elements and gives the buildings an immaterial appearance.

Louis Barillet created the stained-glass windows, Jean Prouvé the entrance doors. A concierge used to live at No. 1, the pianist Madame Reifenberg at No. 8, the sculptors Joël and Jan Martel at No. 10, and Robert Mallet-Stevens at No. 12. In 1932, the architect also built a house with studio for Louis Barillet at Square de Vergennes 15.

Hôtel Lemordant (280)
1927–1931
50, avenue René-Coty / 14e
Jean-Julien Lemordant, Jean Launay

The painter who had lost his eyesight during World War I created the model for the studio himself. It remains unknown

Ateliers d'artistes (279)
(studio apartments)
1926–1928
65, rue La Fontaine / 16e
Henri Sauvage

Sauvage gave up the principle of the terrace house here, in what is one of his latest buildings. The newly retiled structure is well preserved.

The combination of large studio and small apartment windows creates two very different façade compositions underscored using colorful tiles and bay windows.

The colorful structural ceramics already employed elsewhere in the house unfold here to their full effect, transforming the building into a canvas for abstract geometrical patterns.

why he still wanted to build the house as a studio. The asymmetrical structure resembles the bow of a ship, and the lower sections of the walls are closed off as a boat hull.

Central téléphonique (281)
1927–1928
106, rue du Temple / 3e
François Le Coeur

This concrete building by François Le Cœur, the architect appointed by the Ministry of Telecommunications, is somewhat incongruous in the Marais district.

Concrete pilasters divide the façade into five parts, three of which are discreetly rounded above the ground floor. The divisions are so marked that one might mistake them for separate buildings if the monumental cornice did not unite the ensemble.

The façade also illustrates the variety of patterns possible on bare concrete surfaces.

École Normale de Musique – (282) Salle Cortot
1928–1929
78, rue Cardinet / 17e
Auguste & Gustave Perret

A grille-like frieze with ventilation outlets is the sole structuring element of the neo-Classical façade. According to Alfred Cortot, the leading 19th-century piano teacher who commissioned the building, the nine-by-twenty-nine-meter concert hall behind the façade sounds "like a Stradivarius". Covering the concrete walls with vibration-transmitting wood paneling permitted to achieve the excellent acoustics. Furthermore, although Auguste Perret usually left the concrete surfaces visible on his buildings, he also painted the walls of the lobby with a wood-like paint to obtain a stylistic unity in the interior.

Maison de Verre – Dr. Jean (283) Dalsace
1928–1932
31, rue Saint-Guillaume / 7e
Pierre Chareau, Bernard Bijvoet, Louis Dalbet

Pierre Chareau designed this residential house with a ground-floor medical suite in 1925–1928 for Dr. Dalsace, a member

179

of the French Communist Party, and completed it in 1932. On an international scale, the "Glass House" is the most radical example of the modern style of architecture in the early 1930s.

Because the building is in a courtyard, the architect gave it a façade of glass blocks to admit natural light. This solution was unusual at the time, and the manufacturer refused to guarantee that the material was waterproof.

Not only the glass blocks, but all the building materials – including steel beams, rubber floor tiles, perforated metal plates, etc. – are standard industrial products. Inside the building, cables, pipes and other structural elements remain visible, while the metal framework in combination with sliding, folding or rotating glass and steel screens permits variable spatial division. The interior design of the Glass House, a collaboration between Chareau, Bernard Bijvoet (a Dutch architect working in Paris since 1927) and the metal craftsman Louis Dalbet, surpassed all earlier applications of industrial products in residential building development. Another particularity of the building is that it had to be developed under a flat in the upper story of a preexisting structure, as the tenant could not be evicted even after the real-estate had been sold.

Palais des Colonies (284)
(former Musée National
des Arts d'Afrique et d'Océanie)
1928–1931
293, avenue Daumesnil / 12e
Albert Laprade, Léon Jaussely
Léon Émile Bazin

The museum building was one of the main structures developed for the 1931 International Colonial Exhibition. It was originally conceived as a replica of the Angkor-Vat temple, but the authorities ultimately rejected the design as being "not French enough". This building of considerable dimensions with a monumental frieze introduced the pure monumental style in the city, and a variety of similar buildings were built in Paris in the years that followed.

Other structures erected in the neighborhood on the occasion of the Colonial Exhibition – an event that the Surrealists boycotted – include the following buildings: the Église du Saint-Esprit (1928–1935, Paul Tournon) was built to honor the missionaries as the first colonizers, and to remedy the scarcity of churches at the periphery of the city; the Pavillons du Togo et du Cameroun (1928-1931, Louis-Hippolyte Boileau and Charles Carrière) still stand beside Lac Daumesnil and now house the Buddhist Institute; a reconstruction of the

basilica erected under Septimus Severus in Leptis Magna (in present-day Libya) has not been preserved, however. The general idea conveyed by these buildings was to reflect the traditional architecture of the colonies.

Office building (285)
1928–1932
116bis, avenue des Champs-Élysées / 8e
Jean Desbouis

This building – today the home of the Lido (no. 273), one of Paris's most luxurious casinos (Arcades des Champs-Élysées, no. 80) – originally housed the "Poste Parisien" radio station. The building was one of the first modern structures ever built on Paris's most prestigious avenue.

Various details, such as the series of triangular bow-windows of pink limestone in the expressionist style (a rarity in Paris), the window bands in the upper stories, the blue granite facing in the lower stories, and various stainless steel elements, make the structure an unconventional example of the monumental Art Déco style without having to rely on the instrumentation of monumental neo-Classicism. The building's particular personality arises from contrasting materials and the replication of forms ("radiator grille style").

Apartments (286)
1929
89, quai d'Orsay; 22, rue Cognac-Jay / 7e
Michel Roux-Spitz

Michel Roux-Spitz and his "Paris School" played a leading role in the architecture of the interwar period as they attempted a synthesis of classical and modern styles. The use of Hauteville white natural stone, for example, bridges the gap between traditional stone façades and the "white modern" style. The symmetry of the façade and the central bow windows are traditional elements, but the building avoids the profusion of details that characterizes the centuries past. On this narrow but tall structure, the horizontal bands of windows are modern elements that contribute to the harmony of the ensemble.

Notre-Dame du Raincy – hall church in reinforced concrete (287)

This church is the major work of the brothers Auguste and Gustave Perret. The uncompromising use of concrete gives the sacred building an even more revolutionary appearance that the house at Rue Franklin 25 bis (no. 240), which Perret provided with a tiled façade. The extensive glass areas are the reason for the church's nickname, Sainte-Chapelle du béton armé ("the Sainte-Chapelle in reinforced concrete"), which underscores the importance of the building in the history of arts. Moreover, the parish church plays a major role as a monument to the fallen soldiers of the battle of the Marne in September, 1914.

Faced with a limited budget, Abbot Félix Nègre, the parish priest, commissioned Auguste Perret to design a low-cost structure to by erected by his brother Gustave, noted for his capability as a contractor for ferroconcrete construction. The building works took only fourteen months.

A fifty-meter steeple dominates the façade, which is characterized by load-bearing elements that contrast with a variety of infills including modern tracery and a tympanum with a pietà by Antoine Boudelle (added in 1999). Load-bearing elements inspired from Gothic architecture are found inside as well, as Perret favored this style, seeing the Renaissance not as a rebirth, but as the decadent period of architecture whose creations were the leave but a few beautiful ruins. This opinion is evident in Perret's emotional and romanticist approach to the modern style of architecture.

Although the building technology of the 1920s would have made pillars superfluous in a room measuring twenty by fifty-five meters, Perret chose the traditional floor plan of a three-nave church. Other traditional elements include the proportions of the bays in the aisles (half as wide as those in the nave, as was common in Romanesque

churches) and the fluted round pillars without bases or capitals. Moreover, as in the gothique flamboyant, the lateral columns are detached from the walls, making the vault look like a freestanding baldachin. The elevation does not correspond to that of a traditional basilica, however, but rather to that of a hall church, as the aisles are just as high as the nave, although their segmental vaults are perpendicular to that of the nave.

Prefabricated concrete infills and tracery elements of sixty by sixty centimeters make up the building's skin. By using two different kinds of elements, the architect was able to design crosses in each of the bays. The floor gradually lowers itself until it reaches the altar steps, and behind the altar it lightly curves out of the rectangular floor form to form a shallow apse. The figurative representations originate from Maurice Denis, who also determined the color scheme of the entire cycle; the purely decorative elements were designed by Marguerite Huré. Notre-Dame du Raincy was placed under a preservation order in 1966 and restored in 1988 and 1996. Perret created three other versions of this sacred building with its modular design: Sainte-Thérèse de Montmagny (1925), Chapelle d'Arcueil (1927) and Saint-Joseph du Havre (1951). The latter features a mighty central steeple.

The church inside – a modern "Sainte-Chapelle"

The modern single-towered façade

**Cité-Refuge de l'Armée du Salut (288)
(Salvation Army hostel)**
1929–1933
12, rue Cantagrel,
37, rue du Chevaleret / 13e
Le Corbusier, Pierre Jeanneret

The ambitious program developed by the Salvation Army after World War I was aimed not only at providing a sleeping-place for the poor, but also at training them for a new start in life.

This structure, built after the house of the Swiss Foundation at the Cité Internationale Universitaire de Paris, is another effort by Le Corbusier (no. 293) towards his "radiant city".

The main building with 500 beds features a glass façade premiered at Moscow's Centrosoyuz a few years earlier. The linear structure stands on pillars that compensate for the unleveled terrain. Several smaller buildings stand nearby.

Two years after completion of the ensemble, the architect had to provide the south glass façade with ventilation inlets.

The blinds added in the early 1950s, which characterize the building today,

are typical of Le Corbusier's works in the 1930s.

Apartments (289)
1929–1934
3–5, boulevard Victor, rue Lecourbe / 15e
Pierre Patout

On a plot measuring 2.4 by ten meters, Pierre Patout – famous for his interiors of ocean steamers – designed a building that at first glance recalls a ship: Patout had his own triplex apartment in the "bow"; the balconies look like gangways; the top floor suggests a succession of smokestacks.

Designing a building to look like a steamer was not rare in the interwar period. As modern and elegant machines, ocean ships were particularly suitable for Art Déco interiors.

Plain metal rails are likewise common in modern architecture. Yet the association with nautical structures is particularly evident here.

Maison et atelier Perret (290)
1929–1932
51–55, rue Raynouard / 16e
Auguste & Gustave Perret

Auguste Perret built his own house and studio near his major work at Rue Franklin 25 bis (no. 240).

The two buildings are quite similar, although one was erected nearly three decades after the other.

Their similarities include the vertical openings, which contrast with the horizontal windows favored by most of the modern architects. Called "French balconies", these openings rise from the ground floor and are equipped with grilles.

The absence of tiles leaves the concrete skeleton and bricks clearly visible. Perret, a pioneer of the modern style of architecture, created a relatively traditional work here.

Apartments (291)
1931–1933
24, rue Nungesser-et-Coli / 16e
Le Corbusier, Pierre Jeanneret

Le Corbusier used to live and work in the two top stories of this building with a glass façade. Partition walls were originally absent, but added later as the flats were sold. The architect used glass blocks as he already had done in the Maison de verre (no. 283).

The front and back façades are almost identical. They show Le Corbusier's modernism, especially compared with the neighboring structure built one year earlier by Michel Roux-Spitz (Quai d'Orsay, 89, no. 286).

Le Corbusier's apartment can be visited inside.

Saint-Pierre-de-Chaillot (292)
1931–1938
33–35, avenue Marceau / 16e
Emile Bois

This large church incorporates neo-Romanesque and neo-Byzantine elements already found on the Sacré-Cœur (no. 209), as well as the angular shapes and the wealth of details that characterize the Art Déco and Expressionist styles. Moreover, Saint-Pierre-de-Chaillot illustrates the broad capabilities of ferroconcrete.

A sixty-two-meter steeple copied after that of Cluny Abbey dominates the façade coated with natural stones, while the cupola stands forty-six meters above the ground. In the interior, paintings by Nicolas Untersteller adorn the plain concrete walls.

Le Corbusier
*1887 in La Chaux-de-Fonds, † 1965 in Roquebrune (293)

Charles-Édouard Jeanneret, alias Le Corbusier, was born on October 6, 1887, in La Chaux-de-Fonds, Switzerland.

In 1900 he began an apprenticeship as an etcher in his native town, and in 1905 he designed the Villa Vallet for a member at the school of fine arts.

Three years later he began studying architecture and developed a personal style during his training under Auguste Perret, who taught him the principles of ferroconcrete building. In 1910 and 1911 Jeanneret also studied with Peter Behrens in Berlin. During a stay in Hagen, he probably encountered the artist J. M. Lauweriks who might have inspired the idea of modular architecture. After moving to Paris in 1917, Jeanneret adopted a nom d'artiste, an adaptation of his maternal grandfather's name, Lecorbésier. In the French capital, Le Corbusier was in contact with Cubist painters and collaborated on L'Esprit Nouveau, a magazine published by Amédée Ozenfant and himself. The architect compiled his theoretical articles in Towards a New Architecture, a book that remains a must in every architect's library. In 1928, he was one

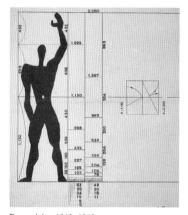

The modulor, 1942–1948

of the founders of the International Congress of Modern Architecture (CIAM). Various periods are discernible in his work, some of which was in collaboration with his cousin Pierre Jeanneret (1896–1967). In his early phase (1914–1915), Le Corbusier favored serially produced residential housing in the international style, exemplified by the "Dom-Ino" system featuring a reduced number of slabs and pillars. In 1920, he designed the initial plans for the "Maison Citrohan", a pun on the name of the French automobile manufacturer Citroën. On the occasion of the 1927 Werkbund Exhibition in Stuttgart, Le Corbusier formulated his "five points for a new architecture": a free floor plan, a free façade design emphasizing function over composition, large horizontal windows, pillars to support the second floor in order to maximize space on the first floor, and

a roof terrace. In the period that ensued, Le Corbusier concentrated on urban development (La Ville contemporaine, 1922) and advocated radically redesigning city centers by demolishing all existing buildings, except for a few landmarks, and replacing them with high-rises such as the 1925 Voisin project or the 1935 Radiant City. In the 1920s he also designed various outstanding large buildings, some of which were erected (Refuge of the Salvation Army, Paris, 1929–1933) while others remained in the projecting phase (Palace of the League of Nations, Geneva, 1927; Palace of the Soviets, Moscow, 1928). In the late 1940s Le Corbusier abandoned the plastered façades and the strict geometry of the international style, favoring more plastic designs and the "brutalism" of bare concrete surfaces ("béton brut"). The Unité d'Habitation in Marseille (1947–1952) originated based on the modulor, and is the first in a series of Unités. This system developed between 1942 and 1948 based on ideal proportions taken from the Golden Ratio, the Fibonacci series, and the height of an ideal human being stretching his arms above his head (2.26 meters). Le Corbusier's most outstanding achievements of his plastic period are the chapel of Notre-Dame-du-Haut at Ronchamp (1950–1954) and the Philips Pavilion at the 1958 World's Fair in Brussels. Last but not least, Le Corbusier implemented his urban development ideas at Chandigarh, India (1951–1955).

He died on August 27, 1965, in Roquebrune-Cap-Martin.

187

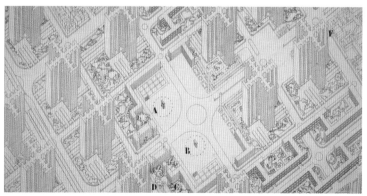

Plan Voisin, 1925: detail with Porte Saint-Denis and Porte Saint-Martin (no. 86 and 88)

Cinéma Rex (294)
1931–1932
1–5, boulevard Poissonnière,
35, rue Poissonnière / 2e
Auguste Bluysen, John Eberson

The building can be easily seen from afar thanks to its corner tower. In contrast to its appearance, this "light house" is just a light structure with a concrete overlay with no independent function besides serving as an advertisement carrier. At the time of its construction the theater was one of the largest cinemas in Europe with 3,300 seats. It was created by Eberson, who specialized in the business and had created more than 400 movie theaters in the USA. On the inside, the hall was decorated with film sets to create a "cinematic atmosphere," a staple of his design. In this case, the set recreates a Spanish town, with a design realized by Maurice Dufrêne.

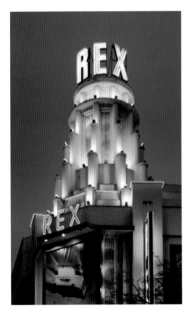

School rue Küss (295)
1931–1934
10, rue Küss / 13e
Roger-Henri Expert

Architects began to give schools a festive appearance only in the 1930s. Roger-

Henri Expert, who designed the main gangway of the Normandie, the most luxurious steamer of the time (1932–1935, in collaboration with Richard Bouwens van de Boyen), developed here a remarkable complex with four rounded terraces that give the building extraordinary energy.

Apartments for the school director and the concierge are situated underneath the terraces. The playful garden strongly contrasts with the monumental school building.

Apartments (296)
1932–1934
42, avenue de Versailles / 16e
Jean Ginsberg, Maurice Breton,
Adolf Franz Heep

The building is one of the most successful corner developments in Paris. With this work, the Polish-born architect Jean Ginsberg, a pupil of Robert Mallet-Stevens who worked for Le Corbusier and André Lurçat, departed from his teacher's monumental neo-Classicist style. The round corner volume can be interpreted as a legacy of the 19th-century corner towers, but in contrast to these it originates on the ground level and does not soar over the rest of the building. Its function is to act as a link between the different designs of the two street façades.

The balconies to the left sculpturally structure the front, while the right side with bands of windows has a flat organization.

The corner volume picks up the window rows that are flush with the façade, but sets them in a sculptural context. This visual puzzle of volume and surface allows the viewer to perceive the corner anew again and again.

Office and apartment building (297)
1932
24, rue Feydeau / 2e
Fernand Colin

As at Avenue des Champs-Élysées 116bis (no. 285), triangular bow windows structure the façade vertically. Because the street is narrow and lined with seven-story

buildings, these windows fulfill more than just a decorative function: they maximize the natural light and direct the tenants' view along the street, not just to the opposite building. The rails of the small balconies are typical of Constructivism.

Immeuble Shell (298)
1932
29, rue de Berri; 45, rue d'Artois / 8e
L. Bechmann, Chatenay

This is the largest commercial building erected in the Art Déco style typical of the interwar period. It contains a large shopping arcade on the ground floor and 60,000 square meters of office space in the upper stories. The use of modern building technology permitted its construction in just twenty months. During his stay in the United States, Lucien Adolphe Bechmann had discovered the great commercial buildings in the Art Déco style that gave major companies a modern, distinctive image. The Art Déco façades can be recognized by their post-and-stall structure, which is incorporated in their decorative design. Moreover, Bechmann outfitted the building with the latest technical equipment, including lifts, ventilators, and heated ceilings.

Villa Savoye – a particular weekend house (299)

The weekend house is one of the main architectural examples of the International Style. The house was built for the insurance manager Pierre Savoye and his wife Emilie, and is located 30 kilometers from Paris in the midst of pastures and orchards, giving it its second name – "Les Heures Claires." The structure exemplifies Le Corbusier's Five Points of Architecture as no other project, and at the same time it marks the end of the heyday of the white villas.

The Five Points – pilotis or pillars, a roof garden, free plan, horizontal rectangular windows and a free façade – are not simply satisfied here, but are exemplarily demonstrated.

The row of second-floor windows features especially prominently on the extremely rectangular building. On the ground floor are the service and domestic staff rooms as well as a large, but comparatively low foyer located to the back of the house.

With the exception of the few closed rooms, the ground floor is largely glazed. Some of the narrow load-carrying pilotis which are placed away from walls on the interior and reveal their retreating sections on the façade, are not incorporated into the building's whole.

They rather seem to piece it as a free-standing scaffolding at points that make little sense in terms of the house's appearance or utility.

Not only does their structural necessity become apparent, but these room "interruptions" must be interpreted as a design principle, as they could have easily been incorporated into the wall using simple casing.

A so-called architectural promenade (named by Le Corbusier, 1930) leads through the house. Following the ramp in the center of the building, one reaches the upper floor from the foyer. A roof garden comprises a part of this stitled story, opening up the living room to fresh air. In addition, this floor contains the master bedroom, guest room, the son's room, kitchen and bath. A second, double-flight ramp leads from the roof garden to the third floor with large terraces. The wall section framed by the two flights is opened up with a large triangular window.

As an alternative to the ramps of the architectural promenade, spiral stairs offer a quicker access and revitalize the environment with their rounded shape. The open spaces of the upper stories are defined as rooms using free-standing walls with unglazed window openings which offer protection from the wind.

This function is especially apparent in the "solarium," a rounded wall shield. From the outside, the spiral stairs and the solarium above enliven the otherwise strictly orthogonal building.

However, so as not to influence the axial structure presented by the villa too strongly, these are located at the back. The ensemble also includes a garden house.

The water supply badly was executed during construction, eventually causing the Savoyes to give up the house entirely. It was even threatened with being torn down in the 1950s. Since 1962, the villa is in state ownership and was placed under historical monument protection in 1965.

Restorations were conducted beginning in the 1980s by Jean-Louis Véret, Jean Dubuisson, Bruno Chauffert-Yvart and Laurence Razy, and today the house is open to visitors.

Representative for Le Corbusier: the elevation by pilotis and the rectangular-shaped windows.

The spiral stairs – short cut of the architecture promenade – set architectural priorities.

Grand Rocher (300)
(Zoo de Vincennes)
1934
Bois de Vincennes,
53, avenue de Saint-Maurice,
route de ceinture du Lac Daumesnil,
avenue Daumesnil (Saint-Mandé) / 12e
Charles Letrosne, Daniel Letrosne

At first glance, the structure resembles a great cliff rather than a building. Following the colonial exhibition with the zoo as its biggest success, a permanent animal park was laid down on adjacent lands to the southeast of the town. At the center of the park is a 65-meter high artificial mountain. Below the 5 cm thick concrete layer resting on a steel framework, the mountain is hollow and houses water tanks and a gallery.

Mobilier National (301)
(national furniture museum)
1934–1936
1–3, rue Berbier-du-Mets / 13e
Auguste Perret

This warehouse for the precious furniture from national palaces replaces another structure that was demolished to make room for the buildings of the 1937 World's Fair. The architect therefore designed it as a palace.

The three-winged palatial complex is higher in the middle, and a curved colonnade with a simple cornice borders the forecourt.

The modern concrete skeleton remains apparent despite the complete covering of the façades.

Palais de Tokyo (302)
(Modern Art Museum)
1934–1937, 2001–2002
11–13, avenue du Président Wilson,
18, avenue de New York / 16e
Jean-Claude Dondel, André Aubert,
Paul Viard, Marcel Dastugue,
rebuilding to museum: Anne Lacaton
and Jean-Philippe Vassal

This building, also built for the 1937 World's Fair, is comparable with the nearby Palais de Chaillot (no. 304), with its two wings and trick fountains.

A colonnade here connects the wings, however, and the fountains are in the cour d'honneur, not near the river.

In 2001–2002, Anne Lacaton and Jean-Philippe Vassal converted the palace into a contemporary art gallery.

Their work was highly controversial, as parts of the palace were purposely left as an unfinished building site due to the limited conversion budget.

However, such an exhibition space could be thought more suitable to underscore the work-in-progress character of

contemporary art than a perfect "temple of the arts".

Fire station Dauphine   (303)
1934–1936
8, rue Mesnil / 16e
Robert Mallet-Stevens

The firehouse reveals none of the desire for representation and Classicism which have usually had a strong influence on the architect. The left, lower side of the building staggers back above the garages. The higher portion of the building on the right unfolds as a free play of volume that is introduced using three small balconies and opens into a tower. The asymmetry and free organization (excluding the tower) of orthogonal volumes display Modernism's intense preoccupation with sculptural architecture.

Palais de Chaillot   (304)
1935–1937
place du Trocadéro, avenue de New York,
avenue du Président Wilson,
rue Benjamin Franklin / 16e
Léon Azéma, Louis-Hippolyte Boileau,
Jacques Carlu

The Palais de Chaillot was built for the 1937 World Exhibition on the foundation of the former Trocadéro Palace. The plan of the predecessor was laid out as a Belvedere with a view out on the Mars Field by Gabriel Davioud from 1878. The new structure consists of two arched wings with pavilions at their extremes, while a square extends towards the terrace facing the Eiffel Tower (no. 218) in place of a third, middle wing. Giant bronze figures stand to the right and left of the Human Rights Square in front of the wings' ends. The terrace, square and both of the projecting wing structures are

elevated using a system of stairs. Fountains as designed for the old Trocadéro Palace are found at the foot of the stairs. The building houses an exhibition space of 55,000 square meters. The ensemble itself, with arched wings and sunken corps de logis, is a paraphrase of Baroque palace architecture, while the façade design is purely neo-Classical.

During the 1937 World Exhibition, the pavilions of various countries stood inside the garden in front of the palace, which acted as the entrance gate. On the bank of the Seine at the end of the premises, the pavilions of Germany and Soviet Union – two likewise monumental buildings by Albert Speer and Boris Iofan – faced each other, separated by the palace axis.

With the addition of Palais d'Iena (no. 306) and Palais de Tokyo (no. 302), Chaillot Hill became the location of the world's most variegated examples of monumental neo-Classical buildings.

Sainte-Odile (305)
1935–1946
2, avenue Stéphane-Mallarmé / 17e
Jacques Barge

This domed church is very unusual, and not just for its 1930s origins. Its seventy-two-meter steeple – one of the highest in Paris – is distinctly rooted in Expressionism, while its three cupolas in a row are taken from the Byzantine tradition.

Windows in the drums below the domes light the interior and recall Istanbul's Hagia Sophia. The arches that separate the

space underneath the cupolas are the sole structuring elements of the interior.

The three gabled façades with window rows follow the dome structure, with each offering generous stained-glass windows.

Palais d'Iéna (306)
(Musée des Travaux Publics, Palais du Conseil Economique et Social)
1937–1943, 1960–1962, 1993–1995
1, avenue d'Iéna, place d'Iéna,
avenue du Président Wilson / 16e
Auguste Perret, Paul Vilmond,
Gilles Bouchez

Although Auguste Perret contributed significantly to the planning of the 1937

World's Fair, he was only commissioned to design one building, a museum exhibiting models of the achievements of French civil engineers.

The structure was intended as a part of the World's Fair, but even the first wing was not completed until 1939. Perret surpassed the requirements of his brief, however, and built a three-winged palace with an impressive entrance rotunda that covers an entire block.

Concrete used to be visible in various textures on the façades. Long exhibition spaces are found inside along with a double curved staircase, reminiscent of Baroque style and unusual for Perret's otherwise conservative use of materials. At the time the staircase, which sets the two stories in communication without any supports, was a unique demonstration of concrete's ability to be freely formulated due to its combination of load-bearing and load-pulling forces.

Collège Néerlandais (307)
1938
61, boulevard Jourdan / 14e
Willem Marinus Dudok

The Collège Néerlandais brought another touch of Modernism into the campus before World War II. The building shows close similarities with a grain elevator in Buenos Aires that Walter Gropius once described. It is made of vertical and horizontal volumes and figures both vertical and horizontal rows of windows with small windowpanes, a typical design feature of the Amsterdam School that decisively influenced Dudok at the beginning of his career. Moreover, the structure shows the rounded shapes – also inspired from the Amsterdam School – that would become part of the Modern style of architecture, as well as the thin protruding roofs inspired by Frank Lloyd Wright and favored by the Amsterdam School and the De Stijl movement.

Cité Internationale Universitaire de Paris (C.I.U.P.) – collection of styles (308)

C.I.U.P. was founded in 1925 on 34 hectares along the city's former fortification grounds. World War I showed that city fortifications like these were no longer capable of defending against modern warfare. According to the specifications of the fortification area development plan, the majority of the area was to be set aside for park zones and sports facilities.

On the edge of these recreational areas are the nation buildings, in some places lining up one after the other in multiple rows.

These houses are occupied in equal parts by the nationals of the corresponding country and citizens of others, promoting cultural exchange.

The first buildings to be erected were the seven Fondation Deutsch de la Meurthe houses designed by Lucien Adolphe Bechmann, built in 1923, which developed the structural plan of the complex.

They are inspired by English colleges and borrow from the Arts and Crafts movement in their adaptation of a countryside Gothic style.

According to the original plan, the nations' buildings should have been built in the style typical for each country. For this reason, most of the successor buildings exemplify a traditional national style, sometimes reduced using neo-Classicism and others featuring Art Déco elements.

Bechmann's later buildings on the grounds are influenced by French tradition, until finally taking a Modernist approach with his post-World War II Fondation Victor Lyon.

Extremely progressive buildings appeared here even before 1939, for example, Pavillon Suisse (1933) by Le Corbusier and the Dutch College by Willem Marinus Dudok (no. 307). Although the Swiss house still shows Le Corbusier's "Five Points", it also clearly deviates from it: it is encased using ashlar panels and even quarry stone on the entrance pavilion. Instead of individual pillars, a link consisting of fused supports is placed underneath the row of the building's volume, where the staircase with a contrasting arched form is also found as an independent body. The building is further proof for the dynamism of form in Le Corbusier's work, which would find its climax in the La Ronchamp church.

The Pavillon Suisse is found at the beginning of the "Residential House Machines", which lead to the Cité radieuse and the Unité d'habitation. Le Corbusier built another one of this main works on the C.I.U.P. campus after World War I: Maison du Brésil (no. 317).

This building is now the successor of the Unité d'habitation (Marseille, 1947). The new street car route T3 Marchéaux, which runs along the Cité Internationale Universitaire to the side of the city, was designed by urban planner Antoine Grumbach and landscape architect Michel Desvigne.

A list with all C.I.U.P. buildings is found in the appendix (A1).

Maison du Brésil, Le Corbusier, 1959

The central administration pavilion of Fondation Deutsch de la Meurthe

Big times after the Second World War – presidents transforming the city (309)

Following Germany's invasion into Western Europe on May 10, 1940, German troops reach Paris on June 14th. The Allies landed in Algiers and Morocco on November 8, 1942, and shortly thereafter Southern France also came under German occupation. On June 6, 1944 the liberation began on the Cotentin peninsula in Normandy under General Dwight D. Eisenhower. Paris was handed over on August 25th without resistance and almost completely undamaged thanks to the German general's refusal to obey orders. After becoming the president of the provisional government, in 1958 de Gaulle became the last prime minister of the economically unstable and mired in colonial crises (Indochina and Algeria) Fourth Republic and the first president of the Fifth Republic. Georges Pompidou (1969–1974), Valéry Giscard d'Estaing (1974–1981), François Mitterrand (1981–1995), Jacques Chirac (1995–2007) and Nicolas Sarkozy (since 2007) succeeded de Gaulle. Modernism was finally able to gain acceptance for state-sponsored commissions (O.R.T.F., no. 311, UNESCO, no. 310, CNIT, no. 315); however, the scene was dominated by modern grid buildings whose proportions and

structure appealed to neo-Classicism using wall templates or window casements within their grids), but especially in Paris, architecture was strongly influenced by the preferences and representation desires of the respective reining head of state. De Gaulle and the minister of culture André Malraux ordered the redevelopment of the old city and the Marais. Additionally, in 1960 they charged city planners to develop a new plan for the Greater Paris regional development, whose first version was hindered by the war; 1965 saw the implementation of the new expansion plan. However, they were missing sufficient infrastructure as well as identification and integration resources. Émile Aillaud built some of the better compositions (La Grande Borne in Grigny; Quartier des Courtillières in Pantin). The new plan ("Schéma directeur d'aménagement et d'urbanisme de la région parisienne") included five suburban recreation areas (Zones Naturelles d'Equilibre or ZNE), a ring expressway (Boulevard Périphérique), freeways along the Seine, airports in Orly (1957–1961 by Henri Vicariot) and Roissy as well as the creation of "villes nouvelles," or

Crowd of french patriots line in the Champs-Élysees to view Allied tanks and half tanks pass through the Arc de Triomphe, after Paris was liberated on August 25, 1944.

planned cities (Sarcelles, Nanterre, Créteil, Marne-la-Vallée, Cergy-Pontoise). These were laid out to form a "crown" at a distance from Paris, and served to unburden the overpopulated city following the example of Britain's New Towns which, in contrast to satellite towns, would offer apartments, workplaces, recreation and all logistics. The new express train (Réseau express régional d'Île-de-France, RER) was to connect them to the transportation system, relieving the old Metro. The construction of the new network fell on the Pompidou presidency, which let the Halls (no. 336), unoccupied since 1969, be torn down to make way for an RER station in 1972. Pompidou continued the rehabilitation of the city and issued a call for a mega-modern architecture, whose culmination is exemplified in the Centre Pompidou (no. 334). Neo-Expressionist buildings like Stade du Parc-des-Princes (no. 333) also distanced themselves from ordinary structural functionalism. This style manifested itself in the first building stage of the office city La Défense (no. 341), planned already in the Fourth Republic, but realized only in the 1960s. At this time, French architecture was not among the world's leaders in the field. Even if Yona Friedman or Paul Maymontfurore created utopian mega-structures, it was still the art (CoBrA), film (Nouvelle Vague), fashion, literature (Nouveau roman), philosophy (Nouvelle Philosophie) and later, cuisine (Nouvelle Cuisine) that made the city a global culture capital. In the meantime, postwar modernism was subject to a fair amount of criticism from architects as well as laymen. The CIAM (Congrès Internationaux d'Architecture Moderne), which had been the unofficial mouthpiece of Modernism and Le Corbusier since 1928, was dissolved in 1969 during a meeting in preparation for a congress in Otterlo (the Netherlands) by the members of Team X; Alison and Peter Smithson (England), Georges Candilis (Greece/France), Jacob Bakema and Aldo van Eyck (the Netherlands). These and other architects who were leaning toward Structuralism or Brutalism demanded that instead of the division of residential, recreation, work and commute spaces as was outlined in the Athens Charter, a hierarchical city structure of clusters, stems and webs with architecture that nurtured such social contact be adapted.

UNESCO (310)
1953–1977
place de Fontenoy / 7e
Marcel Breuer, Pier Luigi Nervi,
Bernard Louis Zehrfuss

The United Nations Educational, Scientific and Cultural Organization is a specialized agency of the UN established in 1945. International architects and artists designed its Paris headquarters. The first three structures – main building, conference hall and permanent headquarters – are works by Marcel Breuer (USA), Pier Luigi Nervi (Italy) and Bernard Zehrfuss (France). The architects' designs were approved by a committee composed of Lucio Costa (Brasil), Le Corbusier (France), Walter Gropius (USA), Sven Markelius (Sweden), and Ernesto Rogers (Italy), who also took advise from Eero Saarinen (USA).Breuer and Nervi styled the "accordion" building – the structure that houses the conference rooms – after their 1958 St. John's Abbey Church in Collegeville, Minnesota. The Y-shaped administrative building, nicknamed the "three-pointed star", fits harmoniously in Place de Fontenoy alongside the École Militaire (no. 118) designed by Ange-Jacques Gabriel. The seven-story structure on pillars conforms to Le Corbusier's "five points towards a new architecture" and features the sun blinds favored by the architect since the 1930s. Twenty-four V-shaped pillars support each of the star's points. The reception hall is located at the meeting point of the three wings, and is accessible both from Place de Fontenoy and the garden. The garden entrance offers the main access, but has

always been reserved for heads of state. In front of it is a low gate arch, which at first glance appears to be a canopy, but a closer look reveals it as an independent structure. A parable-shaped arch carries two projecting bowls, whose inner sides follow the course of the arch starting from the peak until the ground while the outer section proceeds to swing out above the highest point, creating an impression of a stylized wing trajectory. The "back entrance" for visitors is set apart from the building volume, but is less prominent. In subsequent development phases, Zehrfuss working alone designed several additional structures, including the patio and the building at Rue Miollis. The interior decoration includes a mural by Pablo Picasso and works by other outstanding artists, such as Jean Arp, Karel Appel, Alexander Calder, Roberto Matta, Joan Miró, Henry Moore, and Brassaï. Isamu Noghuchi designed the Japanese garden in 1956-1958. Tadao Ando complemented the garden with the Meditation Room (no. 442) in 1996. The new furniture in the conference hall foyers is by Odile Decq und Benoit Cornette (2001).

Maison de Radio-France (311)
Maison de l'Office de Radiodiffusion et Télévision Française O.R.T.F
1953–1963
116, avenue du Président Kennedy / 16e
Henry Bernard

A public monopoly on broadcasting was established in France after World War II, and in 1964 the various services of the national broadcasting agency were grouped

in a circular building with an outside diameter of 175 meters. The façade opposite the Seine rises up to thirty-seven meters. Offices for journalists and administrators are located here. This part of the building also functions as a shield against the noise of the city, protecting the lower circular structure that house studios and broadcasting facilities. The eccentric archive tower inside the circle is seventy meters high, and was intended to be even higher. This spatial organization reflects the workflow in a television and radio station: from program development at the periphery to archives at the center. A hot spring located fifty meters underground provides energy to the building, where some 2,500 people are employed. The aluminum façades of the ensemble dominate the surrounding area in Paris's 16th arrondissement. Architecture Studio redeveloped the building between 2005 and 2013. Near the Maison de Radio France, on an island in front of Pont de Grenelle, stands a smaller version of the Statue of Liberty, a work by Frédéric-Auguste Bartholdi that France donated to the United States in 1886.

Préfecture de Paris (312)
1955–1975
17, boulevard Morland / 4e
Albert Laprade

This building, with its modernist cour d'honneur, pilasters and parapets, re-

produces the megalomaniac style of the 1930s and demonstrates that monumental architecture aimed at legitimizing a government was not confined to the Communist block in the fifties. A monument to bureaucracy, the building clearly dominates its surroundings, while its façade with a strict structural grid underscores the anonymity inherent in a state agency.

Immeuble Fortuny (313)
1956
37, rue Fortuny / 17e
Jean Lefevre, Jean Connehaye

The building focuses the attention on its situation with a rounding-off at the corner, typical for classic Modernism. The horizontal bands underscore this idea while the upright windows were considered fauxpas by the early Modernism, which tried to distance itself from the 19th century (this is the fourth of Le Corbusier's "Five points on modern architecture", cf. no. 84). The load-bearing structure is completely internalized.

203

Paul Andreu
*1938 in Caudéran (314)

Charles de Gaulle Airport in Roissy-en-France near Paris is Paul Andreu's greatest work. As of 1965, the architect developed Terminal 1, directed the other construction phases, and designed the airport's train station and nearly forty other airports.

Located twenty-five kilometers northeast of Paris, Charles de Gaulle Airport covers 3,200 hectares – almost one third of the area of Paris itself – and is thus Europe's third largest airport, after Frankfurt and London Heathrow. The decision to build Terminal 1 was made in the 1960s when it became clear that traffic would exceed the capacity of Orly Airport.

Streets surround and penetrate the circular building tilted outward that features an atrium at its center. Seven boarding pods provide access to the aircraft, making the terminal an autonomous departure, arrival and transfer machine. The initial project called for the construction of five similar structures, but the plans were altered when it became obvious that such "bowls" would have to be developed simultaneously, whereas the airport had to be developed progressively.

Terminal 2 was developed in four sections, A (1981), B (1982), D (1989) and C (1993). The four halls, shaped like concrete vaults along the curving sides of a central oval area, are accessible by car. A railway station was added in 1994, with trains to Paris and shuttles to the parking garages, to Terminals 1 and 3, and to the new E and F halls. Andreu developed the station in collaboration with Jean-Marie Duthilleul, chief architect of the French national railway.

The new halls are shaped like airfoils, and can be seen from the interior to consist of a thin skin. The complicated and expensive design of Hall F made it necessary to find a low-cost solution for Hall E, which was therefore built using a wooden interior vault. However, the 700-meter-long shell without interior pillars still required 91,500 tons of concrete and 6,300 tons of steel. In this hall, as in all terminals at Charles de Gaulle Airport, passengers progress from the semi-obscurity of the check-in areas to the brightly-lit boarding gates.

In 2004, a portion of Hall 2E measuring twenty by thirty meters collapsed as a result of several factors. The entire building was subsequently demolished and is currently being rebuilt.

Terminal 3, which opened in temporary form in 1990 as Aérogare T9, was converted to host low-fare airlines in 2006. The oldest terminals are successively being refurbished and mod-

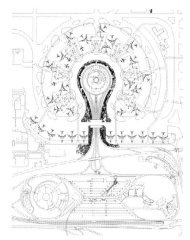

Plan of the airport "Charles de Gaulle", terminal 1

ernized. The four eye-catching information desks of Paris's tourist office were built to plans by soa architectes in 2006–2007.

After the death of his partner Johan Otto von Spreckelsen, Paul Andreu, who for many years specialized in airport construction, finished the Grande Arche de la Défense (no. 341) in the business quarter La Défense to the west of Paris alone.

Since the year 2000, he has been increasingly active in Asia. Among other projects, he has built the Oriental Art Center in Shanghai (2000–2004), the National Grand Theatre in Peking (1999–2007) and the Casino in Macau (since 2006).

In Terminal 3

CNIT, Centre des nouvelles (315)
industries et technologies
1956–1958
La Défense
Robert Edouard Camelot, Jean de Mailly,
Bernard Louis Zehrfuss

The concrete vault, covering 22,500 square meters, was the world's largest when it was built in the 1950s. It rests on three basement blocks joined by steel tie rods. Each of the three sides is 230 meters in length. Jean Prouvé designed the façades suspended between the arches, while the engineer Nicolas Esquillan conceived the shell in collaboration with Pier Luigi Nervi.

Because only a few trade fairs per year were held under the huge, undivided vault, Zehrfuss converted the CNIT into a hotel complex with a shopping center to make the building more profitable.

Office building (316)
1958
37, rue de la Victoire / 9e
Jean Balladur with Benjamin Lebeigle

This corner office building was designed in the "steamship look" typical of the 1930s. The recessed first floor shows Le Corbusier's influence, as do various design details and the building's proportions, shaped according to Le Corbusier's "modulator" principle (cf. no. 293).

Maison du Brésil (317)
1959
4, avenue de la Porte de Gentilly,
7, boulevard Jourdan / 14e
Le Corbusier with Lúcio Costa

In contrast to the building for Salvation Army, Le Corbusier's second work on the grounds of the Cité Internationale Universitaire de Paris (no. 308) is a successor of the Unité d'habitation (Marseille, 1947). Some not-so-sculptural formulations are found in the public spaces of the ground story.

They are comparable to those on the church in Notre-Dame-du-Haut (1955) in Ronchamp, and will become typical for Le Corbusier.

Centre Hospitalier (318)
Universitaire
1960
91–97, boulevard de l'Hôpital / 13e
Jacques-Henri Riedberger

The hospital with a prefabricated metal façade consisting of pillars and balustrades which plainly reveal the absence of any structural function is located close to the Salpêtrière (no. 75). The actual load-bearing structure consists of five-element groups and reveals itself in the recessed zone above the ground floor. To either side of the entrance the ground floor is decorated with a relief of cast stone, which is attached to the structure, and not a part of it.

Tour Albert (319)
1960
33, rue Croulebarbe / 13e
Edouard Albert, Roger Boileau,
Jacques-Henri Labourdette

This twenty-three-story residential building with a height of sixty-seven meters was Paris's first skyscraper. According to the high-rise theory of the time, made it possible to develop recreational areas in the direct vicinity of the tower. The sixth floor is shaped as a terrace and adorned with a black and white ceiling painting by Jacques Lagrange.

Mémorial des Martyrs (320)
de la Déportation
1961–1962
In the east of the Île de la Cité,
quai de Archevêché / 4e
Georges-Henri Pingusson, Olivier Dugas

A memorial to the 200,000 French citizens who died in Nazi concentration camps

stands at the east end of the Île de la Cité. Despite this central location, the memorial remains as inconspicuous as the victims themselves: travelers on riverboats notice nothing but a wall along a quay, while the main entrance remains hidden in a remote corner of the park behind Notre Dame. A flight of stairs leads down to a narrow area surrounded by high concrete walls that barely afford a view of the sky above and of the river visible through a grille. The crypt opposite the opening contains the Tomb of the Unknown Deportee and shining pieces of quartz that symbolize the hundreds of thousands of victims. The original project included a museum that was not developed, however.

Tour Initiale / PB 31 (321)
Tour Nobel / Tour Aventis /
Tour Roussel-Hoechst
1964–1967
La Défense
Jean de Mailly, Jacques Depusse with
Jean Prouvé

This office tower with 25,000 square meters of floor area is the first high-rise

encountered in the La Défense (no. 341) district by those arriving from central Paris. Jean de Mailly, who had traveled throughout the USA, probably designed it after Frank Lloyd Wright's Johnson Tower in Racine, as shown by the rounded corners with curved plate glass imported from the US. Jean Prouvé designed both the load-bearing frame and the metal panels of the curtain wall.

Siège du Parti Communiste   (322)
Français
1965–1971
2, place du Colonel Fabien / 10e
Oscar Niemeyer

Oscar Niemeyer, a staunch Communist, designed this building at no cost in collaboration with Paul Chemetov, Jean Deroche, Jean-Maur Lyonnet and Jean Prouvé. The structure features the rounded forms typical of Niemeyer's developments in Brasilia that introduced a "new plasticity" in modern architecture.

In 1980 Niemeyer added an underground conference hall topped with a dome in front of the main building and its partially underground entrance hall.

Apartments and school   (323)
1965
25, rue Saint-Ambroise / 11e
Louis Miquel, Georges Maurios

Although this ensemble, composed of a residential building and a school, is not located in the park of a "radiant city", it clearly recalls the "unité d'habitation" develop by Le Corbusier (cf. no. 317), the master under whom Louis Miquel studied. The ensemble was developed as part of an extensive construction program initi-

ated after World War II. By doing without pillars under the structure, the project better kept to the initial budget than Le Corbusier's "living units".

Faculté de Jussieu   (324)
Université Paris 6 et Paris 7
1965–1971
place Jussieu / 5e
Edouard Albert, Urbain Cassan, René Coulon, Roger Seassal, Louis Madeline

The campus includes the Zamansky Tower and a large structure on pillars that encloses twenty-one courtyards patterned after the Escorial Palace near Madrid. Over a surface area of 6,000 square meters, 1,750 pillars support the building 4.90 meters above the ground. The extension of the pillars determines

the appearance of the upper stories, yet without suggesting load-bearing elements. The ensemble is thus an excellent example of the large-scale use of metallic modular elements – a characteristic of Édouard Albert's works. Various architects have renovated parts of the campus: Thierry Van de Wyngaert (Tour Albert), Guy Autran and Vladimir Mitrofanov (first sector), Reichen & Robert (second sector). The new atrium building is by Périphériques architectes (2006, no. 481).

Temporary rooms for the renovation period were based on the designs from K. Kalayciyan, J.-P. Djalili, J. Brunet and E. Saunier.

Restaurant Universitaire (325)
1965
3, rue Censier / 5e
Henry Pottier

The building has a closed-off north face, which is additionally underscored with its almost full black ceramic cladding.

Inside, however, a light-filled dining hall bordered by the glazed southern façade greets the visitor.

Synagogue Don Isaac Abravanel (326)
1966
84–86, rue de la Roquette / 3e
Arthur Heaume, Alexandre Persitz

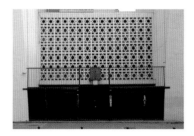

The Sephardic synagogue displays the concrete Star of David as a pattern on its façade made of prefabricated concrete elements, framed by the closed walls. Behind the pattern of the star is a slab of glass, screening the light that falls on it. This filigree pattern is based more on the quamriya, the geometrically structured plaster plates used in Islamic architecture in Egypt, than on a simple transom.

Saint-Marcel (327)
1966
80–82, boulevard de l'Hôpital / 13e
Daniel Michelin, Jean Michelin

This church built in the 1960s replaces a 19th-century building. The various building components – church proper, chapel and community room – are arranged along a longitudinal axis.

In 1993 Jean Michelin redesigned the façade of the building erected by his father thirty years before. The triangular shape fits well in the style of the sixties and gives the building a modern appearance.

Faculté de Pharmacie, extension (328)
1966
63, rue d'Assas / 6e
Pierre Sirvin, Camille Clouzeau

With its style inspired from tradition but never directly quoting historical structures, the extension of the faculty building in the botanical garden clearly recalls works by Louis Khan. For example, the structuring elements are neither columns nor pilasters, but features with a concealed load-bearing function that overlook the ensemble and contribute to the overall rhythm as also did their traditional predecessors.

Saint-Eloi (329)
1967–1968
3–7, place Maurice-de-Fontenay / 12e
Max Leboucher

This church consecrated to the patron saint of goldsmiths and metalworkers makes intensive use of metal – an adequate building material in this case. Its filigree framework, which consists mainly of industrially manufactured metallic parts, permitted the construction of a large hall without pillars.

Maison des Sciences (330)
de l'Homme
1968
54, boulevard Raspail / 6e
Henri Beauclair, Paul Depondt,
Marcel Lods

The light external load-bearing frame recalls those of Mies van der Rohe's postwar buildings. The long succession of high metal shutters, however, is rooted in the tradition of the 19th century. Either open and closed, the shutters form lively, ever-changing patterns on the glass façade.

Apartments (331)
1969
31, rue Saint-Ambroise / 11e
Mario Heymann and Roger Anger

This elongated building with 127 residential units exemplifies the trend toward "new plasticity" in the 1960s. Although the structure integrates the characteristics of mass production, it endeavors to alleviate the resulting monotony by arranging the volumes on different levels. After Team X had dissolved the International Congress of Modern Architecture (CIAM) (cf. no. 309), the structuralists abandoned the totalitarian concept of the "living machine" considered the ultimate form of a residential building, and strove to develop changing structures that would meet the users' needs.

Tour Montparnasse (332)
1969–1973
rue de l'Arrivée,
place Raoul Dautry / 15e
Eugène Beaudouin, Urbain Cassan,
Louis Hoym de Marien, Jean Saubot

The controversial Maine-Montparnasse urban redevelopment project presented in 1958 proposed replacing Montparnasse Station with a slab block 150 meters tall and 100 meters wide. Upon completion of the new station in 1969, however, the project was altered in favor of a 210-meter tower and a lower shopping arcade. Today many people still do not like the complex's long fronts, but the Montparnasse Tower is widely accepted.

The lookout platform atop the office high-rise, with a curtain wall of colored glass, offers a stunning panoramic view over the city, and the best opportunity to appreciate the dimensions of buildings

such as the Louvre (no. 49) or the Centre Pompidou (no. 334).

Stade du Parc-des-Princes (333)
1969–1972
24, rue de Commandant Guilbaud,
rue Claude Farrère / 16e
Roger Taillibert,
Pierre Richard (engineer)

This stadium was the traditional venue for football games of national and international importance before the completion of the Stade de France (no. 429). It replaces a sports field that was developed in the 19th century and demolished to make place for the ring motorway.

Because the main requirement was to provide roofed space for 50,000 spectators without pillars that would impair their view, Roger Taillibert decided to place the supports of the steel cables for the roof and the upper stands at the periphery of the structure. The prefab elements were assembled on the building site using computer technology, a novelty at the time.

Taillibert later designed arenas in the Middle East and in America, including Montreal's Olympic Stadium (1976).

Centre Pompidou – a programmatic corner stone towers the city (334)

The Georges Pompidou National Center for Art and Culture, which Parisians simply call Beaubourg after the site it is built on, houses the National Museum of Modern Art, a public library, and various other cultural institutions. President Pompidou (1969–1974) initiated the urban development project aimed at enlivening the borough between Le Marais and Les Halles (Forum des Halles, no. 336) and at improving the social structure of the neighborhood. The development of the Pompidou Center, which covers a base area of 166 by 60 meters, required the demolition of several blocks of old buildings. With its height of fifty meters, the structure dominates the neighborhood and is visible from afar. In 1971, 680 international architects participated in the architectural competition, and the building was erected the following year in just six months. With 10,000 square meters of exhibition area, the Pompidou Center was to be the counterpart of the Louvre for contemporary art. The winning team of architects therefore proposed a radically modern design. In the aftermath of the French students' and workers' protests of May, 1968, the building was also intended as a provocation to conservatives, a kind of architectural interpretation of slogans such as "Art does not exist," or "Down with the definitive; long live the provisional." The basic structure consists of a steel exoskeleton. Posts every thirteen meters support cantilevered arms and beams that span forty-eight meters, and are braced by a lattice truss system. The floors are suspended from the external posts. This type of construction does away with internal load-bearing elements, so that the space is adaptable for all kinds of uses. Although large spaces without pillars and struts are also found in contemporary office buildings, they always contain service shafts and supply conduits. The architects of the Pompidou Center, however, moved not just the load-bearing structure, but all the fixed installations outside the building. Thus escalators, elevators, ventilation ducts and water pipes dominate both the main and rear façades, becoming ornamental features like the sculptural elements that adorn the stone façades of the Louvre (no. 49). The primary colors of the conduits recall pop-art designs, and are coded to their functions: red for escalators and elevators, blue for forced-air ventilation and heating, green for water and safety equipment, and yellow for electrical power. The Institute for Music/Acoustic Research and Coordination (IRCAM, no. 384) extends underground, underneath the Stravinsky Fountain adorned with sculptures by Niki de Saint-Phalle and machines by Jean Tinguely, as far as the Saint-Merri church (no 36). In 1987–1989, the Renzo Piano Building Workshop (RPBW) expanded the IRCAM with an above-ground building where Place Georges-Pompidou meets Place Igor-Stravinsky. The facade of brick masonry filling in an aluminum framework seems an almost ironic comment on the open steel skeleton of the Pompidou Center. In 1995–1997, RPBW also designed the single-story structure that faces the Pompidou Center and houses the reconstructed studio of the sculptor Constantin Brâncusai. Since its construction, the Pompidou Center has been the object of the same technophobia as the Eiffel Tower (no. 218). Nonetheless, it is now one of the liveliest places in the city, with some 25,000 visitors every day. The sculpture "Le Pot" on the square in front of the center is a golden flower pot set on a pedestal, and is by Jean-Pierre Raynaud (1998).

213

General view

Fire station (335)
1971
37, boulevard Masséna,
16, avenue Boutroux / 13e
Prvoslav Popovic, Jean Willerval

This fire station contains residential units to enable firefighters to reach their vehicles as quickly as possible. The building's forms demonstrate that Le Corbusier's "poetry of the right angle" was becoming obsolete by the early seventies. Instead, the fire station is made of curved prefab elements that were assembled on the building site.

Forum des Halles (336)
1971–1986
rue Rambuteau, rue Pierre-Lescot,
rue Berger / 4e
Claude Vasconi, Georges Pencreac'h,
Jacques Bouton, Paul Chemetov

This gigantic, half-underground complex covers four hectares on the spot where Les Halles (no. 187) used to stand. It includes a shopping arcade, a métro and regional train station, a swimming pool, a cinema, and several libraries. The exterior is characterized by terraces covered by half-cylinders of glass. This part of the complex leads down to the vast interior halls.

Both the areas developed by Claude Vasconi and Georges Pencreac'h in the seventies and the Place Carrée added by Chemetov in 1985 are thoroughly modern, in spite of allusions to traditional barrel vaults and Baltard's covered market. The same can be said of the iron pavilions designed by Claude and François-Xavier Lalanne in the garden above the underground complex (Jardin des Halles). Claude Lalanne also created the

"Children's Garden" in 1986. The locals never really 'warmed to the "Forum", partly because it was built at the cost of the historic covered market, which the novelist Émile Zola had called "the belly of Paris". This in turn explains why several plans were developed for remodeling the complex (no. 489), the latest of which, by Patrick Berger and Jacques Anziutti, is scheduled to be realized in the years to come.

Les Orgues de Flandre (337)
1973–1980
67–107, avenue de Flandre,
14–24, rue Archereau / 19e
Martin S. van Treek

Van Treek developed the design for the housing built in 1950 with the help of an endoscope, using which he could get an idea of the view of the building from the passers-by's perspective at the street level using the model. The rounded forms of the structure make the space found between the volumes more easily perceived as room. In this respect, the design can be compared with Baroque arrangements, with the exception that the modeling stretches itself in the vertical, instead of the horizontal dimension.

Ambassade d'Afrique du Sud (338)
1974
59, quai d'Orsay / 7e
Jean-Marie Garet, Gérard Lambert,
Jean Thierrat

The aluminum plates suspended on the glass façade lend privacy to the interior without impairing the view of the Seine and the building's surroundings. Their crenellated shape underscores their protective function. At the same time, the elongated proportions of the metal plates match those of the windows on 19th-century buildings.

Centre d'affaires George V (339)
1974
30, avenue George V / 8e
Nicola Ilic, Pierre Sicard, Pierre Molins

This building, erected for the French Shoemakers' Association, features varying heights to match the silhouette of the surrounding buildings.

The glass façade – the first ever built in Paris – gave each of the association's seventy members a seven-square-meter display case. As the "displays" protrude, the building seems to be a compound of toy building blocks.

Hôtel Le Méridien (340)
Montparnasse
1974
19, rue du Commandant-René-Mouchotte / 14e
Pierre Dufau

This 116-meter tower, developed by the Sheraton Group, consists of a concrete skeleton entirely covered with white steel plates. The aluminum-framed windows are concentrated on a few vertical strips, which give the building a light, radiant appearance that contrasts with that of the nearby dark Tour Montparnasse (no. 332).

Prefabricated façade elements enabled the architect to minimize the building costs.

215

La Défense – the 21th arrondissement in the west (341)

The construction of a new administrative center to the west of Paris in line with the historical axis on which the Louvre, the small arch, the Tuilleries Garden and Champs-Élysees are all aligned was planned already in the Fourth Republic. The political decisions to erect the office city came only after 1955, and in 1958 saw the founding of the Etablissement publique pour l'Aménagement de la Défense (EPAD), which oversees the district's development to this day. La Défense is not officially a part of Paris, but belongs to the boroughs of Nanterre, Puteaux and Courbevoie; however, it is viewed as the 21st arrondisment. This was formerly the district that contained France's last slums (bidonvilles) and whose residents were resettled to Tours Nuages. The planning principles follow the Athens Charter (1933), which demands the separation of work and living, as well as the designation of vehicular and pedestrian traffic and dense construction of standardized hi-rises. To this end, the pedestrian-only street flanked by skyscrapers extends the Grand Arche, while the automobile traffic is redirected to the Boulevard Circulaire below. Originally, the 860,000 square meters office area was to be built on, with towers each measuring 24 x 42 x 100 meters. Counting a total of 40 million square meters of office space, Paris is Europe's largest office market today. Of that number, only 3 million square meters are in La Défense, but it is only with the creation of this cohesive district and the resurgence of the area since the 1980s did Paris come to investors' attention. More than 1,500 companies have their offices here, and over 160,000 employees work in the neighborhood. At first, numerous apartment buildings for about 20,000 residents were erected (de Mailly: Résidence Bellini Défense, 1957), while the office building development took its time. The first was the Esso building, occupying the lot of today's Coeur Défense (1962) (no. 465). Most of the original office buildings appeared only with the RER link-up in the 1970s, simultaneously with Le Front de Seine in the inner city (Tour Totem, no. 348), and in keeping with the uniform tower dimensions (1972). In the 1980s, after the oil crisis, special attention was paid to engineering savings. A limitation on the district expansion to the west ("Tête Défense") – which turns out to be only temporary – is marked by the Grande Arche de la Défense (no. 377) since 1989. In Rem Koolhaas' 1995 book S,M,L,XL, the arch figures as the actual city's savior as "Tabula Rasa Revisited: Mission Grand Axe, La Défense." Behind it in 1998 the Jardins de l'Arche were built by Paul Chemetov, Borja Huidobro and Atelier Acanthe between the Neuilly and Puteaux cemeteries.

In the 1990s construction started to yield a higher return, a trend that continues today. The district is constantly in a state of further development, however smaller buildings like the Notre-Dame-de-la-Pentecôte chapel (no. 464) or the pedestrian bridge on the rue des Longues Raies by Feichtinger Architekten with Schlaich, Bergermann and partners (2008) are not to be ignored. An additional 850,000 square meters effective area will be added by the year 2015 according to the development company EPAD. Sometime before 2013, the Eiffel Tower of the 21st century, Phare von Morphosis (no. 492), will be erected right next to the CNIT. The highest building in the district, it will have 130,000 square meters of office space. Countless large art pieces like Joan Miro's Quatre Temps are found mostly on the esplanade, but also to its sides, like Caesar's Thumb behind the CNIT (no. 315). In 2001 NOX / Lars Spuybroek ParisBRAIN presented their transurban scheme for the area to the west of La Défense, which imagines a relaxation of the city's periphery.

The buildings and projects as well as their architects are found in the appendix (A2).

217

View from the Arc de Triomphe on La Défense

12ᵉ Arr!

AVENUE
DORIAN

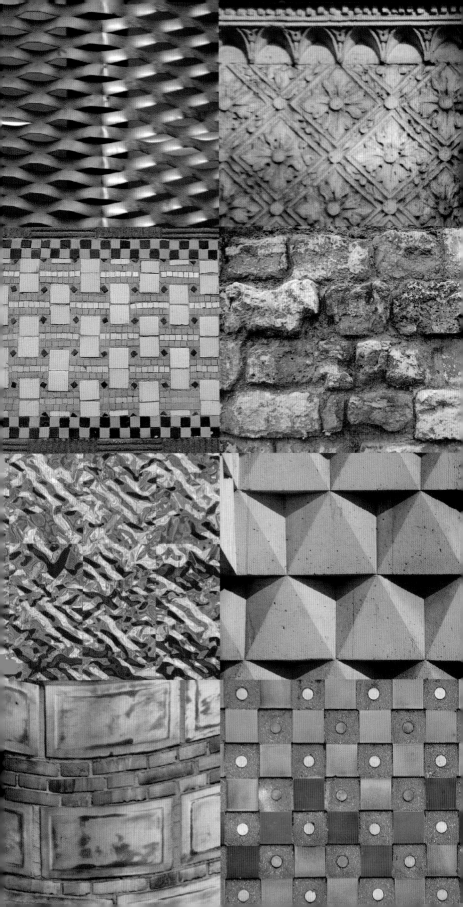

"Grands Projets" and selective urban renewal in the postmodern period and the 1980s (342)

Giscard d'Estaing revised some of his predecessors' plans. The construction of a giant slaughterhouse planned under de Gaulle was stopped in 1974 and rededicated to the Cité des Science et de l'Industrie (no. 404), which offers four times the exposition area of the Centre Pompidou (no. 334). An abandoned train station on the Seine, which de Gaulle wanted to destroy in order to make way for an expressway will become Musee d'Orsay (no. 350). In case of both of these projects and the Institut du monde arabe (no. 361), which was founded by Giscard d'Estaing in 1980, the construction was to start only under Mitterand. In contrast to his predecessors and successors in office, Giscard d'Estaing remained inconspicuous as commissioner and initiator of architectural projects. The disaffection towards postwar Modernism which led to the architects' dissolution of CIAM and public protests against the demolition and new development of the Les Halles site and the Tour Montparnasse led to a Postmodernist breakthrough during his incumbency. Already in 1974 Giscard d'Estaing declared Ricardo Bofill to be "the world's best architect," and hoped that he could "save

Paris from itself." The Spaniard could not implement his Historicist design for the Les Halles quarter, but his apartment building offered an alternative to the featureless residential towers in the 13th Arrondisment. Bofill and his colleagues in Taller de Arquitectura created impressive, low-cost developments that combined rational structural technology (pre-fabricated concrete elements) with wide variation in form. In Cergy-Pontoise (Les Colonnes St Christophe 1986) Saint-Quentin-en-Yvelines (Les Arcades du Lac and Les Temples du Lac, 1981, 1986) and Noisy-le-Grand - Marne-la-Vallée, (Les Espaces d'Abraxas, no. 359) large axial social projects that transform the worker to an occupant of a Baroque palace, complete with all its formal vocabulary. Paris also receives such an ensemble with Les Echelles du Baroque (no. 351), which externally adapts to the perimeter of the block, unfolding its space-filling form in the interior. An additional example of Postmodern revision of an apartment building is the Les Hautes Formes (no. 343) ensemble by Christian de Portzamparc and Georgia Benamo, which also relies on historical formal language, but it is employed less

One of 30 follies in the Parc de la Villette (no. 404), Bernhard Tschumi, 1987–1991

historicistically. The entire ensemble is less monumental, but more intimate and picturesque. This and other similar projects searched for the neighborhood that was dissolved in the postwar period by the construction of tower or row apartment buildings placed along the street, and whose surroundings were lost as social space. In 1977 the capital elected a mayor, like the country's other cities. Until this time, the Préfet de la Seine, the representative of the central state in the department, ruled the city. The Paris police, however, was still subordinate to the police prefect, and due to the city's financial dependency on the state, most structural projects remained "presidential architecture." These grand projets de l'etat experienced an enormous boom under Mitterand and made Paris a center of international architecture yet again. Countless structures that have influenced the city's image have become associated with "Mitteramses I," even though some of the projects (Musee d'Orsay, Institut du monde arabe) were initiated by his predecessor. With the first project, the Arche de la Défense (no. 377), restructuring of La Défense (no. 341) begins. With the

Grand Louvre (no. 49), the former castle is generously but inoffensively expanded to accommodate its "new" role as a museum. The Ministère des Finances (no. 363) and the Opéra Bastille (no. 366) projects prove to be controversial. The Bibliothèque Nationale de France project (no. 408) shows the turnabout to a new architecture defined by large-scale forms. In addition to the grand projects, important reconstruction and renovations of existing buildings in 13e, 15e, 19e and 20e arrondissements were undertaken in 1970s and 1980s (Parc Andre Citroen, no. 399, Parc de la Villette, no. 404). In addition to I. M. Pei (Louvre), Richard Meier (Canal+, no. 401) and Frank Gehry (no. 393) other global players climb Paris's stage. Gehry represents Deconstructivism, the second noose around the Second Modernism, which is implemented in Paris almost simultaneously with the New Elegance of the National Library. While it proves difficult for foreign architects to establish themselves in Paris (from Bernini until today, hardly a dozen notable buildings), French architects increasingly succeed in winning international acclaim and commissions.

La Rue des Hautes-Formes (343)
1975-1979
rue des Hautes-Formes / 13e
Christian de Portzamparc with
Giorgia Benamo

`ENSEMBLE` This urban redevelopment project was among the first manifestations of the postmodern style in Paris. It revives cornices, segmental pediments and Renaissance arches, reducing the traditional architectural elements to mere templates based on geometric forms, yet without degrading them to clichés.

The original concept provided for two low blocks with 209 residential units, but Christian de Portzamparc opted for eight buildings in order to recreate an urban atmosphere. The street, developed in the tradition of Paris's secluded lanes, includes different semi-public spaces. Portzamparc's design transcends functionalism, placing façade, interior and exterior on an equal footing.

Immeuble Matignon (344)
1976
22, avenue Matignon / 8e
Vittorio Mazzucconi,
Jean-Marie Hereng (engineer)

The city voiced its desire that the new building should be well-integrated into the neighborhood while the customer, an advertising agency, wanted something that caught the eye. The architect solved the problem by incorporating a fake spolia into the façade of the modern building. A large cast stone section is positioned above the ground floor, framed unhistorically and with ruin-like outlines, allowing a glass office building to spring up from behind it.

Légation militaire (345)
d'Arabie saoudite
1976
4bis, rue Franqueville / 16e
José Imbert

The building is an example of the increasing rejection of Postwar Modernism. On the one hand, the former long time collaborator of the Perret brothers picks up antique-like vocabulary, but on the other, her arranges it in a uniform, late Modernist system.

Modern projecting elements are missing, and instead rows of loggias ordered in four trusses are placed in front of the actual façade, resulting in 20 compartments. Vertically, the stories are separated by pillars: The shafts on tall bases are on the level of the elevated ground floor; on the three middle stories the pillars have capitals, but these are missing on the top story where they support a terminating cornice. The columns are fluted and are made of concrete with an addition of pulverized marble, resulting in an impression of marble shafts. Behind the terminating cornice are beams which connect it to the façade and act as a pergola.

**Chancellerie de l'ambassade   (347)
de Turquie**
1976
16, avenue de Lamballe / 16e
Henri Beauclair

Sturdy round pillars on the first floor echo the massive appearance of the surrounding traditional structures, as also do the upper stories clad in a light glass envelope forming three slender cylinders. The challenge to the architect was considerably complicated by the requirement to preserve all existing trees and views on the embassy's garden, and by the small dimensions of the lot, which is bordered by the Maison Balzac on one side and an 18th-century city mansion on the other.

Siège BNP   (346)
1976
2, rue Taitbout / 9e
Pierre Dufau

The original design would have demolished a building called "Maison Dorée" to make room for the new bank headquarters. But Pierre Dufau suggested preserving the older building, extending it of two bays along Rue Taitbout, and giving it modern tinted windows to create a harmonious transition to the new structure.

223

Tour Totem (348)
1976–1978
55, quai de Grenelle / 15e
Michel Andrault, Pierre Parat

This tower, which is part of the "Front de Seine" project – a redevelopment program that provided for construction of high-rises in the city center – is contemporary, like most of the skyscrapers at La Défense. The building perfectly illustrates the construction principle based on a load-bearing frame covered with a filling skin. The concrete core, which extends to the top, provides access to 207 living units grouped in threes. Their angular arrangement optimizes the view of the river from each apartment. The functional grouping of apartments and environments as well as structural and visual separation correspond to each other well.

Ambassade Australienne (349)
1978
4, rue Jean-Rey,
9, rue de la Fédération / 15e
Peter Hirst, Harry Seidler
(H. Seidler & Associates)

The large S-shaped building consists of two parts: the half facing the Seine has balco-

nies on the front and almost no openings in the rear, while the other half has balconies all along the façade. The spontaneous appearance of the pillars on the first floor (works by Pier Luigi Nervi) alleviates the otherwise strict geometric design of the ensemble. Marcel Breuer and Mario Jossa collaborated with Peter Hirst and Harry Seidler in the project.

Musée d'Orsay (350)
1978–1986
7, quai Anatole-France / 7e
Renaud Bardon, Pierre Colboc, Jean-Paul Philippon, Gae Aulenti (Interior)

Between 1897 and 1900, Victor Laloux built a railway station for visitors to the World's Fair on the site of a palace that had been destroyed during the Paris Commune in 1871 (no. 226). His iron and glass hall with a neo-Renaissance façade was typical of the civil engineering achievements of the late 19th century. By 1939, however, the station had become too small for modern trains and regular service ended. A 1960s redevelopment project called for the building to be demolished and replaced by a luxury hotel. But the locals, who did not appreciate the destruction of Paris's historic structures such as Baltard's pavilions at Les Halles (no. 187), protested vehemently.

Orsay Station was therefore placed under a preservation order and President Giscard d'Estaing proposed that the building be converted into a museum for 19th-century painting. ACT Architecture won the competition and converted the building in collaboration with Gea Aulenti. The architects preserved the appearance of the former station and partitioned the interior to developed appropriate exhibition spaces.

Les-Echelles-du-Baroque – (351)
L'Amphithéâtre – Les Colonnes
1979–1985
rue de Vercingétorix, place de Catalogne,
place de l'Amphithéâtre,
place de Séoul / 14e
Ricardo Bofill

ENSEMBLE The apartment building ensemble, whose planning started already in the 1960s, begins on the Place de Catalogne with three building sections. The structures are grouped around a fountain by Shamaï Haber and form the city's

largest square since the times of Baron Haussmann. Two additional squares join at the rear side of the middle house. The oval-shaped Place de Séoul stands out as an especially unique, closed-off example of early post modern architecture. While the underlying structure with formally reduced horizontal bays reveals a thoroughly modern structure, the cast stone border is decorated using neo-Classical forms.

The structuring of the walls varies the vocabulary – the bays become column shafts by ending in Doric capitals, although they also house the entrances. The glass façade "carries" the attic story, which along with the remaining walls, niches and window mountings openly consists of prefabricated concrete elements. Two additional columns, built in the style of Historicist architecture in everything except their size, are located at the monumental entrance to the square.

Palais Omnisports (352)
de Paris-Bercy
1979–1984
8, boulevard de Bercy,
rue Romanée / 12e
Michel Andrault, Pierre Parat, Aydin Guvan, Jean Prouvé (engineer)

The arena belongs to the Bercy redevelopment area and was built in support of Paris's bid to host the 1992 Olympic Games. It seats 3,500 to 17,000 and is suitable for a variety of functions. The commission was mainly to design a structure compatible with sports events, rock concerts and trade fairs for optimum commercial efficiency.

Peripheral structures surround the main area covered with a framed roof whose gigantic concrete pillars arise from a base shaped like a truncated pyramid. The greened, sloping sides of the 45-degree pyramid make a smooth transition from the monumental structure beside the Seine to the nearby Parc de Bercy (no. 391), although the greenery is repeatedly interrupted by glazed surfaces and concrete gates and stairs.

Les Arènes de Picasso (353)
1980–1984
place Pablo-Picasso (Noisy-Le-Grand)
Manuel Nuñez-Yanowsky

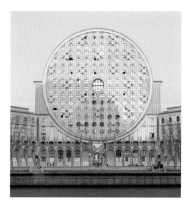

The former collaborator of Bofill takes up historical architectural forms in prefabricated concrete in order to create a building with a large number of residential units that carries a high degree of recognition. However, these two facing volumes with axial symmetry do not refer to neo-Classicism, but treat abstract and geometrical figures as fantastical designs, taking fanciful revolutionary architecture as its example. The two disc-shaped building volumes that appear simply left in place, nicknamed by the occupants the "Camemberts," are inspired by Boullée's design for Isaac Newton's masouleum.

Warehouse-renovation (354)
1980
145, rue de l'Ourcq / 19e
Christian Maisonhaute with
Arnaldo Coutine and Jacques Lévy

This former warehouse converted into seventy-six residential units is the first

Parisian example of a roofed public space uniting private apartments.

The architects used the original load-bearing elements, which remain visible everywhere in the former warehouse. The resulting duplexes thus look like detached houses lining a green lane.

Hotel des Ventes (355)
1980
9, rue Drouot / 9e
Jean-Jacques Fernier, André Brio

The architects worked to create a modern interpretation of the Haussman street front by searching for modern forms which would pick up on the stereotypical

progression and stacking of the boulevard zones without exactly imitating any historical forms. Thus, the crystalline corner composition is a reference to the 19th century corner cupolas with rotundas, but does not actually reveal the original form. Aluminum panels take up the repetitive Haussmann façade sequences without formally quoting them.

Cité des Eiders (356)
1981
145, avenue de Flandre / 19e
Mario Heymann

This residential complex includes 905 low-rent apartments. Heymann opted for a versatile modular system in order to introduce variations, unify the ensemble and reduce the anonymity inherent in many social housing complexes. Their terraced buildings with individual modules on the roof are characterized by rounded angles and bays that enliven the ensemble.

Apartments (357)
1981
11bis, rue Pierre-Nicole / 5e
E. D.

The ceramic façade is to be interpreted as homage to the corresponding material designs of the Art Nouveau. Its relief recalls façades by Lavirotte (cf. no. 234, 246) and the sculptural, asymmetrical resolution of building fronts at the turn of the century. At the ground level, Ngoc

Duong creates a ruinous landscape whose alleged spolia draw the passers-by's attention.

Apartments (358)
1981
3, avenue Boudon / 16e
Bernard Reichen and Philippe Robert

This building with its turret and bow windows revisits the façades developed under Baron Haussmann in an abstract and contemporary style. Moreover, the structure integrates vertical gardens using grids and espaliers.

Place
des Fédérés

Les Espaces d'Abraxas – Palaces for the proletariat (359)

After completing his Arcades du Lac in Saint-Quentin-en-Yvelines (1972–1975), Bofill built five additional social housing complexes in and around Paris. The Abraxas residential ensemble was built in 1978–1982 in the suburbs of Marne-la-Vallée. The ensemble is Bofill's most famous, and not just because it has been inducted into film history – this is where Sam Lowry, the hero of Terry Gilliam's film "Brazil" (1985) lives.

It is here that Bofill developed his style of using prefabricated parts according to historical architectural vocabulary. Almost 600 apartments are grouped in the building surrounding an inner yard, on one side arranged as a green amphitheatre and closed off by a semicircular façade that features monumental columns, while on the other side a rectangular lawn is bordered by an orthogonal building with 19 floors. At the center is a small ten story hi-rise that frees the central axis along seven of its floors. The orthogonal building consist of three wings subdivided into two volume depths separated by a partially covered pedestrian walkway. The lower and middle areas are split vertically using two by two traverses, while the upper section is a continuous bridge. Between the three rectangular wings, the building volume is opened up at the corners, enabling a view inside the complex. In this way, Bofill is successful in sectioning the mass into various depth layers.

Magnified historical structural ornamentation is found as surface decoration at various positions and with variations on their original function. Thus, lightly reliefed, disrupted gables (a Baroque form) grace the top sections of the front of the block and invite a view of the outer layer of the building. Below them are rectangles reminiscent of a triglyph frieze. Further down, above fluted pillars on the buildings' corners are circles, a reference to a warrior's shield. Here, the architecture features a second shallow relief of historicist architecture, in this

"Modern Baroque" across the corner

case with an antiquity-style, undisrupted gable, mirrored by the horizontal sectioning of the yard façades.

The ten-storied triumphal arch (Arc de Triomphe, no. 158) also combines monumental pylons in the stylized columns (which also contain apartments) with paired pilasters in the overlying architrave. Small temples around the ensemble bring the gigantic proportions down to human scale.

Triumphal arch in the courtyard

229

Massive cuboid in the succession to Claude-Nicolas Ledoux and a "negative" clustered pillar

Conservatoire de Musique (360)
Erik-Satie
1981–1984
135, rue de l'Université,
7, rue Jean-Nicot / 7e
Christian de Portzamparc

This ensemble includes a music conservatory and a home for the elderly facing each other across an interior courtyard. The elaborate main façade, characterized by a protruding tower and round pillars on thin bases enlivens the street by giving it a spatial aspect despite the lot's cramped dimensions.

Moreover, the linearity of the triangular and segmental pediments above the cornice strongly contrasts with the sturdy appearance of the lower elements.

Institut du Monde Arabe (361)
1981–1987
11, quai du Monde Arabe,
1, rue des Fossés Saint-Bernard / 5e
Jean Nouvel, Gilbert Lezenes,
Pierre Soria and Architecture Studio

This ensemble is mainly famous for its 27,000 solar diaphragms that underscore the decorative potential of high-tech elements. The diaphragms in various sizes automatically regulate the natural light reaching the interior.

They are arranged on plates that form patterns reminiscent of the qamariya windows (openings with tracery fanlights) common in Arab architecture. The straight lines of the library building with

the diaphragm façades match those of the nearby Faculté de Jussieu (no. 324). The façade of the museum follows the curve of the street and the Seine. Moreover, the patio between the two structures is a typical element of the traditional Arab architecture.

School (362)
1982–1985
rue de la Croix-Saint-Simon,
rue Mouraud / 20e
Architecture Studio

The elongated building plays with recurrent yet varying motifs: on the first floor, a row of pillars emphasizes the horizontal dimension while vertically undulating walls alleviate the impression of endlessness.

The window bands on the upper stories seem to be similar at first glance, but a closer look reveals differences in size and disposition. Finally, the pediment crowning the school echoes that of the neighboring church and divides the building symmetrically.

Ministère de l'Économie, des (363)
Finances et du Budget
1982–1989
1, boulevard de Bercy / 12e
Paul Chemetov and Borja Huidobro

The Ministry had to vacate the Richelieu Wing of the Louvre (no. 49) after President Mitterrand decided to reorganize the museum.

The new premises were conceived as a growth engine in the Bercy redevelopment area (no. 452) and as a modern gateway to the city for those arriving from the east. The building therefore extends over Quai de la Rapée and into the river.

The remarkably long structure with pillars that structure dark glass elements and support a light-colored horizontal bar clearly suggests a bridge. Because of the building's slender shape, all offices enjoy excellent natural light conditions.

Ateliers d'artistes (364)
1982
1, chemin du Parc de Charonne / 20e
Yann Brunel, Sinikka Ropponen

Yann Brunel and Sinikka Ropponen, who had lived in Finland for a time, built one of Paris's few modern timber-framed houses in just four days.

The wood-frame construction is clearly visible and made development of large rooms possible. The staircases, however, are made of stone and thus fire-resistant. The composition of the different volumes underscores the alternation of wood and stone.

Villa dall'Ava (365)
1982–1991
7, avenue Clodoald (Saint-Cloud)
OMA, Rem Koolhaas

Rem Koolhaas designed this villa in dialog with the modern classical style in a genteel suburb characterized by an abundance of 19th-century cottages. The architect was asked to design a glass building in the style of Mies van der Rohe with a swimming pool on the terraced roof. In his design he succeeded by not making the pool the grand finale of an "architectural walk," in the fashion of Le Corbusier's Villa Savoye (no. 299). Instead, Koolhaas built a superstructure for the pool.

Its heavy second floor with the private apartments of the parents and their daughter rests on a base made of glass. Invisible pillars support the pool on the

231

second floor. With this work, Koolhaas turns the usual disposition of elements and materials on its head, so that the villa appears as an ironical comment on the traditional function and design of this type of building.

Opéra de la Bastille (366)
(Opéra National de Paris)
1983–1989
120, rue de Lyon,
place de la Bastille / 12e
Carlos Ott

As one of the "grand projects" initiated by President Mitterrand, a popular opera house was to be built on the former site of the Bastille Station since the old Opéra Garnier (no. 198) had become too small for the French capital. Carlos Ott won the international architecture competition with his design for a vast complex conceived as the new dominant feature of Place de la Bastille.

The circular part of the building indeed dominates the square, but the stylized entrance gate with a great flight of stairs—a characteristic feature of a grand cultural building —respects the height of the surrounding traditional structures. The opera's various components that extend behind the rotunda follow a precise rhythm in order to break up the volume. A shopping arcade within the building functions as a link between everyday life and the rather daunting world of opera.

Hôpital Européen (367)
Georges-Pompidou
1983–2000
20, rue Leblanc / 15e
Aymeric Zubléna

A long covered avenue leads to the various facilities of this large hospital complex. With its cafés, green spaces and rest areas, the avenue connects the medical center with the outside world.

Its glazed shed roof achieves a transition between the surrounding buildings and the parallel structures on either side that are higher and house the hospital facilities.

Le Zénith (368)
1984
Parc de la Villette / 19e
Chaix & Morel

The Zénith hall was originally planned as a temporary multi-purpose venue

during the construction of a rock music theater at Porte de Bagnolet. Since the building project was abandoned, however, the Zénith has become a permanent part of the La Villette Park.

The hall, a work by Philippe Chaix and Jean-Paul Morel, consists of a seventy-meter scaffolding structure designed to support a load of fifty tons and covered with a polyester skin whose curved surface counteracts the forces of the wind.

A second, internal skin improves the acoustics in the hall, and a curtain serves to reduce the interior from its maximum capacity of 6,400 (with 5,800 seats on 6,200 square meters) to about 2,000.

The building is crowned with an airplane, which now serves as the Zénith's logo, marks the spot where a feed silo for the expanded slaughterhouse once stood.

The temporary hall has been so successful that several other "Zéniths" have been built elsewhere in France.

Senior living apartments (369)
1984
120, rue du Château-des-Rentiers / 13e
Christian de Portzamparc

This small building – a home for the elderly – tries to break with the "autism" of the neighboring constructions. It connects with the existing structures by echoing the curves of the building on the left and extending the horizontal window stripes of the one on the right.

De Portzamparc's work unites the street façades by acting as a hinge which sets a highly noticeable point into the architectural flow and gives the street human proportions.

Médiathèque (370)
Jean-Pierre Melville
1984–1989
93, rue de Tolbiac / 13e
Canal (Daniel and Patrick Rubin)

The austere appearance of Paris's first mediatheque reflects the expanded

scope of a modern library: it is no longer a temple of books, but a shell to house information and entertainment media. Likewise, the open ground plan and the transparent façade illustrate that culture is no longer bound to a bookcase, and hence more approachable.

Cité de la Musique (371)
1984
221, avenue Jean-Jaurès / 19e
Christian de Portzamparc

The generous south entrance of the park de la Villette (no. 404) on Avenue Jean-Jaurès, in front of the Great Hall, features the Nubian Lions fountain (Pierre-Simon Girard, 1811) flanked by two modern structures built to plans by Christian de Portzamparc: the National Conservatory of Music and Dance on the left (1984–1995) and the City of Music on the right.

The latter building references of one of Tschumi's follies at the entrance area but continues with a completely other set of forms for the rest.

Various types of ceramic coatings dominate the façade. The spiral-shaped interior of the building is based on the legend of the "Ear of Dionysus", a cave in a Sicilian quarry that is said to amplify sound sixteen times. (According to the legend, Dionysus I of Syracuse came to this place to eavesdrop on the songs of slaves or the conversations of prisoners.)

The interior walls along the curved passageway are shaped like traditional Parisian façades. The City of Music contains a concert hall, the Museum of Music designed by Franck Hammoutène (1997), and the Café de la Musique with an interior by Élizabeth de Portzamparc.

Grand Ecran (372)
1985–1991
18–30, place d'Italie / 13e
Kenzo Tange, Michel Macary, Xavier Menu

This building, located at a major crossroads, links traditional 19th-century structures and 1960s high-rises. The façade that follows the curve of Place d'Italie has a stone facing that quotes Paris's traditional architecture, while the tower is rooted in postwar modernism.

The building's name stems from the 22-meter-wide screen of the cinema inside. Moreover, the recessed and curved façade also evokes a screen and its frame.

School (373)
1985–1988
99–101, rue Pelleport / 20e
Francis Soler

For this nursery school, Francis Soler took over Joseph Cornell's surrealistic boxed bric-à-brac to create unconscious associations from an assemblage of heterogeneous items. Two sides of an

uncompleted metal frame hold the glass façade without bounding its other sides. Aluminum, dark concrete and black metal combine to form a three-dimensional collage. Tilted double pillars support the horizontal portion of the frame at a position determined by nothing noticeable in the overall composition.

Cuisine de l'Hôpital (374)
Saint-Antoine
1985
30, rue de Citeaux / 12e
Henri Ciriani

As the unglazed terrace and the filigree balconies show, this kitchen building forms a transition between the neighboring structures using an architectural system of its own, inspired by the international style of the 1930s. However, Henri Ciriani affirms his independence from interwar modernism by extending both the base and the intermediary cornice of the building to the right on his own stone façade.

Conservatoire Municipal (375)
de Musique
1985
29, rue Baudelique / 18e
Claude Charpentier

The five-storied building takes on the tradition of vertical level-spanning metal window bays, which contrast with the metal panels of the façade surface. The door is framed using playful motifs reflecting the building's musical character.

Apartments (376)
1985–1987
106, rue du Château-des-Rentiers / 13e
Architecture Studio

Triangular lots are not uncommon in Paris. Here the architects developed a residential building with twenty-five low-rent apartments, thus concealing the unaesthetic face of the neighboring structure.

235

The enlarged map of the district that adorns the blind north wall shows the relatively high number of undeveloped lots in the city.

According to Architecture-Studio, developing a thousand such lots to make the urban fabric more coherent would cost no more than one of the many prestigious buildings in the city. In order to simplify the workflow, the architects integrated the tower of the building crane into their design. This part of the machine, set at the acute angle of the lot, now houses the entrance and ends in a tower.

Louvre (no. 49) through the triumphal arch of the Carrousel and the Obelisk at Place de la Concorde (no. 149), the length of the Avenue des Champs-Élysées (no. 80), and through the Arc de Triomphe de l'Étoile (no. 158). From closer up, the arch frames the landscape of office buildings at La Défense.

The building, with a floor area of 115,000 square meters, is a cube without the front and rear faces. The remaining surfaces are beveled inward like a picture frame. Steps in the three-story base provide access to the hollow interior of the "cube". The two vertical sides house offices, while the horizontal top contains conference and exhibition rooms surmounted by a lookout platform.

A series of four concrete frames bear the load of the Great Arch. Concrete beams that form partition walls in the base and the top hold the four frames together. The building is entirely faced with Carrara marble.

The "cloud" that Andreu added after von Spreckelsen's death hangs in the middle of the arch near the panoramic lifts.

Grande Arche de la Défense (377)
1985–1989
La Défense
Johan Otto von Spreckelsen, Paul Andreu

Since 1983, this gigantic arch has terminated the vista that runs from the

Nursery Saint-Maur (378)
1986–1990
56, rue Saint-Maur / 11e
Christian Hauvette

The building itself is hidden behind an extremely closed façade, transforming the day care center in to a childhood fortress. The spacing of the set-in-place, curved concrete slabs is clearly felt thanks to the few wall openings, which provide no functional façade structure.

Only on the left side does the window sequence pick up on the rhythm of the neighboring 19th century house front.

unites modern glass architecture with motifs of known urban landmarks.

Hôtel Industriel Berlier (380)
1986–1990
26, rue Bruneseau / 13e
Dominique Perrault

This building that belongs to the "Rive Gauche" redevelopment (no. 452) project was erected as the city of Paris launched a program aimed at promoting multiple-

Passage Marché Saint-Honoré (379)
place du Marché Saint-Honoré / 1er
1986–1996
Ricardo Bofill / Taller de Arquitectura

The new ensemble on the square consists of two glazed row buildings that form a common passage under a shared roof. As this building type, typical for Paris, is functionally turned into modern architecture, the overall shape of the timeless gabled house model is brought up to date.

The all-covering roof forms a triangular gable known from the times of the antique temple architecture. Bofill's actualization of the basic historical pattern

use construction on low-cost lots at the periphery of the city. Thoroughfares, including Paris's ring motorway, surround the fully glazed building.

The stacking of high windows emphasizes the vertical dimension, while sun blinds and ground plates underscore the horizontal. Minimalism continues in the interior, so that the building can be seen as a pure volume without any particular assignation.

Théâtre des Abbesses (381)
1986–1996
31, rue des Abesses / 18e
Charles Vandenhove with Jacques Sequaris and Prudent de Wispelaere

`ENSEMBLE` This ensemble composed of a dance conservatory and thirty social housing units brings Classicism to the modern period: round pillars without capitals replace the columns, while segmental pediments partially inserted into the walls top the windows.

Further ornamental details are absent, however. The overall composition, with a balanced façade design and a closed forecourt, is thus rooted in the tradition of Paris's city mansions.

Apartments (382)
1986–1991
1–11, avenue du Nouveau-Conservatoire, 33, avenue Jean-Jaurès / 19e
Aldo Rossi with Claude Zuber

The linear residential building near the Conservatoire National Supérieur de Musique et de Danse (no. 388) matches the style of the neighboring 19th-century structures, so that Rossi's work is hard to identify as a new development at first glance.

Only the grids in the façade hint at the building's modernism and manifest the architect's taste for simplified forms: a regular façade, a zinc roof and an arcade on the ground floor that recalls Rue de Rivoli (no. 154).

Îlot Candie Saint-Bernard (383)
1987–1998
rue de Candie, passage Saint-Bernard / 11e
Massimiliano Fuksas

An entire block was redeveloped using concrete and zinc to build residential and commercial buildings of different heights shaped as a wave. The project also included the development of open spaces and altering the plan of a sports hall, partially underground.

Although Massimiliano Fuksas used traditionally Parisian elements such as the perforated façade with vertical windows, his design is clearly rooted in modernism through the use of industrial building materials and contemporary features of unregulated urban development, such as lattice gates and open sports field with high fences like those common in the US.

IRCAM-Extension (384)
1987–1989
1, place Igor-Stravinsky / 4e
Renzo Piano Building Workshop

The building housing the IRCAM institute near the Centre Pompidou (no. 334)was developed by Renzo Piano and Richard Rogers between 1973 and 1977. The architects opted for an underground solution

to avoid impairing the view of the choir of the Saint-Merri church (no. 36). The only visible parts of the building are a glass roof and ventilation ducts. The original building is situated underneath the Stravinsky fountain that was completed in 1983 and is adorned with sculptures by Jean Tinguely and Nikki de Saint-Phalle. The extension southwest of the plaza is a tower-like structure that houses stairs and elevators providing access to the institute's facilities, which are located in a former primary school. Because the local authorities specified a brick façade to match that of the school, Renzo Piano covered the extension with terracotta slabs in brick format, grouped in panels stacked one above the other, which gives a decisively modern appearance to the traditional building material.

Apartments (385)
1987
7, rue Saint-Gilles / 3e
Jacques Vitry, Dominique Hertenberger

This building not only uses the pediments and brick-and-stone façades typical of French Renaissance achievements such as Place des Vosges (no. 45), but also groups the apartments around courtyards, an arrangement common in Paris and the Marais in particular before Haussmann's alterations. Other traditional elements include the building's almost symmetrical volumes, with the façade horizontally divided into the base, the piano nobile and the attic story. The design of the apartments behind the street front does not reflect the social significance implied by the façade.

239

Architecture Studio
*Founded in 1973 in Paris (386)

Architecture Studio sees itself as a collective, much like TAC (The Architects Collaborative, Inc.) founded by Walter Gropius in 1946. Currently, it includes eight partners: Martin Robain (since 1973), Rodo Tisnado (1976), Jean-François Bonne (1979), Alain Bretagnolle (1989), René-Henri Arnaud (1989), Laurent-Marc Fischer (1993), Marc Lehmann (1998) and Roueïda Ayache (2001).

The buildings created by the office should be understood as a communal work of all those involved, not of just one individual. Around 100 architects,

city planners, designers and interior decorators from 25 nations work in the office, and this practically guarantees a constant flow of different currents, manifold approaches and continued innovation by young coworkers. The founding idea states that architecture as an art should be involved in society and consciously design the living environment of people.

The works by Architecture Studio are often large in scale and include the widest range of building types: from apartment houses to educational institutes, company offices to production buildings, recreational structures to city planning. Their international activity spans from Athens to Beirut, to Shanghai and back to Italy. The company has focused on China by opening an office with 20 employees in Shanghai. Although the studio's collective approach has resulted in highly variegated buildings, common features can still be identified. Following a short Postmodern intermezzo in the 1980s (École maternelle et élémentaire, no. 362, 10, rue Mouraud , façade design 9 boulevard de Courcelles), was followed by a return to "simpler" design carried by striking, easily comprehensible forms and ideas (106, rue du Château-des-Rentiers conveys perhaps the most direct meaning of "striking", no. 376).

With the Institut du Monde Arabe (no. 361) built together with Jean Nouvel and others), the office became known in professional circles, whereas the European Parliament Building in Strasburg (1999) made it famous in public. The European Parliament consists of three interacting basic ideas: the primary building volume follows the curve of the river and rises as it reaches the curve's zenith. At this highest point the dome of the plenary hall can be seen on the roof showing from behind the pitch.

On the opposite side, the hollow cylindrical volume housing delegates' offices encroaches on the plenary building whose façade and roof are drastically sunken in the direction of land. Visitors

Renewal of the Maison de Radio France – O.R.T.F., completion 2013 (no. 311)

enter the Olympus of European politics through the rounded structure, like gladiators entering an amphitheatre. The combination of these simple but meaningful forms makes the building a typical Architecture Studio project. Another important work by the office is the reconstruction of Jean Prouvé's Aluminum Pavilion (1954) on the grounds of Parc des Exposition in Villepinte, a Parisian suburb. The project involved the addition of an exhibition hall with a garage (1999).

241

Chambre de Commerce et d'Industrie in Paris (competition 2006)

Centre Commercial Bercy 2 (387)

1987–1990
rue Escoffier (Charenton-le-Pont)
Renzo Piano Building Workshop

The five-story road-side shopping arcade lines an elongated atrium. Despite its location near the ring motorway and the A4 motorway, the building remains noticeable to motorists on the thoroughfares thanks to its "aluminum drop" appearance, inviting them to slow down as they approach Paris.

The aluminum climatic skin covers an area of two square kilometers. Public spaces inside are roofed with plate glass.

Conservatoire municipale (388) de musique et de danse

81, rue Armand Carrel / 19e
1987
Jacques Pouillon

This building is clearly inspired by the revolutionary style of architecture. The gigantic pylons that frame a fountain composed of three column segments of different diameters and a semicircular basin with a sculpted waterfall show

the influence of Ledoux and his fanciful designs.

The progressively recessed door jamb that leads to the entrance and dominates the entire façade also recalls the geometric reductivism of historical motifs in the revolutionary style.

Municipal administrative (389) building

1987–1993
94–96, quai de la Rapée / 12e
Aymeric Zubléna, Sechaud + Bossuyt

The large building presents itself as thoroughly modern, and develops its monumentality using modern elements: two elevator shafts form the axes of the asymmetrical façade and extend over the eave line like masts.

To the left, the façade is concave; to the right – straight. Thanks to a sliding façade plate out of metal and glass, the rounded section can also be closed off and transformed into a foyer.

This leaves the outline of the building open. The window rows become smaller at the top of the building to further underscore the illusion of larger size.

Bibliothèque Gutenberg (390)

1987–1991
8, rue de la Montagne-d'Aulas / 15e
Franck Hammoutène

The black concrete cube of the library is enveloped by metal bands, which make it appear only temporarily approachable.

The library is a hortus conclusus, and it-self encloses an inner garden. The build-ing, which appears so fortified from the outside, is filled with light inside thanks to its transparent roof.

Parc de Bercy (391)
1987–1997
quai de Bercy, rue Joseph-Kessel / 12e
Marylène Ferrand, Jean-Pierre Feugas,
Bernard Le Roy, Bernard Huet,
Ian Le Caisne, Philippe Raguin

GARDEN The park, on an expanse of 190 by 790 meters along the Seine, forms the core of the Bercy urban redevelop-ment area (cf. no. 452). Unlike archi-tecture gardens such as Parc de la Vil-lette (no. 404) and Parc André-Citroën (no. 399).

Parc de Bercy is rooted in the Roman-tic tradition of landscaped gardens. It in-tegrates structures extant from the time when Bercy was Paris's central wine warehouse, and complements them with new buildings. Many old trees have been preserved. Lawns extend near the Pal-ais Omnisports arena (no. 352), while nine thematic gardens form a second zone, and water architecture character-izes the expanses on either side of Rue Joseph-Kessel.

Viaduc des Arts (392)
1988–1995
avenue Daumesnil / 12e
Patrick Berger

The former Daumesnil viaduct, devel-oped by Albert Bassompierre-Sewrin and Marie-Émile Vuigner in 1859, was once part of the railway line connecting the suburb with Bastille Station.

When the later building was de-molished to make place for the Opéra Bastille (no. 366), the local authorities decided to preserve the thousand-meter viaduct, converting its sixty arches into boutiques and studios for designers and craftsmen.

The roadbed atop the viaduct was converted into a garden called theProm-enade plantée (no. 394).

The American Centre – (393)
Cinémathèque Française
1988–1994
51, rue de Bercy,
rue de Pommard / 12e
Frank Owen Gehry, François Jullien,
Roger Saubot

The stone façade of the Bercy redevelop-ment area's cultural center (c.f. no. 452) was a novelty in Frank Gehry's work. The lateral parallelepipeds along the street are a reference to traditional Pa-risian style. The less constrained façade towards Parc de Bercy (c.f. no. 391) fea-tures the curved, collaged and strongly modeled shapes that are characteristic of Gehry, however. According to the ar-

Arts (no. 392) and leads from Place de la Bastille to the Bois de Vincennes. It is connected with other gardens, including the small Jardin Hector-Malot (by Andreas Christo-Foroux) and the Jardin de Reuilly (by Pierre Colboc and Groupe Paysages), which covers a parking garage and is linked to the promenade by a footbridge.

École Spéciale d'Architecture, (395) extension
1988
254–256, boulevard Raspail / 14e
Cuno Burllmann,
Arnaud Fougeras-Lavergnolle

chitect, this underscores the opposition between French tradition and the American way of life.

The building remained unused for several years, but now houses a cinematheque and a film library. Massiomo Quendolo designed the stage, while Dominique Brard, Olivier Le Bras and Marc Quelen created the interior in 2003-2005.

Promenade plantée (394)
1988–1992
avenue Daumesnil / 12e
Philippe Mathieux (promenade),
Jacques Vergely (landscaping)

GARDEN A "planted promenade" starts atop the nine-meter-wide Viaduc des

The style of the annex strongly contrasts with the demure neo-Classical building designed in 1865 by Émile Trélat, the founder of Paris's free architecture school. Indeed, the modern structure emphasizes the design using a visible load-bearing frame and a glass façade. The freestanding staircase and all building materials are likewise visible.

Outstanding architects who have taught here include Auguste Perret, Robert Mallet-Stevens, Paul Virilio and Christian de Portzamparc.

Nursery (396)
1988
10, rue Delbet / 14e
Christian de Portzamparc

In 1884 a banker's daughter commissioned Paul Blondel to design medical facilities for the Furtado-Heine Foundation. Christian de Portzamparc recently developed a day care-center on the same plot, preserving the original portico and adding matching elements.

Portzamparc also used the brick-and-stone pattern and designed horizontal strips, thus creating a foreign principle that contrasts with the new building's elements, such as the staircase in the courtyard.

Scavengery (397)
1988–1989
17, rue Raymond-Radiquet / 19e
Renzo Piano Building Workshop

In contrast to the Centre Pompidou (no. 334), Renzo Piano here used a quiet style, similar to that of the contemporary IRCAM extension building (no. 384). Yet he did not conceal the city cleaning facilities behind a closed façade, but exposed them behind a glass front, as is common for office buildings.

Galvanized steel is another dominant element, as in the fire escape. A central mast and a large entrance gate identify the building as that of a public agency.

Institut National du Judo (398)
1988–2001
25, porte de Châtillon / 14e
Architecture Studio

The complex near the ring motorway consists of two elements: the sphere, which houses the Judo Institute, and a parallelepiped, which houses a budget hotel. A narrow passage between the two provides access to the interior. The high curved roof gives the institute building a distinctive appearance and makes it easily discernible, even from the sunken motorway.

The development phase was exceptionally long, as the plans were repeatedly altered: the arena was enlarged to seat 2500 rather than 1800, and the developers changed the accompanying building from offices to a hotel.

Parc André Citroën (399)
1988–1992
quai André Citroën / 15e
Gilles Clément, Alain Provost (landscaping), Patrick Berger, Jean-Paul Viguier, Jean François Jodry (architecture and viaduct), Patrick Berger (conservatories), RFR (engineers conservatories)

245

GARDEN The plot of the park located on the former Citroën automobile factory

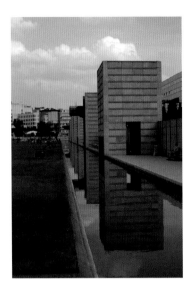

of the enormous growth of the Parisian outskirts during the second half of the 20th century.

After the 1965 expansion plan suggested the creation of satellite towns, the village of Evry was transformed into "ville nouvelle Evry" with 500,000 inhabitants. As in the banlieue itself, inhabitants belonging to the Christian confession make up a minority here, and the cathedral serves not only as a spiritual center of the satellite town, but also as a manifestation of the continuation of French culture. However, the structure's rotunda frees itself from the tradition of French cathedrals at the very first glance, acting as a confession-free focal point in the city's fabric.

Twenty-four linden trees have been planted on the tilted roof of the rotunda. References to the Christian architectural tradition are found only in the details. On the façade, these are the bells hung in a filigree steel framework, a cross and a modern interpretation of a portal. Inside, a wall curving upward into the interior space replaces the vaulting of the choir area. This also provides the building with an orientation. The on the opposite side of the choir is an elevated gallery that can be reached using side ramps and which frames the low entrance into the church.

grounds has a very irregular shape. This isn't immediately apparent because of its division into a large symmetrical section at the center of the park and smaller sections next to it. The central part features a large lawn, marked by the banks of the Seine and Patrick Berger's two green houses. These are constructed as glass versions of Greek temples, and their columns revert to the archetype of all building in their appearance resembling tree trunks. Between these two buildings there is a square with fountains. On the oblong sides of the lawn, small buildings are located along a canal to the north, and various themed gardens, which can be accessed only by a side path, adjoin it to the south. These gardens can be seen from the lawn. Even the irregular, separated areas each have received an independent character.

Cathédrale de la Résurrection (400)
1988–1995
place des Droits de l'Homme et du
Citoyen, cour Monseigneur Romeo (Evry)
Mario Botta

France's 91st cathedral was built for the diocese of Evry, Corbeil-Essonnes, outside the city proper, and is the first new building built for a diocese in more than 100 years. The building is a symbol

Canal+ (401)
1988–1991
2, rue des Cévennes,
quai André Citroën / 15e
Richard Meier & Partners

The headquarters of the Canal+ television station consist of two structures, one for the offices and the other for the broadcasting studios. The office building

the filigree steel cables that support the stadium's roof membrane.The arena is part of a complex that also includes the offices of the French Olympic Committee and various sports facilities with views of the main playing field from the first floor.

Tour Pacific and Pont Japon   (403)
1988–1993
La Défense
Kisho Kurokawa
Hugh Dutton (design concept bridge)

has a convex glass façade overlooking the Seine, while the broadcasting wing is lower with few openings. The white panels of the main façade are a trademark of the famous New York architect.

Stade Sébastien-Charléty   (402)
1988–1994
avenue de la Porte de Gentilly,
boulevard Kellermann,
avenue Pierre de Coubertin / 13e
Henri Gaudin, Bruno Gaudin

A succession of gigantic balancing concrete elements hold the bowl and stretch

The office building is a city gate leading to La Défense (no. 341). Coming from the direction of Valmy, a pedestrian bridge – a modern Taiko Bashi project – leads across the expressway into a hollow opening in the convex stone-clad façade which represents the European tradition. Crossing this entryway changes the perspective completely: The narrow, high slit opens onto a large roofed-over square with glazed façades.

The curtain wall represents shoji, the movable Japanese screens. A presentation of Japanese culture is found on the topmost of the building's 25 floors, and an abstract Japanese garden and a tea ceremony room are found on the roof, 90 meters above ground.

From slaughterhouse to museum's area: Parc de la Villette (404)

The architectural park on fifty-five hectares in the northeast of the city was developed in the 1980s and 1990s around a former slaughterhouse that had been closed down in 1974. The Great Hall, a filigree basilica of iron built by Jules de Merindol and Louis-Adolphe Janvier between 1863 and 1867, covers nearly two hectares alone. To the north of this structure, the architects Fournier, Semichom and Waulan began a larger concrete building in 1964, but the idea of meat production facilities within the city limits was abandoned in the 1980s: increasing delivery traffic to the site had seriously congested Paris' commuter ring. The mutton and veal butcheries were demolished, but the Minister of Culture at the time, Jack Lang, decided

to preserve the Great Hall in order to convert it into an auditorium and exhibition center. Robert & Reichen directed the works in 1985.

The abandoned building and adjoining land were then converted into an experimental park. Between 1980 and 1986, Adrien Fainsilber developed the Museum of Science and Industry (Avenue Corentin-Cariou 30) using the existing concrete shell of the abandoned slaughterhouse. The converted building features marked contrasts between the pre-existing structure and its new extension executed in filigree, high-tech style. RFR (Ian Ritchie, Martin Francis, Peter Rice) designed the supporting frame behind the suspended greenhouse façades. Due to elaborately glazed areas

Cité des Sciences et de l'Industrie

La Géode, a three-dimensional cinema in a geodesic dome

Bernhard Leitner's sound cylinder

gy. However, adults of both playful and serious disposition are also attracted to the permanent and special exhibitions, including those on architecture and design. The enormous interior offers room for large exhibits such as a small space station. Near the museum, Fainsilber and RFR also built a geodesic dome that houses a 3D cinema ("La Géode", 1980–1985).

The park itself, created in 1987–1991 by Bernhard Tschumi, is no less of an attraction. A masterpiece of deconstructivism, it refers to the tradition of "follies," or purely ornamental buildings, in landscape gardening. Tschumi's follies are bright red to complement the color of the lawn, and unlike their historic predecessors, they are not hidden in the landscape, but are set on the nodes of a strict quadratic grid. The thirty buildings, each ten meters on a side, display various shapes deconstructed from the base structure, some postmodern, some reminiscent of Russian constructivism. Unlike traditional gardens, this park is intended not for relaxation, but for activity, and for this reason the "follies"

and to the absence of other urban material in the direct vicinity, the building seems smaller than it is, although its volume is four times that of the Centre Pompidou. The documentation center behind the Cité was realized by Agence Dubesser-Lyon in 1986–1987.

French industrial businesses sponsored the museum in order to stimulate young people's enthusiasm for the multi-faceted world of science and technolo-

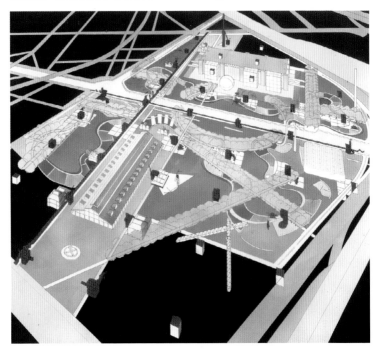

One of the follies

serve a wide range of functions. For example, the chairs designed by Philip Starck (1993), rotate. In contrast to the meandering paths of 19th-century landscape gardens, the walkways leading through La Villette Park are as straight as a ruler. With the exception of the meadows, the plants are either kept to the periphery or sunken into the landscape, like Alexandre Chemetoff's bamboo garden. The Galerie de la Villette with its curved roof extends through the park from north to south, alongside the Great Hall. It crosses the St. Martin Canal that flows through the park, and the bridge affords a particularly clear view of the garden's overall layout with the row of follies along the waterway. Other sights in the park include a decommissioned submarine; Bernhard Leitner's Cylindre Sonore (1987); a sculpture by Claes Oldenburg representing parts of gigantic bicycle wheels rising out of the earth; extensive playgrounds, including a dragon designed by Bernard Tschumi; Oscar Tusquets Blanca's Paul-Delouvrier Pavilion; and north of the museum the former veterinary building (Lundansky, 1867), which was remodeled as an exhibition hall in 1987 by Pierre du Besset, Dominique Lyon and Kazuroshi Morita.

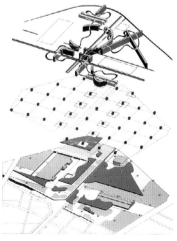

The layers of the parc

251

Residential house (405)
1989
42, rue de l'Ermitage / 20e
Atelier Lab

The architect Christophe Lab is known for his small single family houses found all over the city. They are quite individually formed, but are always guided by a radical basic idea. In this case, the facade appears very industrial, especially on the ground floor level, and is similar to the architect's own studio (21, rue de Tanger / 19e, 2001, no. 478).

Students' dormitory Croisset (406)
1989–1996
4–8, rue Francis-de-Croisset / 18e
Architecture Studio

The student dormitory's 352 rooms and 1-bedroom apartments are found in three sharply pointed wings with convex façades that are positioned in parallel to each other and face the city center. The windows partially protrude from the façade surface in order to improve light entry. At the ground floor level the residential wings adjoin a low perpendicular administrative wing. The fifth volume is shaped as a bar and is placed along the Boulevard Périphérique to act as a noise-blocking wall at the edge of the expressway. The 103 meter long and 33 meter high wing houses a large hall with a giant window facing the road. The sides of the "noise shield" are striped using bright signal colors, as if the building were a road sign.

Centre d'archives de Paris (407)
1989–1992
18, boulevard Sérurier / 19e
Henri Gaudin, Bruno Gaudin

The building near the Boulevard Périphérique with the hermetic structure of an archive presents itself closed off and sealed. The reading room is, however, filled with light and two tilted structural elements on the roof point like arrows down onto the public space. The dominant symmetry is consciously interrupted on the building's sides.

Bibliothèque nationale de France – Cité François-Mitterand (408)
1989–1996
quai de la Gare /13e
Dominique Perrault with
Gaelle Lauriot-Prévost

Highly visible from a long distance, the 100 meter high towers of the Bibliothèque Nationale de France set the rhythm for the redevelopment of the ZAC Rive Gauche. The complex measures 250,000 square meters and is one of the most revered projects of the 1980s and 1990s. Four glazed towers symbolizing opened books are grouped as a four-winged structural ensemble around a green yard. Stairs completely cover the downward sloping plot surrounding the buildings. Without acting as an independent structural element, the stairs function as a krepis, or step podium of a temple. Only after scaling these stairs does it become clear that they are already a part of the library. The towers house the book collection, while the reading rooms surround the yard.

Conservatoire National   **(409)**
Supérieur de Musique et
de Danse de Paris
1990–1995
209, avenue Jean-Jaurès / 19e
Christian de Portzamparc

The National Conservatory of Music and Dance is completely different: where the City of Music stands alone between the park and the street, the conservatory forms a smooth transition between the park and the surrounding blocks. To accomplish this, the building still takes on the orthogonal character of a city block, but its volume appears to dissolve under a large, overarching roof, successively leading it into the distance, away from the diagonally running street. Another wing extends as a terrace along Avenue du Nouveau Conservatoire opposite the Rossi apartments (no. 382). Its curving roof suggests a succession of rising and falling notes in a score. Smaller buildings stand in the courtyard behind the two main buildings. The conservatory facilities include an opera auditorium,

concert halls for organ and symphony orchestra, 105 practice rooms, 79 music classrooms, five dance rooms and residence halls for fifty students.

Tour Crystal   **(410)**
1990
7, quai André Citroën / 15e
Julien Penven, Jean-Claude Le Bail

The building in the Front-de-la-Seine hi-rise area was originally planned as a residential tower, but was converted to an office tower. By borrowing from the form of a crystal, it attempts to override the squareness of the late modernist towers. The completely glazed bronze-toned façade supports an image of a crystal that has grown out of the city.

Patrick Berger

Claude Vasconi

Manuelle Gautrand

Jean-Michel Wilmot

Architecture Studio

Jean Nouvel

Dominique Jacob

Paul Andreu   Christian de Portzamparc

Denis Valode   Jean Pistre

Jacques Anziutti   Renzo Piano

Brendan Macfarlan   Tom Mayne

Current tendencies – Paris is outgrowing itself (411)

Measuring merely 105 square meters, Paris is France's smallest département. More than two million people live within the confines of Boulevard Périphérique, a figure that went down from almost three million in 1901. The city proper lost one third of its inhabitants in the course of the last century while still retaining the world's highest population density of 20,000 persons per kilometer squared. An additional 4 million live in the petite couronne of the Parisienne region (which belongs to the directly bordering départements of Hauts-de-Seine, Seine-St.-Denis, Val-de-Marne), whose population nearly quadrupled in the same time period to reach 4.5 million. The population of greater Paris has also more than doubled, and the city now constitutes only a fifth of the population of the entire metropolitan region. This development did not only create an immense change in traffic volume, which daily congests Boulevard Périphérique with 250,000 vehicles and makes the RER and métro station Châtelet – Les Halles (1977) the city's most important entry point, but also led to the alienation of the so-called banlieue, the swelling "cursed" region located at a

30 kilometers distance from the city. These suburbs and satellite towns have turned into a hotspot of social problems like joblessness, crime and drugs, and came into international focus during the street violence that erupted here in 1993 and 2005. The advancement of these areas is the most important problem that must be solved by the city of Paris in the course of the next decade, although the areas themselves are located in other administrative zones. In the city itself, however, modernization is already in high gear. Following the building boom that took place under Mitterrand, the buildings left by Chirac were cause of considerably less sensation (Musée du Quai Branly, no. 454, restoration of Grand palais, no. 225, redevelopment of Palais de la Porte Dorée for Cité de l'immigration, no. 284). Due to the shortened presidential office tenure, Sarkozy could also end up failing to immortalize himself with a large number of state projects, even though the completion of the Philharmonie (no. 475 and the Jardin des Halles (no. 336) that is finally ready to be realized will fall on his term. During Chirac's office, urban development moved forward using ZAC

left: NOX / Lars Spuybroek, Paris Brain – the
city resolves itself

right: Morphosis, Tour Phare – Working
in the 21st Century

(no. 452) instead of funding single large projects. The completed ZAC Bercy located on the grounds of the city's former wine warehouse (no. 431), as well as the giant ZAC Rive Gauche around the new National Library (no. 408) are milestones in modern restructuring of former industrial areas in their variegated and still comprehensive design. In the course of their completion, the new plan local d'urbanisme went into effect in 2006. In it, a maximum building height of 25 meters is required for the city center, 31 meters for other districts, and 37 at Périphérique. The new National Library, however, is an architecturally postulated building with an exceptional height, which combines an international trend of a new elegance which, following Postmodernism and in parallel to Deconstructivism and BLOB (no. 456), takes up simple forms of classical Modernism and combines them with a refined surface design. Neither the materials and texture of the surface, nor the Postmodern decoration, often double-layered, are used to differentiate individual parts of the building, but instead almost the entire volume seems enveloped, reminiscent of Christo's "wrappings." A wrinkle-free melting together of individual structural parts occurs. In contrast to the bitter style wars of the past decades, this tendency succeeded in incorporating Deconstructivism and Blobitecture; while the first lost its collage-like additive quality and turned to a synthesis of divergent forms under a uniform surface, the second developed its binary multiplicity from the continuum of a uniform skin. In the light of rising environmental awareness, archaic eco-architecture of the 1980s and programmatic high-tech of the 1970s turn to a pragmatic use of sustainable construction methods and technology implementation in order to save energy, a trend which adjusts to any style. Vertical gardens, which simultaneously offer compact greenery and an attention-getting façade texture, are an especially prominent expression of this coming together of different trends in Paris. In August 2008 mayor Bertrand Delanoë enacted a plan, which permitted the construction of high-rise buildings within the city center. As the first one the Triangle Tower by Herzog & de Meuron is supposed to come into being at the external border of the 15th district.

257

Le Monde Siège Social, (412)
former
1990
13–15, rue Falguière / 15e
Pierre du Besset, Dominique Lyon

The building stands on the location of a former garage whose ramp has been reused as an open atrium in the office building. The building façade concavely curves from the street level and back. At the heart of the building is a 600 square meters entry hall which is meant to encourage contact between the employees and readers. The remaining spatial structure is determined by openness and offers room for informal contacts. DEGW/Espace Architecture designed the interior.

Funiculaire de Montmartre (413)
1990–1991
place Suzanne-Valadon,
rue du Cardinal-Dubois / 18e
François Deslaugier, Roger Tallon

The Cogwheel train moving along the long stairs (app. 200 steps) leading to the Sacré Cœur church (no. 209) was constructed in 1900. In spite of 2.5-time increase in capacity, it is often overburdened. Travelling at a 36°, the funicular needs 40 seconds for the 36-meter vertical climb. The train stations are by Deslaugier, who was invited by Roger Tallon to join the project as an architect. Tallon, who designed the TGV and the Météor Métro line, designed the trains.

Fondation Cartier pour (414)
l'Art Contemporain
1990–1994
261, boulevard Raspail / 14e
Jean Nouvel, Emmanuel Cattani & Associés, Ove Arup & Partners (engineers)

The foundation houses an exhibition hall for contemporary art and office space. It is a largely glazed frame construction with two façades – the actual building volume is recessed into the plot, and a second, incongruent glass wall is placed at a distance in front along the street line. Structurally, this free-standing wall references the building. It is hardly possible to talk of a single volume, because all elements except for the floors consist of glass and extremely refined vertical elements. Five thousand meters squared of glass and 650 tons steel were used to build the building volume and the street façade. The existing greenery, including a cedar tree planted by the former resident of the Chateaubriand property, was preserved between the two layers. The building appears to dissolve in a glazed park. Garden design is by Lothar Baumgarten.

Post office and (415)
post apartments
1991–1993
113, rue Oberkampf / 11e
Frédéric Borel

The narrow but deep plot, typical for Paris, has been opened up in the course of this project. Approaching from the street, a small terrace is reached after walking underneath the building volume; this terrace offers access to the 80 residential units and a view of the greened yard located further inside. The yard is surrounded by buildings which, in addition to being formally separated from one another, create distance between them using variegated massing. Asymmetry and variety of forms were used to make the new structure appear as an organic entity.

Nursery (416)
1990–1991
13bis, rue de Rouen / 19e
Pierre Granveaud, Pablo Katz

On a tightly surrounded plot, the building receives light by splitting into two volumes separated by a "light corridor." The façade consists of a black mosaic in a strict metal grid. The free distribution of slightly protruding windows and ran-

domly dispersed white stones breaks out of the grid, loosening it up.

La Tribune (417)
1991
46, rue Notre-Dame-des-Victoires / 2e
Jean-Jacques Ory

The wall of Ory's building located in the financial and news quarter in the 2nd arrondissement is almost fully dissolved into window surface. Nonetheless, the radically modern design fits in quite

well with the surrounding 19th century structures as the strongly sectioned façades appear as a high-tech variation on the theme. Horizontal and vertical grouping continue the rhythm of the pilasters and cornices, and the windows are subdivided similarly to traditional lattice windows.

Senior living apartments (418)
1991–1998
18–20, rue de l'Orillon / 11e
Architecture Studio

The building for senior citizens forms a cour d'honneur: a three-winged ensemble around a closed-off green yard with prominent side wings that reach toward the middle wing in a concave swing. While the middle section containing the main communication structures appears almost completely closed-off, the wing façades are fully glazed.

Behind the glass shield and visible from the street are corridors that form access to the 90 apartments. As in houses with the "golden lane" structure, the apartment doors are placed in well-lit locations. Each unit is individualized using bright colors, strengthening the resident's identification with his or her apartment.

Hôtel de Police (419)
1991
78, avenue Daumesnil,
23, rue de Rambouillet / 12e
Manolo Nuñez-Yanowsky

At first glance, the Police precinct appears to be 1920s Art Déco, but details like the grating on the ground floor inform the viewer of its true time of origin. Truly impressive are the figures that materialize from the recessed upper stories. These are magnified copies of the dying slave created in 1513-1515 by Michelangelo for the grave of Pope Julius II that is found in the Louvre (no. 49). The figures represent the torment of humanity, but by cutting out a triangle on their upper torsos to let in light, Nuñez-Yanowsky included a symbol of hope and redemption into the figures.

Social housing (420)
1992
19, impasse Charrière,
rue de la Chanzy / 11e
Massimiliano Fuksas

In contrast to the redevelopment of the Îlot Candie (no. 383) in the vicinity, Fuksas relies on traditional motifs for filling this gap in the block structure. The original factory façades remaining on the left side are translated into a modern version with glazed fronts. On the right, a clinker façade fits in with the neighboring building.

Here, rounded balconies reach to the middle section and accent the corner situation. The middle is separately de-

seen even in 19th century ground floor compositions. Above a platband, they support merely three bundled pilasters that structure the glazed façade. The cubes mirror the horizontal segmentation of the façade.

Compared to the glazed middle, the sides are massive, the way the façade that is supported by the Atlases is expected to be. However, the cast iron section carried by the figures is executed with Gothic slenderness.

veloped as well, indicating a sectioned-off structure.

Gallery and office building (421)
1992
34, avenue Matignon / 8e
Jean-Jacques Fernier

The building's access is articulated by two Atlas figures of proportions seldom

Postal center (422)
1993
18–20, boulevard de la Chapelle / 18e
Architecture Studio

At the intersection of divergent city spaces (bridge spanning sunken railroad tracks, elevated train, street) the building attempts to position itself as a source of order.

Toward the street, it creates an autonomous black surface with a white wedge and a thin yellow stripe. The emblematic blue-and-yellow client's colors are presented on a large scale in the direction of the rails on the most prominent buildings.

Office building (423)
1993–1999
16–18, quai de Loire / 19e
Philippe Gazeau

This Le Monde building (no. 480) also has a large glazed convex façade that is oriented to the Bassin de La Villette.

Above the fifth floor, the rounding abruptly stops and a new glazed curvature starts above this break, creating an illusion of a roof section above the eave line.

Maison de la Culture du Japon (424)
á Paris
1993–1997
quai Branly, rue de la Fédératon / 15e
Masa Yuki Yamanaka and Armstrong Associates

In contrast to the Australian Embassy (no. 349) across the street, this building is completely transparent. Containing a theater, a library and exhibition spaces on a small plot, the building appears larger than it really is.

This is a result of an overarching form, a curvature that follows the street bend and the filigree, story-spanning round pillars in a wide traverse. In spite of the constricted space, a light-filled atrium could be placed behind the screen façade.

Post office and (425)
post apartments
1993
13, rue Saint-Jean-Baptiste-de-la-Salle / 6e
Canale 3

The building is a part of the postal service's project to provide their em-

ployees with affordable housing built by young architects. The central axis of the aluminum façade is left open, letting in light inside the structure's volume.

Two air shafts flank the passage like columns in the front section of the facade, while the rest of the ground floor is recessed below the upper stories. Apartment layouts are expandable from one to up to three rooms and can adjust to the changing circumstances of young first-time renters.

Holiday Inn (426)
1993
218–228, avenue Jean-Jaurès / 19e
Christian de Portzamparc

Across from the Conservatory and the Cité de la Musique (no. 371), Christian de Portzamparc built a building housing a hotel and offices. Together, these buildings form the gate to the city when exiting Boulevard Périphérique from the Porte de Pantin. The interacting forms prevent the smaller volumes from blocking the access to the Parc de la Vilette. Rounded corners and a light shade of stone that defines the many-storied plinth zone on the hotel take up the height of the buildings along the park.

Collège Georges Brassens (427)
1994
51–55, rue d'Hautpoul / 19e
Manolo Nuñez-Yanowsky

The school building displays a wide range of forms, meant to fire up the students' imagination.
In the context of other references to architectural history, the large 'floating ledge,' a long, purely decorative metal framework, appears as a blending of a jag frieze and a cantilever from Russian Constructivism. It optically closes off the school yard on one of its three sides.

Social housing (428)
1994–1999
131, rue Pelleport,
15, rue des Pavillons / 20e
Frédéric Borel

The apartment tower standing on an elevation at an intersection is a real eye-catcher. A calm façade acts as rue Pelleport's point-de-vue, while the side

views with sections that bear intense colors and are staggered against each other are completely dissolved. The surfaces completed as slants, displacements and cants in yellow, orange and brown and as large metal sections recall a vibrant, organically created conglomerate of buildings. The apartments have very individualized lay-outs and each occupy a whole floor.

Stade de France (429)
1994–1998
Saint Denis La Plaine Cedex
SCAU (Aymeric Zubléna, Michel Macary),
Michel Regembal, Claude Costantini, Rice
Francis Ritchie (engineers)

The 80,000-capacity stadium was created for the 1998 Football World Cup on a plot of industrial waste land to the north of the city. The structure is 35 meters high on the outside, while inside the field is sunken by 11 meters into the ground. The 17,000-ton roof, whose form is inspired by the shape of an airplane wing in cross section, is suspended from pillars standing around the stadium. The shape minimizes the area of wind resistance. Rice Francis Ritchie assisted the architects in the role of an engineer. The stadium's remarkable feature is its lower tribunes, which are movable in a way that was earlier possible only in sports halls. This creates a

263

football field that is narrowly surrounded by tribunes, as was the express wish for the WC, but with the option to easily accommodate other events (light athletics, performances, concerts, etc.).

Post office and (430)
Post apartments – Couple-plus
1994
132, rue des Pyrénées / 20e
Michel Bourdeau

In the context of the apartment construction program of the postal service (cf. no. 425), the architect found a façade which overrides the fine fragmentation of the apartments inside, and gives volume to the street front. The curved fronts shield the apartments from the city and its noise while offering narrow, framed views of it from the inside.

Commercial Center (431)
Bercy Village
1994–2000
Cour Saint-Emilion / 12e
Valode & Pistre

ENSEMBLE In the middle of the ZAC Bercy (no. 452) on Cour Saint-Emilion, a portion of the city's former wine warehouse was preserved. The house from ca. 1880 was used to store wine shipped on the Seine before it passed customs control. Today, the completely restored structure is occupied by restaurants and

stores. While the pedestrian zone at the Cour is dominated by older buildings, the opposite side has taller new structures. They consist of a modern framework with glass and wood infills, but which still maintain their reference in shape to the older buildings. The architects also created the UGC cinema (no. 447) at the end of the Cour.

Le Jardin Atlantique (432)
1994
place des Cinq-Martyrs-du-Lycée-Buffon / 15e
François Brun, Michel Peña

GARDEN A small garden oasis can be found on the roof of the Montparnasse

train station (by Baudoin, Cassan de Marien, Lopez, Saubot). Here, the densely populated 15th arrondissement finds the sorely needed open lawns and various gardens.

The gardens take up the landscape of Southern France as their theme, reflecting the direction in which the trains leaving the station are bound. Despite a limited availability of space, the gardens appear to be large thanks to successful nestling of space.

Street furniture (433)
1994
Everywhere in Paris

The new bus stations, whose predecessors began Jean-Claude Decaux's career in the 1950s, were designed by Norman Foster. The company JC Decaux specializes in free installation, operation, cleaning and maintenance of street utilities and is financed by the associated advertising.

In addition to the bus stations, the company also operates advertising columns, illuminated city maps, fully automatic self-cleaning toilets and tourist signs (design by Philippe Stark). The lat-

est addition to this list is the Vélib. Other well-known architects like Mario Bellini, Philip Cox, Peter Eisenman, Peter Lanz & Horst Weber, Porsche, Martin Szekely and Jean-Michel Wilmotte design for the internationally active group.

Extension, (434)
Palais des Congrès
1994–1999
place de la Porte Maillot / 17e
Christian de Portzamparc

The extention of the conference and convention center erected by Guillaume Gillet in 1969-1974 gave Porte Maillot a new focal point. Being merely a connecting area, the square on the city edge could have hardly developed a life of its own. Christian de Portzamparc adorns

it with a calculated roadside architecture, which can be perceived even from behind the wheel.

The large, outward-turned building is divided into two volumes, between which the auditorium is visible. A wide promenade connects the building horizontally and divides its height like a large city balcony. Several flights of stairs lead down to street level without supports of their own.

Apartments (435)
1995–1996
17–19, rue des Suisses,
4, rue Jonquoy / 14e
Herzog & de Meuron

The unified and minimal façade design make this street corner-hugging residen-

tial block a typical example of buildings by the Swiss architecture office. Folding lattice shutters with a full-story height completely cover the upper floors, interrupted solely by strips of concrete. These are the front edges of the balcony floors. The vertical rectangular grate elements and narrow balconies appear as a modernized version of Haussmann repertoire of forms, while the facade itself is a thoroughly modern glazed front.

Notre-Dame de l'Arche (436)
d'Alliance
1996–1998
81, rue d'Alleray / 15e
Architecture Studio

On one of its sides, the building body is completely closed off – a cube with a repeating façade structure and an access at the top floor. Twelve columns, a reference to the apostles, create the appearance of supporting the upper story above the baptism chapel on the ground floor. On the other side, the building is completely open, but is enveloped by a loose lattice structure, creating the appearance of the inner structure being on display inside the façade's glass case. The belfry consists completely of this lattice element. Thus, the first new church finished after the construction of Saint-Eloi (no. 329) continues in its tradition of modern sacral architecture.

Apartments Totem – (437)
Tour de Flandres
1996
27–29, avenue de Flandre,
6, rue du Maroc / 19e
Tectône with Jean Lamude

The small apartment tower asserts itself in the midst of Flandres Avenue's collection of tall buildings by optically splitting its volume into three slanted tower segments that appear to rotate due to their tilted arrangement. The red, white and gray sections take on the colors of the surroundings. The composition references Suprematism from Malevich's architectons.

Apartments (438)
1996
11, rue Émile-Durkheim / 13e
Francis Soler

In the context of the ZAC Rive Gauche, various apartment buildings could be constructed, such as this one on the side street of the new National Library (no. 452). The completely glazed façade behind the continuous filigree balconies is partially covered with screen prints to reduce sun exposure. Multiple nature motifs as well as details taken from historical art works are found among the featured patterns.

Musée national des Arts (439)
Asiatiques – Guimet, rebuilding
1996–2001
6, place d'Iéna / 16e
Henri Gaudin, Bruno Gaudin

The building was created for the Meeting of Industrialists by Charles Terrier in 1888. After it was turned into a national museum and became fuller and fuller and its appearance aged, reorganization plans were drawn up.

The monumental Hellenic Eclecticist façade was listed, but the architects were given a free hand with most of the interior. As a new main connection, a complex staircase was added behind the rotunda, enabling countless views into the museum's various sections. Openings in the rooms offer views from one culture to the next.

Dominique Perrault
*1953 in Clermont-Ferrand (440)

Dominique Perrault studied architecture, urban planning and history. In 1981 he opened his first office in Paris, followed by branches in Berlin, Luxemburg and Barcelona under the name DPA, Dominique Perrault Architecture.

He quickly gained international fame with his École supérieure d'ingénieurs en électronique et électrotechnique (ESIEE) in Marne-la-Vallée (1984). This building already displays the architect's radical minimalist approach as well as the typical understanding of the building's integration into the urban structure. The access to the flat, pulled-down in the direction of the street building, behind which hide a transverse connecting body and multiple perpendicularly positioned bar volumes, opens up as a semicircle for a traffic roundabout in the style of a Baroque castle approach.

The New National Library (no. 408), whose four corner buildings placed on a step-shaped understructure define an empty space in the middle, is even more radical. At the center of the newly developed area, below the understructure, is a "hortus conclusus," a hidden garden.

The access to the elevated, but hardly perceptible building is also similar in the case of the Berlin Olympic complex of the Vélodrome and the swimming pool (1992-1999). Both sports facilities are enveloped in metal sheeting – one disc-shaped and the other rectangular, and both appear as artificial forms that were sunk into the surrounding gardened development, protruding only one meter above the artificial lawn plateau. Surface unification, as seen here as well as in the Paris library, is an additional typical feature that complements the radical overall geometric shape, even if it is an outlined void.

Perrault, who once wanted to become a physical expressionist artist, now passionately creates buildings whose highly formalized appearance transforms them into artworks within the city's image. In this respect, Théâtre Mariinsky II in Sankt Petersburg alone does not fit into this frame. The design tends to be more deconstructivist with its interruptions in volume, but returns to consistent unification with the forceful pattern of its façade openings. The building could be viewed as a unification of interruptions. This pattern appears like a veil thrown over a building – a twin of the historical theater.

Hiding and obscuring is another motif hinted at by library's void and the sunken forms and metal screens of the structures in Berlin. The Ewha Women's University in Seoul will be recognizable as a building with façades only from a canyon, which is itself created by the structure's volume. Minimalist art is often integrated into Perrault's architecture. There is the large "Earth Axis" looking out from the ESIEE roundabout island by Piotr Kowalski. The expansion of the Innsbruck City Hall (1996-2002) features equally minimalist coloring of glass panels by Daniel Buren on the roof spanning the historical courtyard. The printed glass panels on the central City Hall tower by Peter Kogler resist the uniformity of architecture with their coiling nooses and irregular progression of pipes. If this piece were executed in color, comparisons could be made to the tangles of Centre Pompidou (no. 334), but its purely black design succeeds in integrating its into the controlled architecture.

In 1997, Perault was awarded the Mies van der Rohe Award, and today the multiple branches of his office employ circa 60 architects, engineers and designers. Recently his work has often featured stacking of similar geometric volumes. This is the case in Fukoku Life Tower in Osaka (2007-2010),which starts at the top as an orderly glass tower, but whose panels begin to escape their joints with increasing intensity with each lower story, beginning to rotate and slide behind each other, displacing the lower floors from the façade's perimeter.

Master plan of the thermae in San Pellegrino, Italy

School (441)
1996–2000
6–8, rue de la Moskowa / 18e
Frédéric Borel

The school is the main building located on the new square created by the ZAC Moskova project (cf. no. 452). On top of the base structure encased in slightly buckling granite rests the white orthogonal upper story. The shape and arrangement of windows animate the façade. The volume presentation is more complex on the side streets. For Frédéric Borel, the easy readability of the main view is explained by the fact that the architect wanted to make the building comprehensible even for grade-schoolers down to its details.

Meditation room (442)
for the UNESCO
1996
place de Fontenoy / 7e
Tadao Ando

At the end of the UNESCO headquarters' Japanese gardens, the Japanese architect

has created a non-confessional meditation room. It was built as a symbol of peace to commemorate the 50th anniversary of UNESCO's founding. The rotunda with a diameter of 33 meters displays Tadao Ando's reduced design language. A consciously elongated path leads the visitor from the mundane into a space without doors, and outside again.

In the room, high concrete walls block the outside world almost completely, while the circular layout redirects the visitor back into him or herself. The walls consist of fine, homogenous concrete that is typical for Ando; the floor is of concrete that was exposed to nuclear bombardment in Hiroshima, and later decontaminated.

Passerelle Solférino (443)
1997–1999
Seine / 1er, 7e
Marc Mimram

The bridge closes a gap in crossings over the Seine in the city center. It consists of two arched flights, one at the street level and the other below, connecting to the river promenade.

The arches of different diameter meet at the apex, allowing pedestrians to switch levels.

Fire station Saint-Fargeau (444)
1997–2000
47, rue Saint-Fargeau,
avenue Gambetta / 20e
Vincent Brossy

Following the tradition of engineer-architect collaborations like the buildings from Edouard Albert (33, rue Croulebarbe with engineer Jean-Louis Sarf) or the Centre Pompidou (no. 334), this buildings is readily recognizable as a highly

occupied by the French Electrical Works. The center of this panel measuring 20 meters in diameter marks the meeting point of the esplanade axis and the seven-degree axial deviation of the Grande Arche de La Défense (no. 377). Seen from above, the tower has a corner at this point, but the circle of the canopy cuts into the tower's volume at an angle that results in concave vaulting of the tower. This vaulting begins below the canopy in its full width and tapers off on its way to the top corner of the building.

Notre-Dame-d'Espérance (446)
1998
47, rue de la Roquette,
rue du Commandant Lamy / 11e
Bruno Legrand

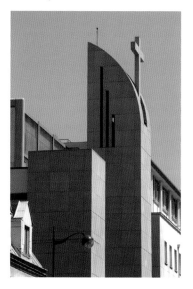

technical construction. The apartments for firemen were created between older structures and were placed on stilts, as the lower level had to continue being used as a firehouse and as a parking and training grounds for the firemen. Two 85 meter-long beams hold up the lightweight metal structure that projects over the street.

Vertical elements (supporting or resting) and horizontal double-T supports create a grid, whose proportions are reminiscent of a column-and-cornice arrangement.

Tour EDF (445)
1997–2001
La Défense
Henry Cobb – Pei, Cobb, Freed & Partners,
Jean Rouit, Roger Saubot

The large, circular canopy is the most prominent element of the office building

The successor of an Art-Déco-church announces its continued function as a parish church with a large cross above the tower. From a close-up perspective, however, it takes more than one glance to recognize this as a sacral structure due to the volume's façades being so strongly integrated into the building line-up of the intersection.

The display containing a Holy Virgin figure (from the predecessor buildings, Mlle Heuvelmans, 1930) and a wide double-leafed door with four evangelist sculptures (Pierre Degraw) reveal the church's identity. Closer inspection reveals numerous details that point to the building's true function: numerous inscriptions cover the building and the glass facade (Guillaume Saalburg): Gospels according to Mark, Matthew and Luke on the exterior, Old Testament along the side street. The calligraphy is by Franck Lalou. The texts are repeated as boustrophedons, changing their direction row by row. Inside, more inscriptions from the Gospel according to John and Pauline Epistles are found.

Additionally, of note are the rounded altar by François Cante Pacos and the cross by Nicolas Alquin, whose horizontal crossbar is indicated solely by three golden fields, the central on the vertical bar, and the lateral on the galleries.

UGC – Ciné-Cité Bercy (447)
1998
114, quai de Bercy,
cour Saint-Emilion / 12e
Valode & Pistre, Alberto Cattani,
Pierre Chican

The cinema is celebrated as a paradigm of 21st century movie theaters. Its 18 halls offer a 450-seat capacity. The large complex concludes the intimate Bercy Village in the direction of the Seine and simultaneously extends the Saint-Emilion through its body, leading up to a platform along the river with the Saint-Emilion.

The building thus split in two, is then further subdivided into additional rooms. However, the individual halls and connective spaces remain clearly

readable within the volume. These individual elements are veiled by uniform façade surfaces. These consist of metal netting and lamellas, which standardizes the appearance at a distance without hiding the complex structure from up close. Luminescent stainless steel mesh panels reveal the inner operations bathed in blue light.

Saint-Luc (448)
1999
passage Wattieaux,
80, rue de l'Ourcq / 19e
Pierre-Henri Montel, Christian Basset

The glazed stairwell inside the façade lets the onlooker assume that the building is an apartment house. The stairs, however, reach only to the gallery on the church's second floor. Only the cross, towering over the neighboring building and the belfry, visible on the upper section of the façade indicate that this is a sacral structure.

A second glance reveals many details that confirm this function: inscriptions from the Gospel according of Luke are on the glass panes; the glass wall is sectioned into four using thin "pillars," creating a window row for each evangelist. The door is found in the Luke section.

On the interior, simple means are used to create a sacral atmosphere in the high-ceilinged hall. Holy water vessels, the lectern, altar and the tabernacle are made of aluminum in a strictly reduced design (Bernard Malaquis Mato).

Passerelle Simone-de-Beauvoir (449)
1999–2006
Seine /12e, 13e
Dietmar Feichtinger Architekten

The pedestrian bridge connects the Quartier Tolbiac, where the new National Library (no. 408) is located, to the ZAC Bercy (no. 452). In contrast to the Passerelle Solférino (no. 443), which connects two arched bridges, this bridge consists of an arch and a suspended construction, which pierce each other twice. The flights also begin at two different city levels, one of the four ramps starting at the base of the new library. Here, arched and suspension bridges – taken individually, both conventional construction types – reciprocally prop each other up. RFR (M. Kutterer, H. Bardsley) architects assisted in planning the load-bearing structure for this project.

Ateliers d'artistes (450)
1999
109–115, avenue de Flandre,
184, rue de Crimée / 19e
Patrick Berger, Jacques Anziutti,
Janine Galiano

At an intersection of two variegated avenues built up with different heights, the orthogonal building with a clear lay-out has a pleasant appearance. Upon closer examination, however, the complex design comes to the fore. The four-meter long window rows of both of the middle stories each consist of two windows, whose lower window leads into the residential area, while the upper provides lighting for the artist's studio. The wood of their frames is repeated on the upper story in dense rows, and is reminiscent of the August Doebel art center in the rue Philidor (2003). The gray border of the upper story windows is picked up in the base story. Studios and artist apartments each have separate entrances in the back.

Office building (451)
1999–2003
148, rue de l'Université,
10–12, rue Surcouf,
1, avenue Robert Schumann / 7e
François S. Braun et Associés

The architectural buro known for its restructuring of historical buildings created an office building here. It is striking due to its narrow façade which develops a slight curve independently from the volume. The actual orthogonal volume becomes visible in isolated strips and on the ground floor.

The outer façade arches outward like a sheet of paper reaching towards a roof that is independent of the building and covers balconies. This quarter-barrel is simultaneously reminiscent of Haussmann-era roofing.

273

The ZACs – reshaping the city (452)

The Zones d'Aménagement Concertées (ZAC, areas of concentrated rebuilding) are a city planning tool based on a 1967 law. They are successors of the successors of the Zones à urbaniser en priorité (ZUP, priority urbanization areas), which especially contributed to the creation of the grands ensembles between the 1950s and 1970s. ZACs, in turn, are characterized by smaller or more fragmented planning. In most cases, the architect creates a master plan and several others execute it. Thus, for example, in ZAC Porte d'Asnieres, the Quartier Hauts de Malesherbes plan (Boulevard Berthier / Avenue de la porte d'Asnières / 17e) was created by Christian de Portzamparc in 2003. It is here that he could realize his idea of the open block construction: separate multi-family homes encircle a common sunk garden and share the free space between them.

The recreation space planning is originally from the Jardin des Hauts de Malesherbes by Arpentère. The best-known structure of the ensemble are Les Jardins de Saussure von Eduard François. At the city "gates" some of the ZACs were turned into GPRUs (Grand Projet de Renouvellement Urbain), where infrastructural renewal played a big role. The most significant finished ZAC is the ZAC Bercy, which was placed in the focus of local politics in the 1970s as part of the "rééquilibrage Paris vers de l'Est," or eastern city renewal. It is divided into an older western section to the north of the Parc de Bercy (no. 391) and a newer eastern section around the Place des Vins de France, including Bercy Village.

The ZAC Rive Gauche is much larger, and its planning has been going on since 1988, but only since 2003 has it been finally taking shape. On both sides of the Avenue de France the district has been split into 7 smaller areas. A lively neighborhood is forming on and around railroad tracks and industrial land, with the New National Library (no. 408) at its center. Living, working and studying are all in close quarters.

Since the completion of this ZAC, inhabitant participation plays a more prominent role than before. The border of ZAC Rive gauche to the Seine blurs with port restructuring by the Port Autonome de Paris and Gare de Austerlitz redevelopment by Arup and Jean Nouvel. The districts and the planers can be found in the appendix (A3).

Masterplan of Quartiers Hauts de Malesherbes, Christian de Portzamparc, 2003

View of the steady growing ZAC Rive Gauche

Tower Flower (453)
Les Jardins de Saussure
1999–2004
8, rue Stéphane Grappelli,
23, rue Albert Roussel / 17e
Edouard François

The apartment building grants the city residents' wish to have a green balcony in an unusual way. The façades with continuous balconies have large flower pots placed along each one. A total of 380 automatically watered plants grow in these containers, most of them bamboo, but one pot is also left at the discretion of the occupants of the 30 apartments. The pots, like the entire building, consist of fine concrete, lending a monolithic appearance to the entire object. Patrick Blanc, the vertical gardens specialist, assisted the architect.

Musée du Quai Branly (454)
(Musée des arts premiers)
1999–2008
55, quai Branly,
198, rue de l'Université / 7e
Jean Nouvel

The new museum brings together art objects from non-European cultures that were earlier distributed among the city's various museums. The building is located in a generous garden and the ground floor remains to a large extent open, letting the gardens connect underneath the building. The 18,000 square meters garden designed by Gilles Clément takes various types of vegetation as its theme. A large glass wall (12 meters high, 200 meters long) shields the garden from the heavily-trafficked Quai Branly.

The 800 square meters of the green wall to the west of the progression of Quai Branly by Patrick Blanc are composed of 15,000 specimens of 150 different plants from Japan, China, America and Central Europe. The wall is located on one of the three new buildings. Inside the main building, a complex path leads through the open exhibition areas and into cabinets that become visible from the outside, appearing as closed, colorful cubes through the glazed northern façade. As a contrast, the red-brown façade on the southern side is characterized by horizontal window blinds.

In the middle of this façade is a rounded element with three rows of windows and aluminum blinds. These

ensure that maximum light reaches the exhibition area with minimum direct sun by rotating in response to the sun's movements. The interior lighting is by Yann Kersalé.

Boutique Momi (455)
2000
29, rue des Saints-Pères / 6e
Yoshio Sakurai

The city's most unusual jewelry boutique is a result of restructuring of a simple house entrance taking up exactly one meter squared.

The tiny space is completely encased in white panels forming a strict square grid along small metal bars. The small sales counter is integrated into the room just like the minimalist display cabinet on top.

The architectural jewel gleams behind a tinted door.

Restaurant Georges (456)
2000
19, rue Beaubourg / 4e
Jakob + Macfarlane

As a free-standing group of small buildings, the Georges is found in the top story of the Centre Pompidou (no. 334). The café is considered an incunabulum of Blobitecture (binary large object). In computer science, this concept represents simply enormous chunks of data and is a metaphor for amorphous and indefinable objects. These buildings are formed in such a way, that their complex

dimensions cannot be described using simple mathematical expressions (formulas, vectors, numbers).

Here, the kitchen, the sanitary infrastructure and cabins are articulated using such BLOBs and are freestanding within the space designed by Piano and Rogers. The architects completed the Pink Bar in 2007.

Kiosque des noctambules (457)
2000
place Colette / 1er
Jean-Michel Othoniel

The sparkling kiosk for night owls was created as a new entrance to the Palais-Royal-Musée du Louvre metro station to commemorate the 100 year anniversary of the Metro. The small building consists of two domes on stilts, a grate and a bench. The complete building is made up of aluminum spheres and circa 800 colorful hand-blown "pearls" and discs of Murano glass. The artist Jean-Michel Othoniel assisted Geoffroy Aurrousseau.

Siège EMI France (458)
2000-2005
118-124, rue du Mont Cenis / 18e
Renzo Piano Building Workshop

Four new buildings have been built on former industrial grounds, whose formulation is based on the typology of Parisian factory houses. Originally, various record companies were to move in here. The façades are clad in terracotta and the interiors are illuminated through large windows and additionally with shed roofs. Bridges form connections to two older buildings above a surrounding garden.

Métro Bibliothèque nationale (459)
de France
2000
13e
Antoine Grumbach, Pierre Schall

The large station was the terminal of the new line 14 until its extension further away from the city in 2007. The Linie Méteor (MÉTro-Est-Ouest-Rapide) is a completely automatically controlled underground train.

Antoine Grumbach's station is the most monumental on the line: segmented arches resting on round pilers in basilica-sized halls, a striated wall, amphitheater-like stairs – these are just some of the architectural historical motifs that are taken up here, creating a festive space able to conduct large streams of visitors, contrasting the narrow walkways of the older stations and the functional sobriety of the postwar ones.

Librairie Florence Loewy (460)
2001
9-11, rue de Thorigny / 3e
Jakob + MacFarlane

The bookstore specializing in art and artist books itself became an 'environment' thanks to an appointed interior design. The voluminous outline shapes of the shelves appear as sections of rope emerging out of the floor and ceiling. Their division into separate shelf boards follows a strict square grid, appearing as if the levels of surrounding coordinates have materialized themselves following Theo van Doesburg's comprehension of space.

However, in contrast to outlines that could have been created from these surfaces by De Stijl, these are organic, flowing forms of BLOB that determine where the grid appears. In places, the forms create secondary rooms.

Mur pour la paix (461)
2001
champ de Mars / 7e
Clara Halter, Jean-Michel Wilmotte

The pavilion by Clara Halter and Jean-Michel Wilmotte in front of the Jaques-Ange Gabriels Military Academy (no. 118) on the Mars exercise field exhorts the wonders of peace.

The word is found here in 32 languages. Visitors can leave their wishes for peace in the crevices of the construction. The architecture of the "wall" makes a direct reference to Gabriel's building. As one approaches from the direction of the Eiffel Tower (no. 218), the vertical column elements and horizontal elements of the airy pavilion overlay Gabriel's heavy façade structure. In the meantime, the Parisian monument has received sisters in Saint Petersburg (Tour de la paix, 2003) and Hiroshima (Portes de la paix, 2005).

Comme de garçon Parfums (462)
2001
23, place du Marché Saint-Honoré / 1er
Rei Kawakubo, Takao Kawasaki
Architectures Associés, Future Systems

The fashion designer Kawakubo creates the designs for her boutique branches herself together with the architect Kawasaki, whereby often other designers lend their assistance.

Here, Future Systems designed the façade, which consists solely of a glass slab set in front of the wide openings of the older building. The building's raw surface remained preserved. The panes

are colored magenta in the lower section and lose their color only in the top third of the window. This way, the street life can't intrude the boutique's "pink glasses." Inside, the effect of the pink light is reduced by using complementary light.

Display cases set on top of pedestals and a rounded, tilted to the back wall are the only space-building shapes.

Nursery (463)
2001
8ter, rue des Récolletes / 10e
Frédéric Borel

The kindergarten with a capacity for 100 is located in a section of a former garden of the Recollete convent.

It is shielded from the street with a glass sluice. The reserved building volume consists of a wood frame and is subdivided into countless small wide-angled sections. The ground floor is generously glazed, while the upper stories are mostly closed-off. Here, the surface is made up of washable orange-toned composite anthracite panels. The restoration and conversion of the convent itself is completed by Robert et Reichen (2003).

Chapelle Notre-Dame- (464)
de-la-Pentecôte
2001
La Défense
Franck Hammoutène

The small church is located on a strip of land between two towers, and using a set-forward façade shield seeks connection to the large office buildings surrounding it. A cross is formed on its entire body. To the side of this "sacral billboard" is an entrance to the main space, which is reached through the low ground floor. The altar is made completely out of translucent glass, which enables the sur-

roundings to be fully suppressed while illuminating the space.

Cœur Défense (465)
2001
La Défense
Jean-Paul Viguier

The complex consists of two main towers, each 150 meters in height, connected by an intermediary tower and three low wings. With 214,000 square meters of office space, this is the largest addition to the office city. The narrow building cross-section enables a window desk for the majority of the 10,000 employees. The project is located on the spot where the district's first hi-rise was opened in 1962.

Comme de garçon (466)
Red Boutique
2001
54, rue de Faubourg Saint-Honoré /8e
Rei Kawakubo, Takao Kawasaki
Architectures Associés, KRD

The boutique consists of two parts, which are located at the opposite ends of a comparatively light backyard of a Parisian house block. Opposite the boutique itself is a resting space for customers. While

The 180 meter tower on a triangular plot connects the existing structures of the Alicante and Chassagne towers to create an ensemble for the Société Générale, forming the border between the Valmy area of the office city and the rest of Nanterre.

The 36 floors offer s total of 70,000 square meters of office space.

Publicis (468)
2002–2004
133, avenue des Champs-Élysées / 8e
Michele Saee

the branch stores in Tokyo and New York were dominated by the colors blue and white, the Parisian space is determined by glaring red fiberglass. The resting space was created by Kawakubo and Kawasaki with Abe Rogers and Shona Kitchen of KRD. Red cubes stand in a bright white room, moving unpredict-ably around, as if pushed by an invisible hand. The entrance to the store on the opposite side is blocked by a red wall, which slides to the side on its own. The interior is structured exclusively using red elements. The table is designed by Christian Astuguevieille, and the wall elements are designed by Red Wave.

Tour Granite (467)
2001–2008
La Défense
Christian de Portzamparc

The linear architecture from the 1970s has been enveloped by a dynamic glass skin created using 700 square meters of curved laminated safety glass.

The glass panes curve with varying radii and culminate in a glass spiral at the building's corner that reaches up to the roof terrace.

The 4,000 square meters interior has also been partially redesigned.

A spiral interconnects the areas and presentation islands on the building's five stories.

C42 – multi-story car park as a shop-window with shelf (469)

The new Citroen flagship store is more than merely a worthy replacement for the large display window that represented the automobile manufacture on Champs-Élysée until now. The store was created in 2001–2006 by Manuelle Gautrand. The latest studies, current models as well as the classics are displayed here as part of the 1,200 square meters store's everyday function. A wall-to-wall faceted glass façade rises above a tall ground floor on a narrow plot, curving into the building and thus creating a roof.

The flow of the façade continues as it lowers itself into the yard, from where it is raised again with a sideward swing. If it were not for the facets, the front could be thought of as a glass drape stretched between the neighboring buildings by the architect.

These crystalline interruptions of the surface are unevenly distributed, and go on to form rhombs in varying heights, widths and depths of protrusion around Citroen's trademark double upward facing wide angles.

The facets' placement and use of clear and reddish glass visually creates five upper stories, allowing the unusual street front to nonetheless offer a horizontal structure continuous with the neighboring buildings.

Inside, however, this sectioning finds no reflection; with just a few exceptions, the building in its entire height, width and depth is just a single space, interconnected by a rising stairwell fastened on the façades and side walls. During the ascent, the stairs circle around a central glowing "shelf" with seven boards. At the back façade, the boards meet with stair landings at four points, where the displayed autos can be viewed from up close.

The three remaining platforms are not accessible and can be merely viewed from the walkway behind the Champs-Élysée façade. With its numerous projecting facets that from the inside appear as large, completely glazed bays, this façade offers head-spinning views of the busy avenue below. Visitors with a fear of heights are encouraged to use the elevator on their way down.

Manuelle Gautrand (*1961) opened her office in 1991 and is one of the young stars on the French scene. As in this case, her work usually features a continuing development of a linear graphic idea – here the transformation of the Citroen symbol into the third dimension, which eventually comes to dominate the design.

These unconventional metamorphoses remain completely flexible, appearing to be born out of playful consideration of an idea, and join unusual spatial forms with extravagant light effects.

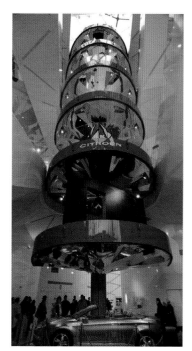

Interior view

The faceted façade

Ministère de la Culture et de (470)
la Communication – Immeuble
des Bons Enfants
2002–2005
192, rue Saint-Honoré; 2, rue des Bons
enfants; 1, rue Montesquieu / 1er
Francis Soler

The new building housing the Ministry
of Culture and Communications was
created using a reconstructed old department store and part of the former
Ministry of Finances. Francis Soler
joined the buildings by covering the
façades in a unifying ornamental web.
The twelve millimeters-thick stainless
steel panels measuring 3.8 x 3 meters
are attached to the load-bearing structure. Viewed from up close, the building appears as if covered by a painting
craquelure, while from afar, the lines of
the web blur and take on the appearance
of a cocoon that reveals only the outline
of the volume. The interior design is by
Frédéric Drout.

Hotel Wagram (471)
2003–2008
37, avenue de Wagram / 17e
Christian de Portzamparc

The building stands on the former location
of the theater. The lower level contains
boutiques and creates a passage through
the large gate arch to Salle Wagram. The
façade of the six upper stories is created
using windows of oscillating concav-
ity, which recalls the stacking façade
structure of the Ceramic Hotel (no. 246)
located diagonally across the street. The
swells function as window bays, revealing
a view of the street below.

MK2-Bibliothèque (472)
2003
128, avenue de France / 13e
Jean-Michel Wilmotte, Frédéric Namur

Along with the National Library (no. 408),
Martin Karamitz's mitiplex movie theater with 14 screens is the second important building in the Quartier Tolbiac
ZAC Rive Gauche (no. 452).

With three restaurants in various
price classes (design: Hervé Bourgeois,

Guillaume Richard), a bar, exhibition space and retail space (design: Gérard Barrau, Stéphane Jardin), it considerably enlivens the area.

In terms of city planning, the elongated building creates a bar between the library and the sprawling rail road tracks at the periphery of the city, enabling a long glazed passage to be created on the ground floor.

The white bar consists of various volumes, whose continuum is interrupted by a small garden (landscaping: Francois Neveu, Bernard Rouyer).

Airy structures extend the building on its narrower sides – on one side, a canopy prolongs the roof surface, while the other is a large pergola.

Both are supported by filigree pillars. The street furniture on the Avenue de France is the work of Wilmotte in cooperation with Paul Andreu.

Lentille Météor St-Lazare (473)
2003
cour de Rome, rue Saint-Lazare,
rue de Rome / 8e
Arte Chapentier et associés, Abbès Tahir

The new design of the four level-deep metro station for the Météor is indicated by a lens-shaped glass dome measuring 17 meters across located on the square in front of the train station. It can be closed using sliding doors with a slender grill.

The light enters the tunnel through a wide shaft. Underground, a lot of attention is paid to dispersion of natural and artificial light, for example using glass stairs. The lens is composed of single panes of glass of varying shapes and sizes.

Magasin Kenzo (474)
2003
1, rue du Pont-Neuf,
75, rue de Rivoli / 1er
Jean-Jacques Ory

In 2003 Samaritaine 1 (no. 247) was partially restructured and expanded to include the Kenzo flagship store, a company that is part of the LVMH group. Restaurants and a beauty center represent the various facets of the Kenzo brand; at the center is the actual store with flowers, greenery and manifold references to Japanese gardens.

The Kenzo store's interior was designed by Deuxl, Lena Pessoa, Vudafieri Partners and Simona Quadri. Emmanuelle Duplay created the La Bulle Kenzo. The Lô Sushi restaurant was decorated by Andrée Putman; the glazed Kong offering a view of the neighborhood is by Philippe Starck and Dorothée Boissier.

Philharmonie de Paris – a new hill in town (475)

The new Philharmonic for Paris has been in discussion for over two years, and ever since Christian de Portzamparc finished his Conservatory (no. 409) and the Cité de la musique (no. 371) on the edge of the Parc de la Villette (no. 404), the adjoining plot has been determined to be the location of the new building.

Shortly before the end of Chirac's office tenure, an international competition selected the project design submitted by Jean Nouvel, the current "national architect" of the city and the laureate of the 2008 Pritzker Prize. With his Musée du Quai Branly (no. 454) he had already created the last completed large-scale project in Paris and was building the Abu Dhabi branch of the Louvre. Nouvel has also built the Culture and Convention Center's concert hall in Lucerne, redeveloped Lyon Opéra, and is working on the Philharmonic in Copenhagen.

And now, Paris's first new concert hall since 1927 will open here sometime before 2012. Standing behind two of the park's signature red "follies" and acting as a barrier from the Boulevard Périphérique, the building will appear as a mountain of aluminum reaching 37 meters in height. Paris's specified building height limit will be overstepped by a projecting sail reaching 52 meters in height.

The lair-like, folded construction will have an accessible exterior, thereby providing not only a functional interior, but also expanding the park with a vertical dimension. In this way, nature acts as an extension of the building, as is typical for Nouvel's current architecture (Fondation Cartier, no. 415, Tour Signal, no. 493). The program on 20,000 square meters consists of two large and six small rehearsal rooms, exhibition spaces and a hall with a 2,400 capacity, which can be refurnished to serve other purposes.

The entrance hall alone measures 4,200 square meters. The EUR 200 mil-

lion budget is provided by the state and city government (45% each) and the Île de France region (10%). The new building for the Orchestre de Paris will have fine-tuned acoustics created with the help of specialists from Marshall Day Acoustics and Yasuhisa Toyota of Nagata and is expected to become one of the leading houses in Europe, placing it in the company of Berlin Philharmonie, Wiener Musikverein and Amsterdamer Concertgebouw.

In contrast to Nouvel's concert hall in Lucerne, the Parisian hall will have a rounded auditorium, like the Berlin Philharmonie (vineyard type). In the case of the Swiss building, acoustics were created with the help of the Russel Johnson, and here the orthogonal, frontal structure similar to the Wiener Musikverein was chosen (shoe box type).

In Paris, the auditorium will be located inside an "oyster" within the building. The rounding of the form and terraced tiers makes it possible to place each audience member within 30 meters of the conductor. Only the oyster's "pearl" – the podium – is rectangular, while the walls and tiers inside the oyster shell all have different curvatures. Adjustable in height, flat cloud-shaped objects suspended from the ceiling can customize the building's acoustics for various performances (classical, jazz, world music).

The "hill"

Inside of the basin

Palace Fouquet's Barrière (476)
2003–2006
91–99, avenue des Champs-Élysées,
46–48, avenue George V; 23–27, rue
Quentin-Bauchart; 2–4, rue Vernet / 8e
Edouard François

The restructuring takes place in a conversation with new and converted buildings with original façades. The new façades pick up on the decorative structure, but distance themselves from the existing buildings by imprinting the façade ornamentation into the modern structure. The façade is likewise forced open by the new inner workings of the house (decor: J. Garcia) – the new windows are placed at locations that are "wrong" according to the historical arrangement.

Pavillon de l'Arsenal (477)
2003
21, boulevard Morland / 4e
LIN Finn Geipel, Giulia Andi,
Christian Biecher with Soizic Lebigot

The pavilion was planned in 1878 by A. Clément as a private museum, but ended up being used mostly as a warehouse. After renovation by Reichen & Robert in 1988, the 3,330 square meters exhibition space became one of the main hubs for interested architects and urban planners in Paris. In 2003 the permanent exhibition was designed by LIN.

At the center of the permanent exhibition is a large interactive city plan (from Electronic Shadow) that presents various current projects in the context of the city's layout. In addition, changing exhibitions and the unusual video loun-

ge by Christian Biecher and Soizic Lebigot (2002) offer an excellent view of the current situation. The lounge consists of glowing arching screens which create cabins without subdividing the space.

Atelier Lab (478)
2004
21, rue de Tanger / 19e
Atelier Lab

The house with the architect's studio of Christophe Lab and Cécile Courtey separates the residential area above and the working area below using an open story. The building framework is especially noticeable here, but can be easily recognized at other locations behind mounted wall elements.

Although the building leans against the wall of the neighboring house on the right, it is completely free-standing structure which disregards its context and appears moveable due to the lightness of its structure.

Nursery Lauzin (479)
2004
22, rue Lauzin / 19e
Shohreh Davar

The restructuring of the child care center improved the overall appearance of the entire nine-story building, which now boasts an attractive eye-catcher on its first floor. The colorful envelope consists of scale-like overlapping reinforced glass plates, story-high but only 60 centimeters wide, mounted on a metal frame. The eight pastel colors immediately indicate that the building is intended for a child target audience, with two differently colored screens found together on one panel. The front's total area of 200 square meters juts over the actual volume of the building and forms a screen toward the garden, which contributes to the weightlessness of the structure's appearance.

Siège Le Monde (480)
(Siège Air France, formal)
2005
74, boulevard Auguste Blanqui; 19, rue Vulpian; 14–18, rue Paul Gervais / 13e
Christian de Portzamparc

The restructuring and expansion of the office building position it as a landmark of the southern section of the inner city and simultaneously as an advertising sign for the newspaper that built it. The front panels of the double-leaf glass façade are printed with a half of a fictional title page above the ground floor. These act as a sun protection. The typical headline section with the name "Le Monde" appears on the panels, and below, instead of real articles, Victor Hugo's text about the freedom of the press appears ruptured by a drawing by Jean "Plantu" Plantureux. The pages are animated by a free alteration of windows and various aluminum panels. The interiors of the upper floors with a restaurant and a winter garden were designed by Elizabeth de Portzamparc.

Atrium building Jussieu (481)
2006
2, place Jussieu / 5e
Périphériques architectes

The new building takes the old mega structure as an example and alters it drastically. The proportions remain the same, the volume is placed on stilts and façades are dominated by panels, mounted on the construction of pillars and baseplates.

But everything else is different: a large atrium with a glass ceiling occupies the interior, and various colors indicate different areas. The façade panels are much

more decorative here, with aluminum plates with circular opening of varying size bending incoming light.

Docks en Seine (482)
Cité de la Mode et du Design
2006–2008
quai d'Austerlitz / 13e
Jakob + Macfarlane

The new multi-function building was created for the Port Autonome de Paris (PAP) in the course of the restructuring of a former warehouse dating from 1907 (by Georges Morin-Goustiaux) with a 280 meter façade facing the Seine. The architects dismantled the building down to its concrete framework and enveloped it with a steel and etched glass construction. Toward the Seine, the façade displays itself with a large green "plug" in the form of abstract waves.

The building's 12,000 square meters on three floors are occupied by Institut Français de la Mode (IFM), an art and design exhibition center, a library specializing on these topics, bars, restaurants and boutiques. A greened roof will be a 24-hour terrace to the Seine. The view toward the street will be blocked off using Pampas grass.

Lycée hôtelier Guillaume-Tirel (483)
2006
237, boulevard Raspail / 14e
Atelier d'Architecture Olivier Brénac,
Xavier Gonzalez

Sporting a completely regular façade with strongly vertical windows in deep soffits, the building is a representative of the New Elegance, which aims to produce a highly structured façade. The volume consisting of multiple orthogonal parts could have come out of Modernism, but the window distribution is turned into a pattern dominated by a uniformity that has nothing to do with Le Corbusier's free distribution. This strictness of repetition transforms functional elements to pure patterns. An almost completely glazed wall screen toward the boulevard includes a massive gate, also a post-war element, where by in this case the variety of used glass introduces clearly playful components.

École d'Enseignement (484)
Supérieur Advancia de Paris
2006–2009
3, rue Armand Moisant / 15e
Architecture Studio

The restructuring and comprehensive extension of the school takes up the height of its surroundings and plays with the bordering forms of historical roof shapes by developing a mono-shed roof that bends out of its street façade. On the reverse side, the façade ends with a horizontal conclusion and the flat roof is covered with a garden.

The yard acts as a generous atrium. The new façades display a unified surface of glass panels in yellow, orange and red tones that in addition to serving as light screens also control incoming views from various perspectives.

Gymnasium Maurice (485)
Berlemont
2006
22, rue de l'Orillon / 11e
Emmanuel Saadi

The sports hall meant for the school and the residents of the Orillon area has been created by the architect as a closed-off playground. An existing open-air sports complex has been walled-in and roofed over. Both exterior walls located on the intersection consist almost completely of glass bricks, which allow a limited view inside, acting as a reminder of the open space that was here before. The glass bricks are matted only in some places. A high, dark roof weighs optically on the fragile walls. The entryway, accented with strong color, leads directly onto the playing field.

Crèche Jean Jaurès (486)
2007
164–168, avenue Jean-Jaurès,
rue Georges Thill / 19e
B.J.A. (Basselier Jarzaguet Architectes)

The architects created a child care center on a narrow plot with a large window facing a busy street.

The acoustically-isolated glass is printed with a colorful pattern and also acts as an optical screen without blocking the view from within. On the opposite side of the building and in the yard, bubble-like story-spanning cocoons emerge from the walls, and are used by the children as play houses.

291

Office building 39 George V   (487)
2007
39, avenue George V / 8e
Athem, Pierre Delavie

For the period of its construction, the future location of the Bleeker real estate firm has been enveloped by temporary architecture, whose PVC membrane was printed with an image of an apparently Surrealist urban development of the site. The architect Antoine Locqueville and the artist Pierre Delavie represented the building as a distorted, bent, liquefied object from a Dalí painting.

The casual passerby notices from afar that something is amiss, without even noticing the screen. Some sculptural details that protrude in front of the screen like the cornice, some stone barrels and a special stacking of the planes increase the effect, letting it behave in a three-dimensional way as the observer moves past it.

BHV Homme   (488)
2007
30, rue de la Verrière / 4e
Franck Michigan, Saguez & Partners

A distinctive store has been created here using simple means. The architecture is influenced by one of the green façades by Patrick Blanc, appearing here as an architecturally framed wall rug. The subdued design is continued in the 5,000 square meters interior.

Les Halles – rebuilding   (489)
2007 (competion)
rue Rambuteau, rue Pierre-Lescot / 4e
Patrick Berger, Jacques Anziutti

In 2004 David Mangin from Seura won the competition to redesign the Forum les Halles (no. 336) area. While his overall plan is pending realization, the glass roof above the forum has been discarded. An additional competition in 2007 decided in favor of a self-supporting double glass dome.

The forum will be shielded by a turned-over glass bowl, and will include an auditorium, a library, a health center as well as many studios and practice rooms.

With an edge length of 100 meters, the dome is only 11 meters high and is irregularly vaulted. It is made up of strips of glass of varying translucency.

Tour Generali (490)
2008–2012
La Défense
Valode & Pistre

The new building to house the Italian Assicurazioni Generali stands on the former location of the Iris Building (1983). The project budgeted at EUR 500 million will rise to a height of 318 meters.

The tower's expressive conclusion results from the X-shaped load bearing structure that is revealed behind the glass façade. The façade is interrupted at certain locations and the openings in the structure accommodate gardens.

Eighteen wind turbines on the roof produce electrical power and are part of the comprehensive energy and air conditioning solution.

Institut de recherche (491)
clinique sur la vision
2008
13–17, rue Moreau / 12e
Brunet Saunier

The street front of the medical institute building is completely covered with glass plates with varying surfaces, opaqueness and size. Some bordering panels share proportions and/or type of glass and sometimes the opposite is the case, creating an irregular patter of different brightness and reflection levels, covering the façade as well as the gable wall and the roof pitch.

Phare – Tour Beacon (492)
2008–2013
La Défense
Morphosis / Thom Myne

Tour Signal (493)
2008–2015
La Défense
Jean Nouvel

The Phare, located in the corner between the Grande Arche (no. 377) and CNIT (no. 315), along with Tour Generali, will lead La Défense to new heights. The unusual volume, named "The Lighthouse," has 68 floors spanning 300 meters. The lower floors are open, responding to the open structure of the surroundings. The façade itself begins higher, resembling a skirt hemline and resulting in a fluid, undulating form.

With its revealed structure at the lower levels and the complex use of engineering concepts, the Phare continues in the tradition of the Eiffel Tower (no. 218). The foyer is located at the height of 60 meters and acts as a public plaza accessed directly from the metro station below CNIT.

The strongly sculpted, double-layered façade on the south side consists of a glass layer underneath a perforated metal skin which blocks the sun rays. The comparatively flat north side consists of double-layered glass to enable climate control. The building is topped by a "wind farm" crown, which contributes to natural ventilation.

When viewed from the direction of the city, the Signal tower is located to the left of the Grand Arch (no. 377) and counterbalances the Tour Generali (no. 490)

and the Phare (no. 492). In contrast to Nouvel's cylindrical Tour Sans Fin, which was planned for La Défense but never completed, this building is strictly cubistic. With an assortment of apartments, offices, a hotel, retail, cultural and public spaces as well as a panoramic terrace distributed on 71 floors, this project will be France's first skyscraper with a high degree of function mixing. The architect underlines this variety using the design, which is an expression of the planned functional diversification of La Défense as a whole. The tower is split into four sections, each with a large sky atrium. The retail spaces are found in the lower block, with the office block, the hotel and apartments stacked one on top of the other. The four patios open up in different directions, and are a part of the building's sustainable air conditioning concept. The ecologically-minded building plan has surely played a big role in Nouvel's receiving first place in the competition, which provided him with a budget of EUR 600 million.

Tour T1 (494)
2008
La Défense
Valode & Pistre

The tower consists of a "conventional" linear façade whose opposite side curves inward much like a vertically placed piece of paper. The 185 meter building appears from the side as a silhouette of a sail. With its vertical façade, Tour T1 lines up with other skyscrapers while

the arched, downward-sloping sides lead connect to the lower structures of the Courbevoie borough. The tower offers 70,000 square meters of office area on 37 floors.

Méridien Hotel (495)
2008
La Défense
Claude Vasconi

On the east near the Boulevard Circulaire, the "small" hotel with 330 rooms nuzzles up to the Esplanade de la Défense. On the narrow plot the thin, glazed bar of rooms forms a pinnacle with a gradually protruding upper conclusion facing Paris. A second building volume retreats backwards and underscores this orientation.

Tips

Tips on the topic of architecture as well as a small selection of restaurants and cafés which are sure to bring a special dose of enjoyment to fans of architecture.

Architecture galleries

La Galérie d'Architecture
11, rue des Blancs Manteaux / 4e
The gallery consists not only of a well-designed exhibition center, but also a forum where people can meet to get information or exchange ideas about architecture and related fields. It supports, exposes and diffuses the contemporary architectural tendencies by displaying French creations as well as international works of landscape architects, designers and urban planners.

La Cité de l'architecture et du patrimoine
1, place du Trocadéro et du
11 Novembre / 16e
The Forum in the east wing of the de Chaillot palace is a new meeting point of architecture fans. It unites monument preservation with modern architecture. This includes a cast collection of Roman and Gothic sculpture and architectural fragments that were amassed at the behest of Eugéne Viollet-le-Ducs for the Musée de Schulpture Comparée. On the other hand, the Institut Français d'Architecture (IFA) takes over the architecture of the 19th century and later. Jean-François Bodin renovated the building for this purpose.

Pavillon d'Arsenal
21, boulevard Morland / 4e
The Pavillon is the leading institution that devotes itself to architecture and urban planning in Paris. The restructuring of the 3,330 sqm space was accomplished by Reichen & Robert in 1988. At the center of the permanent exhibition is a large interactive city plan (from Electronic Shadow) which represents various current projects in the context of the city layout. The video lounge was created by Christian Biecher and Soizic Lebigot in 2002.

Vélibs – Bicycle rental

Since July 2007, Paris has a bike. Everywhere in the city one can find stations (designed by Patrick Jouin) where one of ca. 20,000 Vélibs can be rented using a credit card. Prices favor short-term rents, and start at 30 minutes. In addition, bicycle paths have been created everywhere, taking away precious space away from cars and pedestrians, but ensuring the survival of cyclists in the highly chaotic urban traffic.

Cafés, restaurants

1er
Le Cochon à l'Oreille
15, rue Montmartre
With four large tiled murals on its walls evoking the glory days of the Les Halles produce market which had its origins in the 12th century and functioned continuously until it closed in 1969, the former Café Halles Bar remains a classic Paris bistro named "The Pig's Ear."

Le Pharamond
24, rue de la Grande Truanderie
Picard et Cie
Opened in 1877, this restaurant whose present façade consists of a fake wooden structure imitating Norman architecture. It became well known for its beef stew simmering in cider. The second floor guarantees intimacy and privacy because of its discreet access from the building next door.

L'Escargot Montorgueil
38, rue Montorgueil
Located inside the same historic building since 1875, this restaurant with a black-and-gold lettered facade entrance, a spiral staircase linking two dining levels and a ceiling painting by G.-J.-V-. Clairin is an ideal place to have an escargots tasting and to dine next to well known artists, writers and show businessmen in downtown Paris.

Vélib station

Hôtel Meurice
228, rue de Rivoli
Philippe Starck
Still the same good old Meurice, but even better: The luxurious atmosphere becomes even more elegant due to the little haute couture details of Starck's renovation, like the luminous new passage between the restaurant and the lobby or the swan's head chairs as a reference to Dali.

La Potée des Halles
3, rue Etienne-Marcel
In tribute to bar and coffee maidens of the old Les Halles district, the interior tile murals of this traditional restaurant depict the lively days of the glass-and-iron food pavilions, while its own potée recipe (salt pork, carrots, white beans, cabbage and smoked sausage) dates from 1903.

Le Comptoir
37, rue Berger
For those who are interested in exotic Moorish culture of North Africa, this bar with the iridescent lighting is a must. It is located inside a mid-nineteenth-century Haussmann building.

Café des Initiés
3, place des Deux Ecus
Adrien Gardère (interior),
José Etienne Montiel (decoration)
To eat or have a drink next to famous actors, fashion models and contemporary photographers in Paris, one has to hang out at this renovated dada-style Café with paintings by François Legrand on the wall and chairs signed by Marteen Van Severen.

Different Restaurants and Cafés at the Louvre *compare no. 49*

Lô Sushi and **Kong** *compare no. 474*

2e
Etienne Marcel
34, rue Etienne Marcel
Philippe Pareno, Pierre Huygues
Graphic agency M/M
This luxurious restaurant-bar joins art, technology and design in an interesting

way. The glass front is to be seen as a monochrome negative of a Mondrian's painting, while the chairs in white lacquer by Deeds and Jecky, the juke box and the phosphorescent connecting lighting recompose the ambivalence of the 1960's.

Caffé Santi
49, rue Montorgueil
Monica Santi Bonelli
For those who appreciate mozzarella, cappuccino and design, Santi's Milanese Caffé is the place. Monica's self-designed bar, tables and mirrors together with the Castiglioni's chandelier or the Bertoia's chair offer a promising and yet fruitful combination of trattoria ambience, homemade and imported design.

Bioboa
3, rue Danielle Casanova
Jean-François Delsalle
The first organic fast-food restaurant, opened in 2004 by Marielle Gamboa, keeps on making organic glamorous by having successfully combined food quality with design. Wooden tables, floor in cement, bar in stainless steel and the chairs signed by Charles and Ray Eames are there to prove it.

3e
Murano
13, boulevard du Temple
Vincent Bastie
Situated in a creative district of the city, this first urban resort in Paris belongs to a new hotel concept designed for guests that appreciate modernity and luxury as well. Its fifty-two bedrooms and suites, high-tech equipment, controlled daytime lighting and slate on the bathroom floors are worthy of a mention.

Andy Wahloo
69, rue de Gravilliers
Hassan Hajjaj
With a name meaning "I have nothing" in Arabic, Andy Wahloo is here to prove how an alternative bar design can be made from a relatively small budget. Colorfully filled bottles as light filters, paint cans with pillows as stools and road signs as tabletops set the tone.

Andy Wahloo

Café Baci
36, rue de Turenne
Ideal either for a romantic evening or for a big party, this Italian restaurant with its cream leather stools, baroque chandeliers with pearls and ribbons and old Venetian scenes framed on the walls remains open seven days a week for breakfast, lunch and dinner.

4e

Brasserie Bonfinger
3, rue de la Bastille
Being the oldest brasserie in the city and the first to having served draft beer on tap in 1870, this Parisian restaurant consists of a genuine article from the Belle Epoque. Besides its traditional onion soup, choucroute and crème brûlée, the spectacular stained-glass cupola is definately a reason to pay a visit to this place.

Chez Julien
1, rue du Pont Louis-Philippe
Combining the old hotel "Au pigeon blanc" and a former bakery, the façade of this Parisian restaurant with glass-painted landscapes and a 1820's grill-

work consists of a unique national landmark. The painted ceiling and the view of the Seine and two islands contribute to the building's charm.

Restaurant Georges
compare no. 456

5e

Le Piano Vache
8, rue Laplace
Located in a 16th century building next to the Pantheon, this legendary bar exemplifies the rock'n'roll attitude in Paris for over 40 years. Densely filled with smoke, gathered students and alternative crowds that love new wave, punk, rock or even gothic music, the walls of the bar's asymmetrical rooms boast posters from the 1970s.

Atelier Maître Albert
1, rue Maître Albert
Jean-Michel Wilmotte
Tradition and modernism cross paths in the architecture of the Atelier's cigar salon, its elegant rotisserie and the Vinotheque. Delicious foie gras with celery or

magret de canard make this restaurant a feast not just for the eyes.

6e

Le Bar Dix
10, rue de l'Odéon
Frequented by French hipsters and international students, this Art Nouveau Bar remains famous for its sangria as well as for the juke box full of classic rock and French favorites. The decoration consists of vintage record covers and old theatre bills, while the maroon-painted façade of the 18th century stone building identifies this small dark place simply with "Bar."

Brasserie Lipp
151, boulevard Saint-Germain
A meeting point for writers and theater groups till this day, the former Bords du Rhin dates from 1880, when the Alsatian refugee Léonard Lipp settled in Paris. In 1958 it was considered the best literary salon in town. Its Belle Epoque interior with the exotic ceramics by L. Fargue was expanded in 1920 with a second room, whose painted ceiling represents African scenes.

Le Bistro de la Gare
59, boulevard du Montparnasse
Originally opened as a restaurant in an oil merchant's shop near Gare Montparnasse, the former Chartier Bouillon is the Bistro of choice on the train station since 1923. Its Art Nouveau interior with wooden decoration, mirrors and painted ceramic scenes of floral motifs and French landscapes turn this place into an historic landmark.

La Cantine du Faubourg

Café de Flore
172, boulevard Saint-Germain
Definitely the most famous spot in Paris, Café de Flore harks back to the 1887 and takes its name from a small divinity sculpture on the other side of the boulevard. Authors and philosophers (Sartre, de Beauvoir) have written volumes on its marble-top tables, while poets like Apollinaire, artists (Picasso, Chagall, Dali), communists (PCF members, including Hemingway) and psychoanalysts (Lacan) exchanged their political views and founded groups or movements here. Stars, actors and writers of today have taken their place – Cher, Tim Burton, Coelho or Sharon Stone.

7e
Gaya
44, rue du Bac
Christian Ghion (design)
For those who are in mood to experience the Seine's high and low tide, this restaurant on its left bank shows up as the perfect choice. Projecting moving reflections of fish, its gray space recalls a sardine's silver tones and the tables by Corian_ are decorated with seaweed motifs.

8e
Plaza Athénée
25, avenue Montaigne
Patrick Jouin
The luxurious Plaza Athénée restaurant and the luminous bar invite their guests to a unique and interactive experience, while the bar in sculpted glass lights up when touched.

La Cantine du Faubourg
105, rue du Faubourg-Saint-Honoré
Axel Schoenert, cabinet ROOM (architecture), Pira (interior)
A bar, restaurant and lounge in one, la Cantine du Faubourg has a 500-person capacity appropriate for concerts and other events. With its open kitchen looking out into the dining room, this restaurant offers a variety of ambiences due to the projectors reflecting images on silk screen walls and different ceiling levels playing with subtle displays of lighting.

Häagen-Dazs
49-51, avenue des Champs-Élysées
Saguez & Partners
Opened in Champs-Élysées in May 2007, this 12,000 sqm store is designed not only for ice cream lovers but also for those seeking to settle down in somewhere different for a coffee break: The collection, the Daily Café, the Golden Room or the Ice Bar.

La Suite
40, avenue Georges V
Imaad Rahmouni
Offering a great view to avenue Georges V and widely exposed to Parisian sun, this "deluxe suite" is kept in white and dark brown tones with the horizontal leather upholsteries covering all furniture, including chairs, benches and stools.

Flora Danica
142, avenue des Champs-Élysées
Claire Euvrard (decoration), Helle Damkjaer (design), Eric Picard (landscaping)
Known for its excellent salmon since 1973, this restaurant belongs to the Danish institute and combines in its winter garden Franco-Danish design with the 1960's aesthetic of chairs, cutlery and lights.

Maison Blanche
compare no. 256

Fouquet's Barrière
compare no. 476

Le Senderens
9, place de la Madeleine
Noé Duchaufour-Lawrance
A visit to Le Senderens is a must not just for the famous Art Nouveau sycamore wood carvings designed by Louis Majorelle in 1910. The light pouring from the cocoons on the ceiling, chandeliers and translucent tables make dinner here a memorable experience.

9e
Demets
26, boulevard Poissonnière
Clément Bataille (design), Dominique Palatchi & Philippe de Potestad (architecture)

303

Imagine a giant picnic basket with wooden cutlery, a space in stainless steel and polished concrete that offers delicious seasonal dishes at low prices.

Flood
58, rue de Chateaudun
Matthieu Lehanneur
Combining healthy food with organic design, this new fast food chain illuminates its space with blown glass lights, while 100-liter aquariums filled with spirulina plantensis, a seaweed species that produces oxygen to compensate for its lack in big cities, are well as PVC tables and chairs.

10e

DeLaVille Café
36, boulevard Bonne Nouvelle
Périphériques architectes
The cafe and concert hall are divided into three individually designed areas: Café Charbon emanates a historical coffeehouse atmosphere, an area in the back is a satirical interpretation of a hunting cabin decorated using deer heads and deconstructivist furniture, while the main hall is dominated by furniture with a technical flair and colorful light.

11e

Place Verte
105, rue Oberkampf
Adict
The latest bar-restaurant by the owners of Café Charbon and Café DeLaVille offers the ambiance of a building's entrance hall, as it combines a restaurant, a take away, a photo kiosk and a terrace. Contemporary art on the walls, furniture designed by Aalto and Colombo and reinterpreted objects (like flower boxes) turn this bar to an experimental space.

Le Nouveau Casino
109, Rue Oberkampf
Périphériques architectes
Conceived as urban refuge, we find ourselves feeling tiny in the darkened

DeLaVille Café

Les Grandes Marches

space of this bar-restaurant, its only light emanating from lasers. The space was designed on a Macintosh computer. hammered on a block and veneered in 3D wood.

Le Réfectoire
80, boulevard Richard Lenoir
Located in Oberkampf, this restaurant looks for an audience with those who, while enjoy being connected to the Internet, feel nostalgic for the time when friends ate together in small canteens. Oversized lights in pink, black and white by Douglas Mont and graphics on walls set the tone.

Restaurant El Unico
15, rue Paul Bert
Marcelo Joulia (architect), Enrique Zanoni (photographer)
The 70's decoration, orange walls, chairs by Eames and a table by Foster have turned this former butchery into one of the hottest spots in town. The restaurant serves select Argentine meat while its cellar offers a great variety of wines from Argentina and Chile.

12e
Le Train Bleu compare no. 222

Les Grandes Marches
6, place de la Bastille
Elizabeth de Portzamparc
Asymmetrical forms, dynamic curves and obloquies in both architecture and furniture build up the expressionistic and yet charming atmosphere of this restaurant, whose name is an indirect reference to the large steps of a spectacular spiraling staircase. Its underside, reproducing the chairs' elongated triangular shape, serves as the restaurant's trademark.

13e
Docks en Seine compare no. 482

MK2-Bibliothèque compare no. 472

14e
Apollo
3, place Denfert-Rochereau
François & Eric Walper
"For all travelers coming from or going to..." this restaurant offers both world food and traditional dishes. Its shaded

Café des Deux Moulins

terrace is oriented to the south and can fit a whole wagonload of people; 1970's decoration sets the scene.

15e

Le ciel de Paris

After a short elevator ride of 38 seconds, visitors can enjoy the view upon the city from the 56th floor of the Tour Montparnasse (no. 332.)

16e

Nespresso
45, avenue Victor Hugo
Francis Krempp

Situated next to the Arc de Triomphe, this elegant boutique measuring 200 sqm blends together coffee aroma, accessories in wangé and polished metal, brown and golden chamois, floors in Castille stone and diffuse yet overwhelming light.

Cristal Room, Baccarat
11, place des Etats-Unis
Philippe Starck

Frequented by the cosmopolitan crowd and available for private parties, this former dining room of Marie-Laure de Noailles preserves its original design while displaying a touch of modernism given it by Philippe Starck. A glamorous table, flawless crystal glass and stunning mirrors set the scene for a sophisticated dinner.

Bon
25, rue de la Pompe
Philippe Starck

Ideal for a Sunday brunch or just for a cup of tea, Bon does not perform as just a conventional restaurant – the gray and silver decoration by Philippe Starck turn the space to an alternative and vivid theaterical anti-chamber.

17e

Café Nescafé
15, avenue de Wagram
Michele Saee

Conceived as a symbol of the brand, the glass front building stretches into the interior, where the graphic ribbons pass through the rooms, integrating both floors and seating, and (re)defining different micro zones.

18e

Le Moulin Rouge
82, boulevard de Clichy

The Moulin Rouge was built in 1888 and after it burned down in 1915 it was rebuilt until 1925 with an Art Déco auditorium. In 1929 the theatre was converted to a cinema. In the 1950s it turned into a 1500 seats cinema with new, minor cabarets called Locomotive and Moulin Rouge. Nowadays the cabaret Moulin Rouge uses the most important space in the building again.

La mère Catherine
6, place du Tertre
The most typical restaurant of Montmartre welcomes you with red checkered tablecloths and with the words Danton had scrawled on its wall in 1793 "Let's drink and eat, because tomorrow we will die." This motto was representative of the clientele of this bistro at the time of its founding during the French Revolution.

Café des Deux Moulins
15, rue Lepic
The Art Déco café is not just for "Amelie" fans; the heroine of the film is employed in this establishment. Café des Deux Moulins is located on the section of the street that sharply bends south of the rue des Abbesses.

19e

Café de la Musique
compare no. 371

20e

Aux Troubadours
70, boulevard de Ménilmontan
The toubadours offer dinner concerts with lutes in an early-modern ambience and unusal dishes.

Le Soleil
136, boulevard Ménilmontant
The bar plays world music for the cosmopolitan city.

Le Moulin Rouge

APPENDIX

Supplemental lists

Additions to the three topics found in the main part of the book, whose immense architectural spectrum cannot be inspected one by one, are found below in the following lists that display additional details. These are the projects in the Cité Internationale Universitaire de Paris (no. 308) and La Défense (no. 341), with their buildings listed according to year, as well as a list of urban development areas according to their Arrondisements as an addition to the special on ZACs (no. 452).

A1: Cité Internationale Universitaire de Paris C.I.U.P. (308)

Buildings listed according to year and architect

1923 Fondation Deutsch de la Meurthe: Lucien Adolphe Bechmann
1926 Maison des étudiants canadiens: Olivier Le Bras
1927 Fondation Biermans-Lapotre: Armand Guéritte
1927 Collège d'Espagne: Modesto López Otero
1928 Maison d'Argentine: René Betourné, L. Fagnez, Tito Saubidé
1928 Maison de l'Institut national Agronomique: René Patouillard
1929 Fondation danoise: Kaj Gottlob
1929 Maison du Japon: Pierre Sardou
1930 Maison des étudiants arméniens: Léon Nafilyan
1930 Maison des étudiants de l'Asie du Sud-Est: Pierre Martin, Maurice Vieu
1930 Fondation des Etats-Unis: Pierre Leprince-Ringuet
1931 Maison des étudiants suédois: Peder Clason, Germain Debré
1932 Fondation Rosa Abreu de Grancher: Albert Laprade
1932 Fondation Hellénique: Nicolas Zalhos

1933 Résidence Honnorat: Lucien Adolphe Bechmann
1933 Fondation Suisse: Le Corbusier
1933 Maison des Provinces de France: Armand Guéritte
1935 Maison internationale: Lucien Adolphe Bechmann, Jean-Frédéric Larson, Harris
1935 Collège d'Espagne: Modesto López Otero
1936 Collège Franco-Britannique: Pierre Martin, Maurice Vieu
1936 Church du Sacré-Cœur: Jean-Pierre und Pierre Paquet
1937 Fondation de Monaco: Julien Médecin
1938 Collège Néerlandais (no. 307): Willem Marinus Dudok
1948 Maison du Liban: Jean Vernon, Bruno Philippe
1949 Résidence Lucien Paye: Albert Laprade
1950 Fondation Victor-Lyon: Lucien Adolphe Bechmann
1953 Maison du Mexique: Jorge L. Medella
1953 Maison de la Tunisie: Jean Sebag
1954 Maison de Norvège: Reidar Lund
1954 Maison des Industries Agricoles et Alimentaires: F. Thieulin, X. de Vigan
1956 Maison Heinrich Heine: Johannes Krahn, Paul Maître
1957 Maison du Cambodge: Alfred Audoul
1958 Maison de l'Italie: Piero Portaluppi
1959 Maison du Brésil (no. 317): Le Corbusier, Lúcio Costa
1960 Residence André de Gouveia: José Sommer-Ribeiro
1961 Nouvelle maison des Arts et Métiers: Georges Paul, Max Bourgoin, Urbain Cassan
1967 Maison de l'Inde: J.-M. Benjamin, H.-R. Laroya, Gaston Leclaire
1968 Fondation Avicenne (former Maison de l'Iran): Claude Parent, Heydar Ghiai, Moshen Foroughi

The Fondation Suisse, 1933, Le Corbusier

A2: La Défense (341)

Buildings listed according to year and architect

1957 Résidence Bellini Défense:
J. de Mailly

1958 CNIT (no. 315): Robert Camelot,
J. de Mailly, Bernard Zehrfuss

1966 Tour Initiale (Nobel, no. 321):
J. de Mailly, Jacques Depussé,
Jean Prouvé

1966 Résidence Boieldieu:
Gilbert et Rabaud

1966 Résidence La Défense (Exprodef):
Plancon

1967 Tour AIG: Xavier & Luc
Arsène-Henry, Bernard Schoeller

1969 Tour Europe: J. R. Delb,
M. Chesneau, J. Verola

1969 Résidence Lorraine:
R. Camelot, Jean-Claude Finelli

1970 Tour Atlantique: M. Chesneau,
J. R. Delb, J. Verola, B. Lalande

1970 Tour Aurore: Claude Damery,
Pierre Vetter, Gilbert Weil

1970 Central téléphonique: J. de Mailly

1970 Tour Les Poissons: Henri Pottier

1971 Tour CB16: Roger Saubot, Arsac,
Gravereaux et Cassagnes

1972 Tour Europlaza (Septentrion):
Pierre Dufau, Jean-Pierre Dacbert,
Amsler & Stenzel (renovation
B&B Architectes)

1972 Tour Franklin: M. Chesneau,
J. R. Delb, J. Verola, B. Lalande

1972 Résidence Corvée: J.-C. Finelli

1972 Résidence Louis Pouey:
Société Civile d'Architecture et
d'Urbanisme

1973 Poste EDF: Penso, Natchez et Cleret

1973 Tour France: J. de Mailly

1973 Résidence Vision 80: Jean-Pierre
Jouve, Andreï Frieschlander,
Charles Mamfredos

1974 Tour Areva: Skidmore & Associates, R. Saubot, François Jullien

1974 Tour AXA (Assur, UAP):
P. Dufau, J.-P. Dacbert,
Michel Stenzel

1974 Tour Défense 2000:
Michel Proux, Jean-Michel
Demones, Jean-Michel Srot

1974	Ellipse: Grison, Moritz, Ristorcelli	1982	Le Galion: X. & L. Arsène-Henry
1974	Tour Ève:	1983	Iris: Jean Balladur
	Jean-Baptiste Hourlier, Ivan Gury	1983	Tour Pascal: H. La Fonta
1974	Tour Gan: Max Abramovitz,	1983	SCOR: G. Lagneau, M. Weill,
	Wallace K. Harisson,		J. Dimitrijevic
	André Fouilhoux	1983	Tetris: agence KLN
1974	Résidence Les Dauphins:	1984	Tour AGF – Athéna:
	M. Chesneau, J. Verola		Jean Willerval
1974	Résidence de l'Ancre: CGAU	1984	Bureau Veritas: R. Saubot, F. Jullien
1974	Résidence Maréchal Leclerc:	1984	Frasersuites: J. Binoux,
	Daniel Badani, Pierre Roux-Dorlut		M. Folliasson, A. & H. Kandjian
1974	Tour Winterthur: J. R. Delb,	1984	Ibis Novotel: J. Binoux,
	M. Chesneau, J. Verola, B. Lalande		M. Folliasson, A. & H. Kandjian
1974	Préfecture des Hauts-de-Seine:	1984	Les Platanes: Rophe
	André Wogenscky	1984	Résidence Minerve:
1975	Tour AGF – Neptune: Jacques		X. & L. Arsène-Henry
	Binoux, Michel Folliasson et Ass.	1984	Résidence Neuilly Défense:
1975	Tour Ariane: J. de Mailly,		H. La Fonta und Kaminski
	Robert Zammit	1984	Utopia: Alliaume
1975	Résidence la Sirène:	1985	Acacia: Valle
	Gillet, Cayla, Bonpaix, Niogret	1985	Ampère: R. Saubot, F. Jullien
1975	Tour Manhattan: Herbert et Proux	1985	Tour Total: R. Saubot, F. Jullien,
1975	Tour Gambetta: D. Badani,		Menkes, Webb, Zerafa
	P. Roux-Dorlut, Mestoudijan	1985	Tour Michelet (Total):
1976	Berkeley Building:		J. Willerval, H. La Fonta,
	Decaux et Appert		Michel Andrault, Pierre
1976	Damiers d'Anjou: J. Binoux,		Parat, Godet
	M. Folliasson, Abro S. &	1986	Arkema: M. Andrault, P. Parat
	Henri A. Kandjian	1986	Balzac: Agence MBA
1976	Damiers de Bretagne:	1986	Coface:
	J. Binoux, M. Folliasson,		M. Andrault, P. Parat, Godet
	A. & H. Kandjian	1986	Total (Galilée): Valle
1976	Damiers du Dauphiné: J. Binoux,	1988	Tour Descartes (IBM):
	M. Folliasson, A. & H. Kandjian		Fernando Urquijo, Giorgio
1976	Manhattan Square: Henri-Bernard		Maccola, J. Willerval
1976	Tours Aillaud (Nuages):	1988	Lavoisier: Cabinet SOPHA
	Emile Aillaud	1988	Le Linea: M. Andrault, P. Parat
1978	Damiers de Champagne:	1988	Le Triangle: H. La Fonta
	J. Binoux, M. Folliasson,	1988	Tour Voltaire: H. La Fonta
	A. & H. Kandjian	1989	Jean Monnet: Agence MBA
1978	SGAM: R. Saubot, F. Jullien,	1989	La Fayette: Cabinet SOPHA
	Skidmore & Associates	1989	Grande Arche de la Défense
1980	Monge: Henri La Fonta		(no. 377): Johann Otto von
1981	Les Miroirs: Henri La Fonta		Spreckelsen, Paul Andreu
1981	Les Quatre Temps: Guy Lagneau,	1989	Newton: Agence MBA
	Michel Weill, Jean Dimitrijevic	1990	Collines de l'Arche:
1981	Lotus: J. R. Delb		Jean Pierre Buffi
1981	Maison de La Défense: H. La Fonta	1990	Tour Séquoia (Bull, SFR, Cegetel):
1982	Élysées La Défense: R. Saubot,		M. Andrault, P. Parat,
	F. Jullien, Whitson Overcash		Nicolas Ayoub
1982	France Télécom: R. Saubot,	1990	Passage de l'Arche: J. P. Buffi
	François Jullien	1990	CBC: M. Andrault et P. Parat
1982	Résidence Île-de-France:	1992	Colline de La Défense:
	R. Saubot, F. Jullien		Philippe Chaix & Jean Paul Morel

1992   Facto Kupka: M. Andrault, P. Parat
1992   Tour Pacific (Arcelor), (no. 403): Kisho Kurokawa
1993   Les Saisons: Dacbert et Chauvel
1995   Tours Société générale (Chassagne et Alicante): M. Andrault, P. Parat, N. Ayoub
1996   Tour GAN Eurocourtage: J. Willerval et Associés
1996   Hôtel Le Renaissance: M. Andrault, P. Parat
1997   KPMG: M. Andrault, N. Ayoub
1998   Tour Cèdre: Agence Conceptua, M. Andrault, N. Ayoub
1998   Tour Kvaerner (Prisma): J. Willerval
1998   Le Vinci: Partenaires Architectes
2000   Tour Égée (Ernst&Young): Agence Conceptua, M. Andrault, N. Ayoub
2000   Notre-Dame-de-la-Pentecôte (no.464): Franck Hammoutène
2001   Tour EDF: Pei, Cobb, Freed and partners, Saubot – Rouit
2001   Le Palatin: Turner et Arte Charpentier
2001   Triangle de l'Arche: Valode et Pistre
2001   Cœur Défense (no. 465): Jean-Paul Viguier
2002   Tour Adria (Technip): Agence Conceptua, M. Andrault, N. Ayoub
2002   Guynemer: Rouit et Metge
2004   Défense Plaza: Skidmore, Owings and Merrill, Cabinet SRA
2004   Tour Opus12 (PB12, Crédit Lyonais): Valode et Pistre
2005   Tour CBX: KPF Kohn Pedersen Fox, Rouit Cabinet SRA
2006   Tour Exaltis: Bernardo Fort, Brescia Arquitectonica, Bridot-Willerval
2007   Pyramidion: Pei, Cobb Freed and Partners
2008   Tour T1 (no. 494): Valode et Pistre
2008   Tour Granite (no. 467): Christian de Portzamparc
2009   Praetorium: Arte Charpentier
2010   Tour Axa: KPF Kohn Pedersen Fox
2010   Méridien Hotel (no. 495): Claude Vasconi
2011   Salle des Marchés Société Générale: Jean Mas, Francois Roux
2011   Tour Air2: Arquitectonica
2011   Tour Majunga: J.-P. Viguier
2012   Tour Generali (no. 490): Valode et Pistre
2012   Tour D2: Anthony Béchu, Tom Sheehan
2012   Tour Phare (no. 492): Morphosis
2012   Tour Carpe Diem: Robert A. M. Stern
2013   Tour Signal (no. 493): Jean Nouvel

La Défense, View from the Arc de Triomphe (no. 158)

A3: The ZACs   (452)

The ZACs listed according to arrondis-
ments with date, planers respectively
coordinators and building area:

1er ZAC Les Halles:
     2002-2012
     SEURA architectes /
     Phlippe Raguin
8e   ZAC Beaujon:
     2005-2012
     LLTR Architectes
     Landscape architecture:
     Philippe Hilaire
     20,000 m^2
12e ZAC Chalon:
     1993-1998
     Stanislas Fiszer
     140,000 m^2
12e ZAC Bercy:
     Western area
     1988-2005
     Jean-Pierre Buffi
     Eastern area
     1994-2000
     Michel Macary of SCAU
     601,000 m^2
12e ZAC Reuilly :
     1990-1994
     Roland Schweitzer
     184,950 m^2
13e ZAC Chateau des Rentiers:
     1997-2004
     LLTR Architectes
     169,000 m^2
13e ZAC Tage-Kellermann:
     1998-2003
     Pierre Gangnet
13e ZAC Rive-Gauche:
     Austerlitz Nord:
     2000-2008

Christian Devillers
Austerlitz Sud:
2003-2015
Reichen et Robert
Landscape architecture:
Jacqueline Osty
Tolbiac Nord
1994-2003
Roland Schweitzer
Tolbiac Sud:
2012
Pierre Gangnet
Landscape architecture:
Empreinte
Massena Nord:
2000-2010
Christian de Portzamparc
Landscape architecture:
Thierry Huau
Massena Sud:
1995-2012
Bruno Fortier
Landscape architecture:
Jean-Claude Hardy
Massena Bruneseau:
2006-2015
Ateliers Yves Lion
2,255,000 m^2
13e ZAC Gare de Rungis:
     40,000 m^2
14e ZAC Didot:
     38,500 m^2
14e AC Alesia-Montsouris:
     2000-2007
     G. Charlet, D. Chevalier
     Landscape architecture:
     Michel Desvigne,
     Christine Dalnoky
     96,000 m^2

15e ZAC Dupleix:
1993–2000
Jean-Paul Viguier

15e ZAC Vaugirard:
2002–2005
B. Dubus-Richez, Bertrand
Dubus, Thomas Richez
54,000 m²

16e ZAC Citroën-Cévennes:
Îlot Gramat:
1988–1999
Roland Schweitzer
625,000 m²

17e ZAC Clichy-Batignolles:
2005
François Grether
Landscape architecture:
Jacqueline Osty
536,000 m²

17e ZAC Porte Pouchet:
Michel Guthmann, Pierre-
Alain Trévelo, Antoine
Viger-Kohler
62,000 m²

17e ZAC Porte d'Asnières:
2000–2007
Christian de Portzamparc
Landscape architecture:
Méristème
73,000 m²

18e ZAC Moskowa:
2000–2002
André Vaxelaire
70,000 m²

18e ZAC Porte de Clignancourt,
Porte de Montmartre,
Porte des Poissoniers
172,250 m²

18e ZAC Pajol:
2005–2011
Janine Galiano, Philippe Simon
31,800 m²

18e,
19e ZAC Claude Bernard:
François Leclercq
92,400 m²

19e ZAC Porte d'Aubervillers:
2000–2008
G. Charlet, F. Grether
Landscape architecture: TER
1997–2004
81,800 m²

19e ZAC Bassin de la Villette:
1988–2007
APUR Patrick Céleste
157,000 m²

19e ZAC Manin Jaures:
1989–2000
Alain Sarfati-Sarea

19e,
20e ZAC Flandre Sud:
51,300 m²

19e,
20e ZAC Porte des Lilas:
1993
LLTR Architectes
Landscape architecture:
Philippe Hilaire
131,000 m²

20e ZAC des Amandiers:
1998–2002
Antoine Grumbach

20e ZAC Réunion:
1992–2006
Bernard Bourgade
99,735 m²

*The Docks en Seine
(no. 482) by Jakob + Macfarlane
in front of the ZAC Rive Gauche*

Index of Objects

The black numbers listed in the index refer to the property numbers.

INDEX OF OBJECTS

Index of objects by arrondissements

INDEX OF OBJECTS BY ARRONDISSEMENTS

INDEX OF OBJECTS BY ARRONDISSEMENTS

INDEX OF OBJECTS BY ARRONDISSEMENTS

Index of streets

1, 2, 3

rue 8 Mai 1945: 181
place du 11 Novembre 1918: 181

A

rue de l'Abbaye: 5, 15
rue d'Abbeville: 235, 238
rue des Abesses: 217, 381
rue Agar: 254
rue Albert Roussel: 453
rue d'Alexandre: 151
rue d'Allemagne: 145
rue d'Alleray: 436
place Alphonse Laveran: 67
rue Amelot: 183
rue des Amiraux: 265
place de l'Amphithéâtre: 351
quai Anatole-France: 226, 350
quai André Citroën: 399, 401, 410
place André-Malraux: 144
quai d'Anjou: 73
rue de l'Arbre Sec: 12, 247
rue Archereau: 337
quai de Archevêché: 320
rue des Archives: 21, 28, 69, 99, 100
rue des Arènes: 2
place Armand Carrel: 200
rue Armand Carrel: 388
rue Armand Moisant: 484
rue de l'Arrivée: 332
rue de l'Arsenal: 255
rue d'Artois: 298
rue d'Assas: 328
rue Auber: 198
boulevard Auguste Blanqui: 480
boulevard d'Aurelle-de-Paladines: 177
quai d'Austerlitz: 482

B

rue de Babylone: 220
rue du Bac: 90, 103, 206
rue de Bagnolet: 24
porte de Bagnolet: 368
rue Baillet: 247
rue de la Banque: 61, 165, 182
place de la Bastille: 20, 164, 366
rue Baudelique: 375
rue Beaubourg: 456
rue de Beauce: 100
boulevard Beaumarchais: 87
rue Beauregard: 59
rue Belliard: 262

rue Benjamin Franklin: 240, 251, 304
rue Berbier-du-Mets: 301
boulevard de Bercy: 352, 363
quai de Bercy: 391, 447
rue de Bercy: 393
rue Berger: 39, 336
rue Bergère: 211, 258, 298
rue Bichat: 48
rue Blaise-Desgoffe: 245
rue des Blancs-Manteaux: 94
place Boieldieu: 219
rue Boileau: 221
rue Bonaparte: 5, 172
rue des Bons enfants: 470
rue Botzaris: 200
rue Boucher: 247
avenue Boudon: 358
rue du Bouloi: 170
boulevard Bourdon: 255
rue de Bourgogne: 109
rue de la Bourse: 150
place de la Bourse: 161
avenue Boutroux: 335
quai Branly: 424, 454
rue Brillat-Savarin: 268
rue Bruneseau: 380
rue Buffon: 175
rue de la Butte-aux-Cailles: 264

C

place du Caire: 151
rue du Caire: 151
rue Cambon: 82
Canal Saint-Martin: 164
rue de Candie: 383
rue Cantagrel: 288
boulevard des Capucines: 263
rue du Cardinal-Dubois: 413
rue du Cardinal-Lemoine: 77
rue Cardinet: 282
rue des Carmes: 115
place du Carrousel: 49
rue las Cases: 180
rue Cassini: 81
place de Catalogne: 351
rue Caumartin: 139
rue Cavier: 175
quai des Celestins: 51
rue Censier: 325
rue de la Cerisaie: 255
rue des Cévennes: 401
Champ de Mars: 218, 461
avenue des Champs-Élysées: **80**, 140, 189, 273, 285, 377, 468, 469, 476
rue de la Chanzy: 420

INDEX OF ARCHITECTS

Index of architects

A

Abadie, Paul: 209
Abramovitz, Max: A2
Acanthe, Atelier: 341
ACT architecture: 226, 350
Adict: Tips p. 304
Agence Conceptua: A2
Agence KLN: A2
Agence MBA: A2
Albert, Edouard: 319, 324, 444, A2
Albert, Jean-Max: 404
Alby, Amédée: 223
Aldrophe, Alfred Philibert: 202
Alliaume: A2
Allio, René: 215
Alphand, Adolphe: 138, 185, 200, 203
Amsler & Stenzel: A2
Andi, Giulia: 477
Ando, Tadao: 310, 442
Andrault, Michel: 348, 352
André, Louis Jules: 215
Andreu, Paul: **314**, 377, 472, A2
Anger, Roger: 331
Anglart, Pierre: 36
Antoine, Jacques-Denis: 16, 131, 133
Anziutti, Jacques: 336, 450, 489
APUR: 336, A3
Architecture Studio: 311, 361, 362, 376,
    386, 398, 406, 418, 422, 436, 484
Arfvidson, André: 268
Armstrong Associates: 424
Arnaud, Edouard: 229
Arpentère: 452
Arquitectonica: A2
Arretche: 336
Arsac: A2
Arsène-Henry, Xavier & Luc: A2
Arte Chapentier et associés: 473, A2
Arup & Partners, Ove: 414, 452
Astruc, Jules: 231
Astuguevieille, Christian: 466
Atelier d'Architecture Olivier Brénac:
    483
Atelier Lab: 405, 478
Ateliers Yves Lion: A3
Athem, Pierre Delavie: 487
Aubert, André: 302
Aubert, Jean: 113
Audoul, Alfred: A1
Aulenti, Gae: 226, 350
Aurrousseau, Geoffroy: 457
Auscher, Paul: 245

Autant, Alexandre: 235, 238
Autant, Edouard: 235, 238
Autran, Guy: 324
Ayoub, Nicolas: A2
Azéma, Léon: 304

B

B&B Architectes: A2
B.J.A. (Basselier Jarzaguet Architectes):
    486
Badani, Daniel: A2
Bailly, Antoine: 185
Bakema, Jacob: 309
Balladur, Jean: 316, A2
Ballu, Théodore: 35, 180, 191, 197,
    202, 208
Baltard, Victor: 17, 32, 37, 94, 185,
    187, 195, 201
Baraguey: 134
Bardon, Renaud: 226, 350
Bardsley, H.: 449
Barge, Jacques: 305
Barrau, Gérard: 472
Basset, Christian: 448
Bassompierre, Joseph: 268
Bassompierre-Sewrin, Albert: 392
Bastie, Vincent: Tips p. 300
Bataille: 156
Bataille, Clément: Tips p. 303
Baudoin: 432
Baudot, Anatole de: 217
Baumgarten, Lothar: 414
Bazin, Léon Émile: 264, 284
Beauclair, Henri: 330, 347
Beaudouin, Eugène: 332
Bechmann, Lucien Adolphe: 298, 308, A1
Behrens, Peter: 293
Bélanger, François-Joseph: 136, 213
Bellini, Mario: 49, 433
Benamo, Giorgia: 343
Benjamin, J.-M.: A1
Berger, Patrick: 336, 392, 399, 450, 489
Berger, René: 215, 273
Bernard, Constant: 211
Bernard, Henry: 311
Bérnard, Joseph: 150
Bernier, Stanislas Louis: 219
Bernini, Gian Lorenzo: 76, 82, 84, 115
Besset, Pierre du: 404, 412
Betourné, René: A1
Biecher, Christian: 477, Tips p. 298
Biette, Louis: 232
Bigot, Alexandre: 238, 239, 240,
    246, 251
Bigot, Paul: 274

333

APPENDIX

INDEX OF ARCHITECTS

INDEX OF ARCHITECTS

Picture credits

All pictures which are not separately listed in the following, stem from Chris van Uffelen; not listed historical pictures from the archives of the authors. If not otherwise indicated reference is made to the consecutive numbers of the properties. Portraits not listed in the following, stem from the architects.

Paul Andreu: 314 Plan – Architecture Studio: 386, 484 – artefactory: 475 l. – Patrick Berger & Jacques Anziutti architectes: 489 – Luc Boegly: 481 – Marie-Eugénie Cisternas p. 254 Berger – Nicolas Borel: p. 255 de Portzamparc – Jack Downey / Library of Congress, Prints & Photographs Division, FSA-OWI Collection LC-DIG-fsac-1a55001: 309 – EPAD: 493, p. 254 Nouvel and Wilmotte – © FLC/BILDKUNST, 2008: 293 – Gamma, Raphael Gaillarde: p. 254 Gautrand – Gianni Berengo Gardin: p. 255 Piano – Markus Golser: 49 floor plan, 98 floor plan, 102 – Parish Saint-Joseph des Carmes: 50 – Jacob+Macfarlane: A3 – Fred Kihn: 314 l., p. 255 Andreu – Gérard Laurent / Pariscool: 231 – Mark Lyon / Maison de Verre: 283 – Veronique Marc: p. 254 Anziutti – Jacques Mossot / Structurae: 77 – Roland Nizet: 108 – Ateliers Jean Nouvel: 475 r. – NOX/Lars Spuybroek: 411 l. – Elia Ntaousani: 192, 203, 350 – Peter Olsen: 285, 316, 321, 385, 453, 458 – Dominique Perrault Architecture: 440 r. – 440 l. Perrault Projects – Atelier Christian de Portzamparc: 452, 467, 471 – Agence Rudy Ricciotti 49 – Bernhard Tschumi Architects: 404 plans – Unibail-Morphosis: 411 r., 492 – Valode et Pistre: 490, 494 – Vasconi Associés Architectes 495

The authors

Markus Sebastian Braun (editor), born in 1966, studied history, German language and literature, and economics. From 1993 to 1995 he was editor of copernicus, a popular scientific magazine. Today he is a publisher and lives in Berlin.

Markus Golser, M.A., born in 1968, is a freelance art historian whose interests emphasize Early Modern, Byzantine and Medieval architecture as well as early Modernist buildings. In addition to German-speaking territory, France occupies the center of his activities as author and contributor, and is frequently the destination of educational trips guided by him.

Chris van Uffelen, M.A., born in 1966, is a freelance art historian whose interests focus on medieval architecture and the period following neo-Classicism. He operates an editorial office for publications on the topic of modern architecture. Countless stays in Paris with renowned professors in the course of his studies brought him intimate knowledge of the city, whose architectural activities he follows fervently to this day.

Literature

Albrecht, Uwe: Von der Burg zum Schloss. Die französische Schlossbaukunst des Spätmittelalters, Worms 1986

Aulanier, Christiane: Histoire du Palais et du Musée du Louvre, 10 volumes, Paris 1947–1968

Ayers, Andrew: The Architecture of Paris, Stuttgart 2004

Babelon, Jean-Pierre: François Mansart. Le génie de l'architecture, Paris 1998

Bartz, Gabriele; Eberhard König: Louvre. Kunst und Architektur, Königswinter 2005

Berger, Robert W.: A Royal passion. Louis XIV as patron of architecture, Cambridge 1994

Berger, Robert W.: Versailles. The Château of Louis XIV, London 1985

Beutler, Christian: Paris und Versailles. Reclam Kunstführer, Frankreich, Vol. I, Stuttgart 1979

Borrus, Kathy: One Thousand Buildings of Paris, New York 2003

Borsi, Franco; Ezio Godoli: Pariser Bauten der Jahrhundertwende, Stuttgart 1990

Braham, Allan; Peter Smith: François Mansart, 2 volumes, London 1973

Chadyc, Danielle; Dominique Leborgne: Atlas de Paris. Evolution d'un paysage urbain, Paris 2007

Christ, Thomas: Die Schlösser der Île-de-France, Basel 1994

Cleary, Richard Louis: The Place Royale and urban design in the Ancien Regime, Cambridge 1999

D'Archimbaud, Nicholas: Versailles, Munich 2001

Dictionnaire des monuments de Paris, Paris 2003

Droste-Hennings, Julia; Thorsten Droste: Paris. Eine Stadt und ihr Mythos, DuMont-Kunstreiseführer, Cologne 2000

Erlande-Brandenburg, Alain: Notre-Dame de Paris, Paris 1991, germ. Freiburg i. Br., 1992

Fichet, Françoise (Hg.): La théorie architecturale à l'âge classique. Essai d'anthologie critique, Brussels 1979

Gady, Alexandre: De la Place Royale à la Place des Vosges, Paris 1997

Gady, Alexandre: le Marais. Guide historique et architectural, Paris 1994

Gallet, Michel: Ledoux et Paris, Paris 1979

Gleininger, Andrea; Gerhard Matzig, Sebastian Redecke: Paris. Architektur der Gegenwart. Munich 1997

Hesse, Michael: Klassische Architektur in Frankreich. Kirchen, Schlösser, Gärten, Städte 1600–1800, Darmstadt 2004

Hesse, Michael: Klassizismus als Auflösung des klassischen Architekturkonzepts, In: Gottfried Böhm u.a. (ed.), Studien zu Renaissance und Barock, Frankfurt / Main 1986, 197–220

Jordan, David: Die Neuerschaffung von Paris. Baron Haussmann und seine Stadt, Frankfurt / Main 1996

Kimpel, Dieter: Paris – Führungen durch die Stadtbaugeschichte, Munich 1982

Kimpel, Dieter; Robert Suckale: Die gotische Architektur in Frankreich 1130–1270, Munich 1985

Lablaude, Pierre-André: Die Gärten von Versailles, Worms 1995

Lubell, Sam: Paris 2000+. New Architecture, New York 2007

Martin, Hervé: Guide de l'architecture moderne à Paris. Paris 2003

Mignot, Claude: Grammaire des immeubles parisiens. Six siècles de façades du Moyen Age à nos jours , Paris 2004

Münchhausen, Thankmar von: Paris. Geschichte einer Stadt – Von 1800 bis heute, Munich 2007

Perouse de Montclos, Jean-Marie; Robert Polidori: Versailles, Cologne 1999

Pinon, Pierre; Bertrand Le Boudec, Dominique Carré: Les plans de Paris. Histoire d'une capitale, Paris 2004

Poisson, Michael: Paris Monuments, Paris and Turin 1998

Poisson, Michel: Façades parisiennes. 1200 immeubles et monuments remarquables de la capitale, Paris 2006

Poisson, Michel: The Monuments of Paris. An illustrated Guide, London 1999

Sutcliffe, Anthony: Paris. An Architectural History, New Haven 1993

Texier, Simon: Paris. Grammaire de l'architecture XXe-XXIe siècles, Paris 2007

Texier, Simon: Paris contemporain. De Haussmann à nos jours, une capitale à l'ère des métropoles, Paris 2005

Thomson, David: Renaissance Paris. Architecture and Growth 1475-1600, London 1984

Uffelen, Chris van: Paris. Architecture & design, Kempen 2004

Viollet-le-Duc, Eugène-Emmanuel: Le dictionaire d'architecture, Wavre 1995

Wachmeier, Günter: Paris mit Saint-Denis, Versailles und Fontainbleau (Artemis-Cicerone Kunst- und Reiseführer), Zurich and Munich 1984